Title IV-E Child Welfare Education

BSW/MSW education funded by Title IV-E of Social Security Act ("Title IV-E Child Welfare Education") is an important incentive to encourage social workers to stay in the child protection field. It aims to demonstrate a training partnership between universities and public child welfare agencies.

This book contains essential research results with a focus on the impact of Title IV-E Child Welfare Education to improve worker capacities and case outcomes, as well as on the process and results of social work education in promoting public child welfare work. There are an introduction and nine chapters written by 32 renowned researchers in public child welfare who applied rigorous quantitative and/or qualitative methodologies to clearly describe measures used, data sources, outcome variables, and implications for education, practice, policy, and research. These evidence-based studies address the following child welfare topics: training partnerships and worker outcomes, effective pedagogy and online education, workplace climate and retention factors, and other topics connecting BSW/MSW education to public child welfare practice. Future child welfare education will need to further expand child welfare knowledge and skills, strengthen worker competencies with a strong commitment to social work values and ethical practice principles, and develop a cohesive supervisory network to build a workforce with positive attitude toward child protection programs.

This collection will inform child welfare educators, administrators, and legislators regarding the impact of Title IV-E Child Welfare Education on the development of public child welfare and make recommendations to improve the child welfare curriculum in social work education.

This book was originally published as a special issue of the *Journal of Public Child Welfare*.

Patrick Leung, PhD, is Gerson & Sabina David Endowed Professor for Global Aging and the Director of the Office for International Social Work Education at the Graduate College of Social Work at the University of Houston, USA. Dr. Leung is a Principal Investigator and Evaluator of numerous research projects in child welfare and family services.

Monit Cheung, PhD, LCSW, is Mary R. Lewis Endowed Professor in Children & Youth at the Graduate College of Social Work at the University of Houston, USA. She is the Director of the Child & Family Center for Innovative Research and Principal Investigator of the Title IV-E Child Welfare Education Project in Houston, Texas.

Title IV-E Child Welfare Education

Impact on Workers, Case Outcomes and
Social Work Curriculum Development

Edited by
Patrick Leung and Monit Cheung

Routledge
Taylor & Francis Group

LONDON AND NEW YORK

First published 2020
by Routledge
2 Park Square, Milton Park, Abingdon, Oxon, OX14 4RN

and by Routledge
52 Vanderbilt Avenue, New York, NY 10017

Routledge is an imprint of the Taylor & Francis Group, an informa business

First issued in paperback 2021

British Library Cataloguing-in-Publication Data
A catalogue record for this book is available from the British Library

ISBN13: 978-0-367-43813-5 (hbk)
ISBN13: 978-1-03-208411-4 (pbk)

Typeset in Minion Pro
by codeMantra

Publisher's Note
The publisher accepts responsibility for any inconsistencies that may have arisen during the conversion of this book from journal articles to book chapters, namely the inclusion of journal terminology.

Disclaimer
Every effort has been made to contact copyright holders for their permission to reprint material in this book. The publishers would be grateful to hear from any copyright holder who is not here acknowledged and will undertake to rectify any errors or omissions in future editions of this book.

Contents

Citation Information

The chapters in this book were originally published in the *Journal of Public Child Welfare*, volume 12, issue 3 (July–August 2018). When citing this material, please use the original page numbering for each article, as follows:

Introduction
Title IV-E education: Past, present and future of public child welfare
Patrick Leung & Monit Cheung
Journal of Public Child Welfare, volume 12, issue 3 (July–August 2018) pp. 233–237

Chapter 1
What's in an MSW? Graduate education for public child welfare workers, intention, engagement, and work environment
Ericka Deglau, Ayse Akincigil, Anasuya Ray, and Jennifer Bauwens
Journal of Public Child Welfare, volume 12, issue 3 (July–August 2018) pp. 238–263

Chapter 2
"I was prepared for the worst I guess": Stayers' and leavers' perceptions of their Title IV-E education
Amy D. Benton and Michelle Iglesias
Journal of Public Child Welfare, volume 12, issue 3 (July–August 2018) pp. 264–280

Chapter 3
Preparing Child Welfare Practitioners: Implications for Title IV-E Education and Training Partnerships
Austin Griffiths, David Royse, Kristine Piescher, and Traci LaLiberte
Journal of Public Child Welfare, volume 12, issue 3 (July–August 2018) pp. 281–299

Chapter 4
The role of Title IV-E education and training in child protection workforce diversification
Kristine N. Piescher, Traci LaLiberte, and Mihwa Lee
Journal of Public Child Welfare, volume 12, issue 3 (July–August 2018) pp. 333–353

Chapter 5
IV-E or not IV-E, that is the question: Comparisons of BSW Child Welfare Scholars and matched trainee confidence and retention
Greta Yoder Slater, Marissa O'Neill, Lisa E. McGuire, and Elizabeth Dickerson
Journal of Public Child Welfare, volume 12, issue 3 (July–August 2018) pp. 300–316

Chapter 6

Factors affecting turnover rates of public child welfare front line workers: Comparing cohorts of title IV-E program graduates with regularly hired and trained staff
Anita Barbee, Corrie Rice, Becky F. Antle, Katy Henry, and Michael R. Cunningham
Journal of Public Child Welfare, volume 12, issue 3 (July–August 2018) pp. 354–379

Chapter 7

Views on workplace culture and climate: Through the lens of retention and Title IV-E participation
Sandhya Rao Hermon, Michael Biehl, and Rose Chahla
Journal of Public Child Welfare, volume 12, issue 3 (July–August 2018) pp. 380–397

Chapter 8

An effective pedagogy for child welfare education
Virginia C. Strand & Marciana Popescu
Journal of Public Child Welfare, volume 12, issue 3 (July–August 2018) pp. 398–410

Chapter 9

The future of online social work education and Title IV-E child welfare stipends
Kate Trujillo, Lara Bruce, and Ann Obermann
Journal of Public Child Welfare, volume 12, issue 3 (July–August 2018) pp. 317–332

For any permission-related enquiries please visit:
http://www.tandfonline.com/page/help/permissions

Contributors

Ayse Akincigil, School of Social Work, Rutgers, the State University of New Jersey, New Brunswick, USA.

Becky F. Antle, Kent School of Social Work, University of Louisville, USA.

Anita Barbee, Kent School of Social Work, University of Louisville, USA.

Jennifer Bauwens, School of Social Work, Rutgers, the State University of New Jersey, New Brunswick, USA.

Amy D. Benton, School of Social Work, Texas State University, San Marcos, USA.

Michael Biehl, California Social Work Education Center, University of California, Berkeley, USA.

Lara Bruce, Department of Social Work, Metropolitan State University of Denver, USA.

Rose Chahla, California Social Work Education Center, University of California, Berkeley, USA.

Monit Cheung, PhD, LCSW, is Mary R. Lewis Endowed Professor in Children & Youth at the Graduate College of Social Work at the University of Houston, USA. She is the Director of the Child & Family Center for Innovative Research and Principal Investigator of the Title IV-E Child Welfare Education Project in Houston, Texas.

Michael R. Cunningham, Department of Communication, University of Louisville, USA.

Ericka Deglau, School of Social Work, Rutgers, the State University of New Jersey, New Brunswick, USA.

Elizabeth Dickerson, Marion County Department of Child Services, Indiana Department of Child Services, Indianapolis, USA.

Austin Griffiths, Department of Social Work, Western Kentucky University, Bowling Green, USA.

Katy Henry, Kent School of Social Work, University of Louisville, USA.

Sandhya Rao Hermon, Social Services Agency, County of Santa Clara, San Jose, California, USA.

Michelle Iglesias, School of Social Work, Texas State University, San Marcos, USA.

Traci LaLiberte, Center for Advanced Studies in Child Welfare, School of Social Work, University of Minnesota, Minneapolis, USA.

Mihwa Lee, School of Social Work, East Carolina University, Greenville, USA.

Patrick Leung, PhD, is Gerson & Sabina David Endowed Professor for Global Aging and the Director of the Office for International Social Work Education at the Graduate College of Social Work at the University of Houston, USA. Dr. Leung is a Principal Investigator and Evaluator of numerous research projects in child welfare and family services.

Lisa E. McGuire, Department of Social Work, James Madison University, Harrisonburg, USA.

Ann Obermann, Department of Social Work, Metropolitan State University of Denver, USA.

Marissa O'Neill, Department of Social Work, Humboldt State University, Arcata, USA.

Kristine Piescher, Center for Advanced Studies in Child Welfare, School of Social Work, University of Minnesota, Minneapolis, USA.

Marciana Popescu, Fordham University Graduate School of Social Service, West Harrison, USA.

Anasuya Ray, United Nations Counter-Terrorism Committee Executive Directorate.

Corrie Rice, Training Resource Center, Eastern Kentucky University, Richmond, USA.

David Royse, College of Social Work, University of Kentucky, Lexington, USA.

Greta Yoder Slater, Department of Social Work, Ball State University, Muncie, USA.

Virginia C. Strand, Fordham University Graduate School of Social Service, West Harrison, USA.

Kate Trujillo, Department of Social Work, Metropolitan State University of Denver, USA.

Title IV-E education: Past, present and future of public child welfare

Patrick Leung and Monit Cheung

Public child welfare (PCW) is always seen as a state concern. This Special Issue addresses child protection issues from the angle of analyzing the educational preparedness of child protection service (CPS) workers and the nation's readiness for building a strong workforce through Title IV-E support. Its content is examined with a connection between the past as a link to the present and the future.

The past

History has set the stage for improvement. In 1961, the federal government sought to standardize support through the creation of the federal foster care system and the enactment of Title IV-E entitlement programs. Since 1980, Title IV-E has been an entitlement program for state-managed foster care or subsidized adoption (Valentine, 2012). Within this funding mechanism, state-university partnership has been the Title IV-E training arm aiming to increase the skill level of PCW workforce for the prevention of out-of-home placements.

Even though the funding formula for training and education has been and continues to be determined by the reimbursement rate a state can receive to provide out-of-home care for children under state custody, this rate with state variations has dropped from 70% in the 1980s to 30–50% in the recent decade. This decreasing trend has affected not only workforce planning but also Title IV-E budget on training and education (Children's Defense Fund, 2018). In 1995, as a bridge to initiate a block grant concept for services, the reenactment proposal in Child Abuse Prevention and Treatment Act was vetoed by the President (CWLA, 2018). Since then, legislature has focused on how deal with PCW workforce issues, with research supporting social work education's role (Zlotnik, 2003). In 2006, similar discussions about IV-E eligibility were brought back regarding the possible impact of block grants on administrative and training cost reimbursement (Whitaker & Clark, 2006). The history highlights the importance of education and training for improving services.

The present

Now is the time to act. The landscape of government funding has changed its direction, particularly with the recent passing of the Family First Prevention Services Act in 2018 ("Family First") that may change and limit the service scope under Title IV-E reimbursement. Outcome evaluation is a required step in persuading legislators with evidence that educational training is an essential preventive element in combating child abuse and neglect problems.

This Special Issue of the *Journal of Public Child Welfare* includes contributions from diverse scholars in the child welfare field who have studied the impact of Title IV-E partnerships on PCW development. Diverse themes are examined in nine refereed articles regarding Title IV-E projects' educational principles and tested outcomes. From the abstracts of these 9 articles, a word-cloud analysis shows 10 popular words: Title IV-E (29), Educate (23), Child (23), Welfare (21), Train (17), Work (13), Workforce (11), Agency (10), Employee (9), and Retention (9). While these words connect child welfare education with workforce retention, they also specify research findings in three categories: education and training outcomes, child welfare workforce culture and environment, and retention and turnover issues.

Education and training outcomes

Strand and Popescu in their article entitled "An effective pedagogy for child welfare education" describe the intersection of social work education with child welfare. With results from 29 schools of social work, Title IV-E curriculum was tested with positive outcomes that increased workers' confidence and preparedness to work toward improving the goals in child protection. This study can be used to advocate the inclusion of trauma-informed training so that the preventive nature of social work education can be highlighted.

The process of education and preparedness is also reported in "What's in an MSW?" by Deglau, Akincigil, Ray, and Bauwens. These authors address the use of educational and workplace experiences to influence MSW graduates' career aspirations for the professionalization of PCW practice. Their findings address the intentions to stay as this variable is associated with opportunities for growth and stress manageability.

Child welfare workforce culture and environment

With advances in technology, it is crucial to examine how the IV-E community will respond to the online delivery of social work education. Trujillo, Bruce, and Obermann provide a conceptual framework for analyzing an online platform for Title IV-E education in their article, "The future of online social work education and Title IV-E child welfare stipends." The best support for students is the creation and implementation of a support network to help them balance their time while studying. Online social work programs that provide a flexible opportunity for PCW workers, particularly those working in rural counties, must also provide learning support so that they would use innovative methods for reaching out to their clientele.

Title IV-E education is designed with an aim of promoting workforce diversification. In "The role of Title IV-E education and training in child protection workforce diversification," Piescher, LaLiberte, and Lee identify ways to reduce racial/ethnic disparities in the CPS system. Their research from a survey of 679 child welfare workers shows that children of color have been disproportionately overrepresented in the CPS, while professionals of color are disproportionately underrepresented. Having a realistic expectation of the work environment and job demand is essential to combat work-related alienation.

Turnover within PCW

With a focus on individual-system connection, Griffiths, Royse, Piescher, and LaLiberte in "Preparing child welfare practitioners" report the responses from a national sample of the Title IV-E academy. Turnover can be prevented if the workers maintain positive attitudes about their work. In "Views on workplace culture and climate," Hermon, Biehl, and Chahla further illustrate individual differences that may lead to job factors and complex attitudes toward the workplace. Compared to Title IV-E graduates who stayed, those who left the agency had significantly lower supervisor satisfaction and worse efficacy scores; in contrast, these differences were not found among non-Title IV-E stayers and leavers. Interpreted with a positive note, these findings show that Title IV-E graduates with a high level of service satisfaction are likely to stay.

To address concerns of those who had intent to leave, Benton and Iglesias in their article, "I was prepared for the worst I guess," address the chronic high cost of turnover. Their qualitative interviews aimed to distinguish the differences between stayers and leavers with the hope to find effective retention strategies. However, once training and payback are fulfilled, the credentials for professionalizing child welfare will become the reason and opportunity to exit the CPS workforce. From another perspective, Barbee, Rice, Antle, Henry, and Cunningham in "Factors affecting turnover rates of public child welfare front line workers" discuss the impact of constant high turnover. While most impact studies in the literature have focused on the workers' intent to leave, these authors address the importance of studying the actual exit.

In a longitudinal study, "IV-E or not IV-E," Slater, O'Neill, and McGuire examined the effectiveness of training on BSW IV-E scholars ($n = 52$) as compared with a matched cohort of traditionally trained employees ($n = 57$). Their results included: (1) preparedness and (2) retention in the first 5 years of employment. If IV-E education is a confidence booster, the question is no longer about retention, but instead regards leadership training.

The future

The future of Title IV-E education is based on evidence. Research evidence in this Special Issue points at the connection between social work education and PCW workforce. However, additional research is still required to identify the complexities surrounding workforce issues, particularly when child welfare workers turn to other employment after obtaining their advanced degree. These complex issues are related to workload, staff-client ratio, supervisory relationship, and other systemic barriers and motivators (Leung & Cheung, 2017).

According to Torres and Mathur (2018), the passing of "Family First" aims at preventing children from entering foster care by allowing states to use IV-E reimbursement to pay for substance abuse, mental health, and parenting skill programs. Child welfare advocates have argued against the form of a block grant (Children's Defense Fund, 2018; Harfeld, 2017) in anticipation that preventive service funding may not be sufficient to reach the educational needs of frontline staff (CWLA, 2017). In the foreseeable future, it will be more imperative than ever that the Title IV-E education partnership programs justify continued federal support, showing effective outcomes to prevent or reduce congregate placements and improve child and family well-being.

Outcome evaluation is crucial to support educational work as preventive. Although this Special Issue contains diverse topics on Title IV-E stipend students' learning outcomes and retention within CPS, no studies were submitted concerning how to use research data to testify. One important finding, however, as related to the turnover cost and retention capacities of CPS, has provided evidence about the opportunity benefit of maintaining Title IV-E education and a workforce that enjoys having a sense of belonging to work together for the welfare of children and their families. As witnessed by a CPS investigator, "The families are more open; they're actually asking us to go back out again" (DFPS, 2018), it is time to use evidence to testify on behalf of our nation's PCW workforce and our CPS families to build a network of togetherness.

References

Child Welfare League of America. (CWLA). (2017). *The danger of block grants.* Retrieved from https://www.cwla.org/wp-content/uploads/2017/03/The-Danger-of-Block-Grants.pdf

Child Welfare League of America. (CWLA). (2018). *Could the family first act passage protect title IV-E from block grant?* Retrieved from https://www.cwla.org/could-the-families-first-act-passage-protect-title-iv-e-from-block-grant/

Children's Defense Fund. (2018, February 19). Family First Prevention Services Act implementation timeline. Retrieved from http://www.childrensdefense.org/library/data/ffpsa-implementation.pdf

Department of Family and Protective Services. (DFPS). (2018 April 18). DFPS on Facebook. Retrieved from https://www.dfps.state.tx.us/

Family First Prevention Services Act, The. ["Family First"] (2018, February). *Historic reforms to the child welfare system will improve outcomes for vulnerable children.* Retrieved from http://fosteringchamps.org/wp-content/uploads/2018/02/ffpsa-short-summary.pdf

Harfeld, A. (2017, February 1). *IV-E change needed, but not in block grant form.* Retrieved from https://chronicleofsocialchange.org/opinion/iv-e-change-needed-not-block-grant-form

Leung, P., & Cheung, M. (2017). *DFPS compensation assessment and employee incentives review.* Retrieved from https://www.dfps.state.tx.us/About_DFPS/Reports_and_Presentations/Agencywide/documents/2017/2017-02-20_DFPS_Compensation_Assessment_Employee_Incentives_Review-Formal.pdf

Torres, K., & Mathur, R. (2018, March 8). *Fact sheet: Family First Prevention Services Act.* Retrieved from https://campaignforchildren.org/resources/fact-sheet/fact-sheet-family-first-prevention-services-act/

Valentine, C. (2012, March). Child welfare funding opportunities: Title IV-E and Medicaid. *The State Policy Advocacy and Reform Center and First Focus.* Retrieved from http://childwelfaresparc.org/wp-content/uploads/2014/07/22-Child-Welfare–Opportunities-Title-IV-E-and-Medicaid_0.pdf

Whitaker, T., Clark, E. J. (2006). Social workers in child welfare: Ready for duty. *Research on Social Work Practice, 16*(4), 412–413.

Zlotnik, J. L. (2003). The use of Title IV-E training funds for social work education: An historical perspective. *Journal of Human Behavior in the Social Environment, 7*(1/2), 5–21. doi:10.1300/J137v07n01_02

What's in an MSW? Graduate education for public child welfare workers, intention, engagement, and work environment

Ericka Deglau, Ayse Akincigil, Anasuya Ray, and Jennifer Bauwens

ABSTRACT

This study employs a mixed methods analysis of exit survey data gathered from public child welfare employees at their completion of a Title IV-E funded MSW program, distinct because it was initiated during a period of major reform and permitted students to continue employment during their studies. Findings suggest that opportunities for growth and manageable levels of stress were associated with intentions to stay and engagement with the work, reflected in respondents' positive perceptions of their roles in the work environment and their retrospective assessments of the impact of their social work education.

Introduction

The principle objectives of Title IV-E partnerships between social work educational institutions and state public child welfare agencies are to enhance the skill level of the workforce and to improve retention. A fairly extensive literature, described by Zlotnik, DePanfilis, Daining, and McDermott Lane (2005), examines outcomes in both these areas. Parallel work has delineated factors antecedent to turnover in the wider workforce (Benton, 2016; Mor Barak, Levin, Nissly, & Lane, 2006) and led to the exploration of employee engagement or withdrawal from the job, the latter often a precursor to leaving. These studies suggest that work environment, the presence or absence of social supports, and stress levels are inherent both to intentions to leave or stay (Nissly, Barak, & Levin, 2005) and to engagement with the work (Travis, Lizano, & Mor Barak, 2016).

The present study seeks to explore career intentions and engagement among public child welfare employees who obtained their Master of Social Work through a IV-E partnership. The program was unique in that it was launched during a period of major reform for its partner agency and designed to permit participants, who attended classes exclusively with other public child welfare employees, to continue full-time employment while in school (Deglau et al., 2015). Programmatic outcomes have been examined for IV-E partnerships that include employees among their participants. However, the particular circumstances of the program reviewed here make the translation of previous findings problematic and dictate the need for separate study.

The objective of the study is, through secondary analyses of data collected in an exit survey administered to program participants as they completed their MSWs, to examine relationships between participant career intentions, work environment, and engagement with the work. This objective is achieved through quantitative analysis of career intentions, workplace environmental variables and personal characteristics, and qualitative analysis of participants' responses to open-ended questions concerning their future plans and their reflections about their workplace and educational experiences.

Literature review

This study builds on work that has examined the effects of workplace environment on retention and engagement, as well as a smaller body of qualitative research on the experiences and motivations of public child welfare employees who have sought advanced social work education.

Retention, intention, and engagement

Research on retention, for both specially educated social workers (Cahalane & Sites, 2008; Dickinson & Perry, 2002; Gansle & Ellett, 2002; Jones, 2002; Scannapieco & Connell-Carrick, 2003) and the general child welfare workforce, seeks to predict turnover by examining how environmental factors, such as work conditions, organizational culture and climate, and personal characteristics combine to create conditions in which public child welfare workers might stay or leave (Bednar, 2003; Blome & Steib, 2014; Ellett, 2009; Faller, Grabarek, & Ortega, 2010; Lee, Forster, & Rehner, 2011; Scannapieco & Connell-Carrick, 2007; Shim, 2010; Williams, Nichols, Kirk, & Wilson, 2011; Yankeelov, Barbee, Sullivan, & Antle, 2009; Zeitlin, Augsberger, Auerbach, & McGowan, 2014). Attention to supervisory and work group support, the organizational environment in proximity, has demonstrated effects on turnover, although these have not always been uniform (Collins-Camargo & Royse, 2010; Kruzich, Mienko, & Courtney, 2014; Landsman, 2007; Smith, 2005). Several researchers (Johnco, Salloum, Olson, & Edwards, 2014; Thompson, Wojciak, & Cooley, 2017; Westbrook, Ellis, & Ellet, 2006) provide insight on retention factors by examining public child welfare employees' perceptions directly.

Much of the work on retention and turnover relies on data about *intention*, rather than actual departure, a relationship that is not necessarily

congruent. Recent work raises the equally important construct of engagement with the work, whether or not actual departure ensues. Drawing on
research focused on the antecedents of leaving, particularly as they relate to
job stress, job satisfaction, and the presence or absence of social and relational support (Lizano & Mor Barak, 2012; Mor Barak, Levin, Nissly, & Lane,
2006; Nissly et al., 2005), some researchers have begun to distinguish varying
levels of intention with action (Fernandes, 2016; Griffiths, Royse, Culver,
Piescher, & Zhang, 2017).

Interest in the circumstances under which child welfare workers assume
active and engaged roles in the workplace or withdraw and disengage (Travis,
Gomez, & Mor Barak, 2011; Travis & Mor Barak, 2010) has initiated a new
direction in the research that is of particular interest to this study.
Organizational supports that encourage engaged practice (Kim & Mor
Barak, 2015) and workplace inclusion (Brimhall et al., 2017; Mor Barak
et al., 2016) have evident implications for sustaining quality practice.
Closely related to the notion of active engagement in the workplace is that
of the social capital achieved through inclusion in decision-making, professional autonomy, and relational supports, which can mean the difference
between thriving in the organization and just persevering (Boyas & Wind,
2010; Boyas, Wind, & Kang, 2012; Boyas, Wind, & Ruiz, 2013, 2015).

Public child welfare employees and social work education

Social workers appear to have several advantages over their nonsocial work
peers in terms of both retention and preparation, performance, and overall
confidence in their abilities to meaningfully affect families (Bagdasaryan,
2012; Hartinger-Saunders & Lyons, 2013; Jones & Okamura, 2000; Mathias,
Gilman, Shin, & Evans, 2015; Reed-Ashcraft, Westbrook, & Williams, 2012).
Among MSW graduates, public child welfare employees may have additional
advantages over their less experienced peers. Because of their familiarity with
the work and the organization, they may be better equipped to tolerate
potential dissonance between what they learned in their MSW education
and the experience on the ground, have greater facility to find allies and
supports within the agency, and thus be better able to exercise influence
(Lewandowski, 1998; Whitaker & Clark, 2006).

Some studies suggest that public child welfare employees who pursue
social work education develop relationships, networks, and social capital
during their studies that may contribute to their later roles in the agency.
Altman and Cohen (2016), for example, note the importance of relational
aspects of studying together in cohorts. Studies by Auerbach, McGowan, and
Laporte (2008), Hopkins, Mudrick, and Rudolph (1999), and Mason,
LaPorte, Bronstein, and Auerbach (2012) echo similar findings among public
child welfare employees who pursued an MSW.

Public child welfare employees with social work training appear to be more favorable to organizational efforts to implement family-centered practice and other reforms (Ahn, Keyser, & Hayward-Everson, 2016). MSW graduates, who were public child welfare employees among a large sample of social work students, fully expected to use their skills on the job and to expand their leadership roles in their agencies (McCrae, Scannapieco, Leake, Potter, Menefee, Schudrich, & McGowan, 2014). McGuire, Howes, Murphy-Nugen, and George (2011) report leadership by public child welfare employees in furthering systemic reforms, a finding also emphasized by Deglau et al. (2015), who conducted focus groups with students about their roles in case practice change.

Despite evident advantages in investing in graduate social work education for public child welfare employees, with respect to workforce development and staffing stability, maintaining commitment to and engagement with the difficult work of child welfare can represent considerable challenges (Scannapieco, Hegar, & Connell-Carrick, 2012), even for employees. The present study seeks to examine the experiences of one such group of specially trained public child welfare employees and their intentions to leave or stay. Because of their tenure and the context in which they embarked on their studies, their career intentions become a veritable proxy for engagement.

Methods

Participants and design

A brief description of the MSW program in which public child welfare employees participated is provided as a context for the study. The program, initiated in 2006 by New Jersey's largest school of social work, in partnership with its public child welfare agency, was hybrid in design. Monthly weekend classes facilitated continuation of employment as did one day a week, year round internship, comprising both internal and external placements. Classes in the intensive weekend program were taken as a cohort, with a curricular focus that combined management and direct practice, and incorporated child welfare content. To be eligible, candidates were required to have at least 2 years of qualified employment in public child welfare, extended to 3 years after the program's first year, and to return 2 years of service to the agency postgraduation. Actual service averaged 5–7 years, with a range from 2 to 20 years (Deglau et al., 2014). Open to direct service as well as supervisory and management staff, the program enrolled 164 employees in staggered intervals from 2006 to 2009 and graduated 152, including 1 posthumously, through 2012. One-third were supervisory or management staff and the rest evenly divided between caseworkers and specialized caseworkers.

The exit survey that provided data for this study was developed for purposes of program evaluation a few years into the program and administered as cohorts of students met degree requirements and graduated. Development of the survey was informed by focus groups with the program's first 60 students during its initial year and a subsequent survey with students' workplace supervisors the following year (Deglau, Meyers, & Cho, 2009), as well as exploratory interviews with the program's first two graduates. These early evaluative activities suggested the primacy of the workplace environment both to students' MSW experience and to the facility with which they were able to transfer their learning to the workplace. Portions of Nissly's (2004) workforce survey were incorporated into the survey to address these issues. Prior to its launch, the exit survey was further reviewed for content by child welfare experts from academic and public sectors.

The survey centered on five broad categories of inquiry: (1) competencies acquired during MSW study, (2) workplace environment, (3) future intentions, (4) explorations of educational experience and application to practice, and (5) demographics and employment information. The mixed-methods study presented here explores respondents' future intentions with respect to career commitment to child welfare in the context of their respective struggles and achievements in the workplace and their reflections about their social work education. The principal research question is: how does work environment influence employee engagement and future intention to remain in child welfare?

Study sample and survey administration

Following IRB approval in March of 2010, the anonymous exit survey, using the Survey Monkey platform, was sent out to 151 graduates of the program at staggered intervals, between 2010 and 2013, as successive cohorts completed their studies. Graduates were sent an e-mail with a link to the survey and a request to review, complete, and return an attached informed consent; once the participant clicked on the survey link, a time stamp was automatically generated to indicate the date of the survey, allowing researchers to distinguish the interval between graduation and the completion of the survey. Participants received reminders to complete the survey every 3–6 months.

The current study is limited to participants who answered questions pertaining to their intentions to stay or leave the public child welfare profession and their title or position at both the start of their studies and at survey completion. Given these criteria, 24 survey records were excluded from among the total 128 surveys submitted, resulting in a sample size of 104 useable records and an effective response rate of 69%.

Of the 104 respondents in the study sample (Table 1), more than 90% were female. There were 30 Blacks and 23 Hispanics. Almost half of them were born between 1970 and 1980, and 23 of them were born after 1980. At the

Table 1. Characteristics of the study participants.

	Number of participants	%
All	104	100
Gender		
Male	11	10.6
Female	93	89.4
Race/Ethnicity		
White/Other	51	49.0
Black	30	28.8
Hispanic	23	22.1
Birth cohort		
1950–59	5	4.8
1960–69	13	12.5
1970–79	47	45.2
1980 or later	23	22.1
Supervisor/Manager[a]		
Yes	53	51.0
No	51	49.0

[a]At the time of survey.

time they completed the survey, 53 of the respondents were in a supervisory or managerial position.

Quantitative analysis

The dependent variable, a binary variable indicating intention to stay, was derived from the module regarding future plans (worded as *Thinking about when you complete your two-year commitment, we'd like to ask you about your future plan*). Response to the question *I'd like to work in this organization until I reach retirement age* was used to derive the dependent variable. Survey responses of four or more on a Likert scale of 1–6 (strongly disagree to strongly agree) were dichotomized as "intending to stay." Right-hand side variables included gender, race/ethnicity, age (10 year increments), and supervisor/manager status at the time of the survey. Work place environment was assessed on six domains: organization; peers, stress and tension; growth; supervisor; and conflict (Table 2), with summated responses to questions in a Likert-scale response format.

Analyses were conducted with Stata software. In order to test the bivariate associations between individual characteristics (demographics and supervisor status) and intention to stay (Table 3), *Pearson chi-square* statistics were used (*tabulate* command with *chi* option). Bivariate associations between workplace environment summary scores and intention to stay were tested by *t* statistics (Table 4, *ttest* command with *by* option). A multiple logistic regression model was estimated to predict intention-to-stay outcome (*logistic* command, Table 5). The explanatory variables of the model included individual characteristics (gender, race/ethnicity, age strata, and supervisor status) and standardized workplace environment summary scores (organization, peers, stress, growth, supervisor, conflict). Workplace environment summary

Table 2. Items generating workplace environment summary scores.

Organization (M = 20.6, SD = 5.3)
   I am able to influence decisions that affect my organization
   I am usually invited to important meetings in my organization
   I feel valued in my interactions with managers higher than my immediate supervisor
   I am often asked to participate in activities not directly related to my job function
   I am well informed of what is going on in my organization
   I have access to enough resources to be effective in my job
Peers (M = 29.2, SD = 4.0)
   I have a say in the way my work group performs its tasks
   My coworkers openly share work-related information with me
   I feel that I have the cooperation of the people in my work group
   My contributions are recognized by my peers at work
   In meetings, I feel that my opinions are valued and respected
   I have excellent working relationships with colleagues and peers
Stress, tension (M = 25.6, SD = 7.7)
   I have much freedom and control in my job
   The level of stress associated with the immediate work environment of the office is reasonable
   The level of stress associated with my job is reasonable
   There is tension at the workplace because of the difficulty of the cases*
   There is tension at the workplace because of organizational change*
   There is tension at the workplace because resources do not meet the level of need*
   There is tension at the workplace because of a high level of staff burnout*
Growth (M = 22.4, SD = 3.7)
   I do not have enough opportunity to use my knowledge and skills in my present job*
   I feel underutilized in my present job*
   I feel that I can practice my profession the way I think it should be practiced within this organization
   I feel that I have the opportunity for professional growth within this organization
   I feel that I have the opportunity for promotion within this organization
   I feel that the organization values my position relative to other positions in the organization
Supervisor (M = 23.3, SD = 4.5)
   My supervisor asks for my opinion before making important decisions
   My supervisor communicates information clearly
   I feel valued in my relationship with my supervisor
   I have excellent working relationships with supervisors
   My contributions are recognized by my supervisors at work
Conflict (M = 14.0, SD = 3.2)
   I am usually among the last to know about important changes in the organization immediate workgroup*
   I experience frequent conflict with supervisors in my organization*
   I experience conflict between my values and what I have to do in my job*
   I experience frequent conflict with coworkers on the job*
   There is tension between me and coworkers because of different approaches to the work*

Potential responses for each question was based on a 6-point Likert scale. Summary scores were generated by summation of the responses. *Inverted, i.e., higher scores represent favorable work environment (e.g., more opportunities to grow, less stress, etc.).

scores were rescaled to have a mean of zero and a standard deviation of one before being entered in the logistic regression model (*std* command).

Qualitative analysis

Open-ended items permitted examination of respondents' views about their future career intentions, aspects of their social work education (field, academics, and cohort experience), and the opportunities and challenges they perceived in using acquired MSW knowledge and skills. Following multiple close readings of respondent entries, a thematic analytic framework was used to develop codes, which arose from the response entries. Each response was assigned up to three codes based on themes elicited by the data, deemed to adequately cover topics in comment texts of one to three sentences or phrases. Codes were distinguished according to the positive or negative attributes of the responses. For example, intentions to stay, ability to apply skills, and satisfaction with the organization were deemed positive (+), while intentions to leave, inability to apply skills, or displeasure with organizational circumstances were characterized as negative (−).

Codes A–Q were assigned to *reasons to stay* (+) and *reasons to leave* (−). A–D denoted themes related to financial and other job benefits and work conditions; E–F to the mention of satisfaction with the job and coworker relationships; G–K to career and growth opportunities, feeling valued or underutilized, personal efficacy or lack of agency, autonomy or voice, and opportunities to use skills or lack thereof; and L–Q to systemic issues or overall impressions of self/related to the organization, such as the ability to affect system change, belief in mission or disjuncture with personal values, obligation to give back or disengagement and burnout, alignment with personal and career goals or desire to use skills in another job or field. Responses to *plans to use the skills acquired* were assigned a Y+/N− (yes and no) and *challenges in applying skills* were assigned a NC+/C− (no challenges; challenges), with designated positive and negative attributions. Theme-based, lettered coding was appended for further specification and a similar strategy was used for questions that addressed participants' experience in pursuing their MSW degree in the program.

The data were reviewed by a total of three coders, two of whom were involved at the onset of the project. Coders conducted autonomous line-by-line coding of the data, followed by discussion until agreement on code assignment was reached. The third coder, who was independent of the project, subsequently reviewed the coded data in order to reduce potential researcher bias. Responses were reviewed and themes discussed again, until agreement could be reached to ensure an accurate depiction of the data. Based on the final coder's analysis, no changes were deemed necessary to the salient aspects of the data reported in the study.

Once the open-ended responses were coded and reviewed, the full data set was sorted by the dependent variable, *I'd like to work in this organization until I reach retirement age*, and by the major position categories, designated as supervisor/manager and caseworker/caseworker specialist. Next, coded responses were tallied by subgroups designated as MStay (supervisors/managers with intent to stay), MLeave (supervisors/managers with intent to leave), CWStay (caseworkers with intent to stay), and CWLeave (caseworkers with intent to leave). Analysis proceeded by examining the distribution of particular themes and thematic groups within each subgroup and comparison of similarities and differences between the groups. After close reading and review by the coders, thematic distributional results were regrouped according to broader categories, to permit a closer examination of response patterns, and the regrouping reviewed for accuracy by the three coders. As part of the analysis, horizontal observations were made across demographic (birth cohort, ethnicity, gender), employment (position, promotion, tenure), and education-related variables (graduation year and interval to the survey), as well as response patterns and aggregates of close-ended items concerning workplace environment and tension in the workplace.

Results

Quantitative results

More than two-thirds of the respondents reported that they intended to stay (68%, Table 3). Among supervisors, the intention to stay was 79%; 57% of the case workers reported they intended to stay, and the difference was statistically significant ($p < 0.014$). As expected, rates of intention to stay increased with age ($p < 0.001$). There were no statistically significant differences in rates by race/ethnicity. With respect to gender, 71% of the females and 46% of the males reported that they intended to stay, but the difference was not statistically significant at 95% level of confidence ($p < 0.086$).

Intention to stay was statistically significantly associated with all workplace environmental variables; average scores of workplace environment subscales were significantly higher for all six domains (Table 4) representing more favorable work environment. For example, the summated organization rating, on average, was 21.9 for those who intend to stay, versus 17.8 for those who did not intend to stay ($p < 0.001$). Those intending to stay reported more opportunities to grow at their institution (25.8 vs. 19.6, $p < 0.001$), lower stress at work (27.9 vs. 20.7, score inverted, $p < 0.001$), more acknowledgment of the supervisor (23.9 vs. 21.8, $p < 0.020$), less conflict (24.7 vs. 22.5, score inverted, $p < 0.005$), and better relationship with peers (30.1 vs. 27.3, $p < 0.001$), compared to those intending to leave.

Table 5 reports the adjusted odds ratios from the multiple logistic regression predicting the intention to stay. Females had higher odds to stay, compared to males (OR = 2.42, $p < 0.016$). Odds of intention to stay increased with age: one decade increase in age was associated with approximately 50% higher odds of staying (OR = 1.49, $p < 0.028$). Race, ethnicity, or supervisor status was not statistically significantly associated with intention to stay after age, gender, supervisor status, and work environment summary scores were controlled for.

Table 3. Bivariate associations between intention to stay and respondent characteristics.

	Rate of respondents intending to stay (%)	x^2	p Value[b]
All	68		
Gender		2.96	0.086
Male	46		
Female	71		
Race/Ethnicity		0.14	0.931
White/Other	68		
Black	70		
Hispanic	65		
Birth Cohort		19.9	0.001
1950–59	100		
1960–69	92		
1970–79	79		
1980 or later	41		
Supervisor/Manager[a]		6.0	0.014
Yes	79		
No	57		

[a]At the time of survey.
[b]p Value of Pearson chi-square test statistic, testing presence of subgroup differences in the rates with an intention to stay response.

Two domains of workplace environment were significant predictors of intention to stay: level of stress and opportunities to grow. One standard deviation of improvement in the summated score of stress was associated

Table 4. Average workplace environment summary scores, stratified by intention to stay.

	Not intending to stay (n = 33)	Intending to stay (n = 71)	t Test	p Value
Organization	17.8	21.9	−3.89	0.001
Peers	27.3	30.1	−3.55	0.001
Stress	20.7	27.9	−4.93	0.001
Growth	19.6	25.8	−4.77	0.001
Supervisor	21.8	23.0	−2.35	0.020
Conflict	22.5	24.7	−2.87	0.005

Numbers represent the average of the summated scores across participants, stratified by intention to stay. Higher scores represent favorable work environment (e.g., more opportunities to grow, less stress, etc.). t Test represents the statistic testing whether the mean among those indenting to stay is equal to the mean among those who are not intending to stay.

with fivefold increase in the odds of intending to stay (OR = 5.04, $p < 0.001$). One standard deviation increase in the summated score representing opportunities to grow was associated with 3.5-fold increase in intention to stay (OR = 3.46, $p < 0.004$). Summary scores representing relationship with supervisors, peers, conflict, and organization rating were not statistically significantly associated with intention to stay.

Table 5. Multiple logistic regression modeling intention to stay.

	Odds ratio	z	p > |z|
Female[a]	12.8	2.42	0.016
Black[a]	0.30	−1.59	0.112
Hispanic[a]	0.73	−0.41	0.684
Birth cohort	1.49	−2.20	0.028
Supervisor/Manager[a]	1.63	0.74	0.460
Organization	0.43	−1.52	0.129
Peers	2.28	1.60	0.110
Stress	5.04	3.38	0.001
Growth	3.46	2.90	0.004
Supervisor	0.87	−0.38	0.701
Conflict	1.43	1.23	0.218

[a]Reference groups are male, white/other race and caseworker. Reported numbers are odds ratios from a multiple logistic regression model that predicts intending to stay (vs. not intending to stay), z test statistic and p value for each coefficient. Workplace environment summary scores were standardized (rescaled to have a mean of zero and a standard deviation of one).

Qualitative results

Analysis of open-ended questions descriptively expands on elements of the quantitative investigation of respondents' work environment and adds a second dimension: how respondents' views of their social work education factored into their perceived abilities to apply their knowledge and skills to the workplace. The numerical distribution of themes and the nature of comments entered in response to prompts about the reasons to stay or leave, thoughts about secondary employment, challenges and opportunities to use skills, taking classes with a cohort, and reflections on educational experience provide insight into how these MSWs, with distinct career intentions, envisaged their work and their role within the agency. Together, their perceptions provide an overall picture of their engagement as child welfare employees. The themes are summarized in Table 6, the column designated as (−), denoting a negative or adverse experience.

Reasons to leave and reasons to stay

Although there were some commonalities across subgroups in the reasons given to stay or leave, discreet differences appeared in responses, according to both inclination and position. Respondents expressing commitment to stay among both managers and caseworkers responded nearly unanimously, with multi-themed comments in two-thirds of instances. By contrast, only half the managers and one-third of caseworkers who disagreed with intentions to stay offered comments, most of which were single themed. Conversely, responses by managers and caseworkers intent to leave were more prolific with regard to *reasons to leave*, offering multi-themed comments in more than half of their responses; managers and caseworkers intent

Table 6. Open-ended response distribution.

Theme	MStay	(−)	MLeave	(−)	CWStay	(−)	CWLeave	(−)
Reasons to stay/leave	53	10	8	8	40	11	10	26
A–D financial/work conditions	17	2	4	−	18	2	5	5
E–F job satisfaction; relationships	13	1	2	−	7	1	−	2
G–K person/work	18	−	−	3	11	−	2	9
L–Q person/system	5	7	2	5	4	8	3	10
Secondary employment	26	−	5	−	15	−	5	−
Financial reasons	11	−	1	−	4	−	1	−
Growth opportunities; use clinical skills	12	−	2	−	9	−	4	−
Expand or replace	3	−	2	−	2	−	−	−
Use of skills/challenges in using kills	73	35	15	13	42	23	7	25
Reform related	6	−	2	−	−	−	−	−
To transform practice	20	−	3	−	6	−	7	−
Individual practice challenges	−	17	−	3	−	10	−	11
Systemic challenges	−	11	−	6	−	10	−	9
Cohort	102	4	16	3	40	6	−	5
Cohort relationships	41	3	12	−	21	2	18	4
Networking opportunities	12	−	3	−	4	−	7	−
Child welfare focus	16	1	1	3	15	4	6	1
Educational experience	116	4	39	1	87	5	47	4
Field education	36	4	8	1	17	3	13	5
Academics	26	−	8	−	35	−	15	−
Program structure	20	−	16	−	12	−	12	1
Supports	17	−	3	−	12	−	6	−
Appreciate opportunity	11	−	3	−	8	−	6	−
Transformative	7	−	1	−	3	−	1	−

Notes: (−) denotes a negative attribute or challenge. Totals reflect counts for all themes in the group, but only thematic categories of interest with several responses were included as subcategories.

to stay responded only sparsely. The distribution of responses also varied according to the broad characterizations assigned.

Financial/Work conditions

Financial considerations and favorable job conditions were prominent among themes associated with reasons to stay for all subgroups. Respondents across all subgroups cited job security, benefits, and salaries higher than in the private sector as reasons to stay. Difficult working conditions, perceived unfairness in promotional decisions, stress, and burnout appeared among reasons to leave for respondents, even when they expressed satisfaction and commitment to the job:

> **CWLeave**: I enjoy this job. However, the level of stress whether you are a worker or a supervisor, is very high. I plan to stay for a few more years. I hope to find employment that is relevant to helping children and families in our communities.
> **MLeave**: The amount of stress associated with being an effective employee in this agency is too great and I feel burnt out. I would like a job where the level of stress, anxiety and liability is much less.

Job satisfaction

Satisfaction with the job and the nature of relationships with coworkers and supervisors were closely related to personal fulfillment in respondent comments. Noticeably absent among those intent to leave, the comments were frequent among managers and caseworkers who expressed intentions to remain on the job:

> **MStay**: I actually enjoy my job. I always have. I believe in our mission and vision and want to instill in my staff the best possible case practice skills and that hard work pays off.
>
> **CStay**: I truly love and believe in what I do! The time and energy I have devoted to this career is not something that can easily be replaced and the children and families that I serve deserve to have the best available to them.

Relationship of person/work

Feeling valued and the presence of opportunities for advancement were prominent themes associated with commitment to the work and staying on the job:

> **CStay**: I believe in the work we do and I feel valued as an employee.
>
> **MStay**: I will remain ... for the foreseeable future since I enjoy my current position and feel valued at the office. I feel stable and content in my position, and I feel confident in continued success and promotional opportunities at my current office.

Lack of recognition and limited ability to utilize skills were among the themes recorded by managers and caseworkers inclined to leave:

> **CWLeave**: I plan to leave because I am not putting my skills to practice and feel that I am devalued by the organization ... I prefer to work somewhere where my skills are put to use and where I feel more important.
>
> **MLeave**: I do not feel I can really use my MSW and feel unappreciated and unrecognized for my work.

Organizational relationships: person/system

Themes relating to the relationship of person/system appeared in comments by a few respondents across all four subgroups as both *reasons to stay* and *reasons to leave*. Discordance between what respondents had learned in their MSW studies and actual practice on the ground, despite the reforms of case practice, was a common theme viewed in organizational terms:

> **CWLeave**: ...The reality is that in order to work from this [social work] mindset, the entire agency needs to support this change ... while the Division has supported engagement, many supervisors, casework supervisors, and managers are still operating from a forensic or old framework and if they are not accepting [of] the Division's new approach, then no significant changes will be made in working with families.

This was echoed in a perceived lack of professional autonomy by some caseworkers:

> **CWLeave**: Even though the Division has been improving in service delivery to families, it is still a place where workers do not have a say in how cases should be handled. Too often in my experience have I been forced to deal with problems with families in ways that are not congruent with social work ethics and my knowledge of this field and experience is not taken into account ...

Respondents committed to a career in public child welfare were more apt to offer positive comments about system changes and their perceived role within the agency's changing orientation:

> **MStay**: There is opportunity ... to shape case practice in an effort to mold it so it mirrors social work. I have a chance to teach and model behaviors to staff and change the approach used when dealing with clients.

Plans and challenges in the application of skills

Respondents across all subgroups answered most of the questions about their MSW educational experience and its relationship to their current work and ability to apply skills with near unanimity. While responses were generally short and to the point, many addressed multiple themes, sometimes adding detail to previous responses. Respondents across all subgroups mentioned the ability to apply what they had learned in their day to day work and also addressed various challenges in applying those skills. Indications of no challenges were proportionately higher among those intent to stay and challenges, signified as (–) in Table 6, more prevalent among caseworkers.

Reform, case practice change, and passing it on

Themes referenced the relevance of what respondents had learned to positive changes in case practice at the agency and to their own efforts to transform practice among coworkers and fellow managers. These transformative aspects were particularly prevalent among managers and caseworkers intent to stay:

> **CWStay**: I have already begun to use my skills. The way I approach children, families, and co-workers has changed. My perspective is guided by more compassion, critical thinking, and listening/assessment tools.
>
> **MStay**: ...My experiences will allow me to assist other co-workers, who were not fortunate enough to complete the program, progress in their skill set.

Caseworkers and managers inclined to leave also mentioned their use of skills, if less frequently:

CWLeave: The skills I learned in my Program I use every day while I am in the field. I also share my knowledge with coworkers so that they may better serve their families.

MLeave: I use the skills I have acquired to complement our case practice with families through direct supervision and modeling of behavior/language.

Challenges in applying skills

Caseworkers and managers inclined to leave tended to express the constraints they were confronted with in applying skills learned in graduate school more than their peers who were intent to stay. Many affirmed that they used social work skills in individual practice with clients but were not as confident about the broader change project at the agency. Lack of management support or differences with peers or supervisors was also prevalent in comments, particularly among caseworkers:

CWLeave: Despite all the knowledge learned in the [...] program, management still does not validate that front line workers have the knowledge to make better decisions for families ... [The] other important challenge is that my supervisor does not have a MSW and many times we do not agree with ways to work with families.

While managers inclined to stay were most effusive about their use of knowledge acquired through their supervisory role, some inclined to leave saw their abilities as constrained:

MLeave: Being able to help families in their best interest is challenging when policy does not allow you to help in a way that would be beneficial.

Perceptions of challenges in applying skills were ubiquitous among most caseworkers and among supervisors intent to leave but were not absent among managers inclined to stay, about half of whom registered at least some challenges in applying MSW skills:

MStay: [Applying the skills] ... is not always easy to do; it may be one of the most challenging things about the experience ... that the learning can't easily be used to influence the organization.

Yet, managers committed to staying in child welfare frequently noted both commitment to and upper management support for practice change. While challenges were evident, those inclined to stay among caseworkers and managers tended to express confidence that their persistence in overcoming those challenges would ultimately impact the nature of practice:

CWStay: [Despite] resistance from supervisors or peers who are not educated in the SW field, [I] continue to advocate for families and case plans that are consistent with what I believe will have the best impact on the family.

MStay: The challenges I face in applying my skills are widespread ... [but] I have been using my skills to help staff think differently about what case practice used to look like and where it must be in the future. Change is slow; however, I am starting to see some changes within my office.

Educational and field experiences

Although not formally included as part of this study, respondents' ratings of their relative competency before and after MSW study indicate progressive confidence in their abilities after graduation, with little or no differences between those who expressed intentions to stay or to leave. The differences appeared, however, in how respective respondents portrayed their educational experiences in their open-ended question responses. The distribution and nature of themes among those strongly committed to a career in public child welfare and those who indicated a desire to leave provide additional insight into how respondents conceived of their MSW education in relationship to their work. For those intent to stay, responses to questions about their education were more often multi-themed and expansive. They tended to gravitate, in their responses, toward aspects of their education that enhanced knowledge of child welfare and professional opportunities within this domain. They were, overall, somewhat more positive about the nature of their educational experience, offering details about professors or courses important to their professional development, or examples of field experiences that were particularly meaningful, including those within the agency. Respondents among managers and caseworkers with intention to stay were also more likely than their peers to seek out opportunities for secondary employment that were oriented toward their further professional growth.

The cohort/child welfare focus

Overall, respondents commented extensively and nearly all commented positively about the central role of their cohort as both supportive and professionally useful. Comments were most often expansive among respondents inclined to stay and touched on the advantages of meeting and working with peers from different regions of the state and from a diverse range of positions:

> CStay: I enjoyed taking classes as part of a cohort. It was a good opportunity to get to know DCF employees from other parts of the state and other areas of child welfare practice.
> MStay: Working with a cohort gave me the opportunity to learn about different case practice and needs in other parts of the state. It also gave me the opportunity to create working relationships with others in the same agency that have enhanced my resources after the completion of the program. I strongly believe that a cohort

is beneficial not only for the student but also for the agency as a whole, as it creates a group of staff that have invested in the work and beliefs of the agency ...

The role of these relationships with respect to later career opportunities was not lost:

> **MStay**: ...[I] learned more about the organization than I would have if I didn't enter ... [the] program—built relationships for advancements within the organization.

While managers and caseworkers who indicated a greater predisposition to leave were also generally positive about the advantages of their cohort experience, there was a tendency among these respondents to be more circumspect:

> **CLeave** The cohorts were fine. [I] ... had the opportunity to learn how other areas within the organization function and/or at least what staff's perspectives were with regard to [agency] policies and practices ...

The social bonds seemed less strong for at least some inclined to leave. A few case workers intent to leave would have preferred to take classes with students not exclusively employed in child welfare:

> **CWLeave**: Positive: you get to form relationships with those in your cohort ... negative: not enough exposure to other opinions and professions.

Field education

Most comments were positive about field internships, particularly those outside the agency, which tended to be more clinically oriented. However, caseworkers inclined to leave tended to be most critical about in-agency placements:

> **CWLeave**: Internal [division] placement was redundant and virtually useless. However, I gained so much knowledge from my external placement.

By contrast, managers and case workers intent to stay, while they were not uncritical of placements within the agency, often registered their appreciation of internal field experiences as opportunities to broaden their knowledge about the work of the agency and as favorable to later career advancement:

> **CWStay**: My in [division] field placement also was very helpful to my professional development, as I was able to do my placement out of my office and in a different position.

> **CWStay**: I feel that I had the opportunity to work closely with a very dedicated and talented [in-agency] Supervisor, who has long since become my mentor and guide in my career.

Transforming practice

While comments about the educational and field experience and the structure of the program were positive overall, they tended to be more plentiful and multi-themed among managers and caseworkers intent to stay. The notion of the educational experience as transformative was taken up particularly by managers and caseworkers who had expressed commitment to a continuing career in public child welfare. The theme carried over from these respondents' earlier comments on their reasons to stay—their full engagement in extending their acquired knowledge and skills to others in order to transform practice:

> **MStay:** As I was completing each course, I would pass the knowledge down to my unit. I would constantly evaluate the practice in my unit and how we worked with families. I have been able to provide knowledge and answers to questions that I was not able to before. Meshing this knowledge in a supervisory level allows me to influence my staff with social work values which they hopefully filter to their peers.
>
> **MStay:** ... [The program] has made me a better employee, supervisor and most important of all, advocate for the children and families we serve. I believe that the learning process is essential to our growth as social workers and that this program will have a lasting positive impact on the case practice of the Division.

Discussion

This mixed-methods study has provided an opportunity to examine relationships between future career intentions, workplace environment, and employee engagement (Travis & Mor Barak, 2010) among specially selected public child welfare workers who pursued an MSW while they worked full time and their agency instituted major reforms. The study also demonstrates the utility of combining qualitative and quantitative strategies of analysis to explore complex problems relevant to both practice and research. Indeed, researchers moved between quantitative qualitative results to inform complementary aspects of the research, as well as to query the meaning of the results overall.

Among respondents in the sample, intention to stay in child welfare was favorable, at 68%, and higher among supervisors/managers (79%) than caseworkers (57%). Once personal and work environment variables were controlled for, however, supervisor/manager status had no significant effect on intention to stay. Multivariate analyses identified four variables that made it significantly more likely for respondents to stay: female gender, older age, lower stress levels, and opportunities for growth.

Qualitative results complemented and expanded on the results of quantitative analysis, while providing a more nuanced picture of the motivations and circumstances surrounding career intentions. For example, supervisor/manager status may not itself have been a significant factor in intentions to stay or leave, but observations of qualitative data show that greater levels of autonomy, authority, recognition, and opportunities for growth were often integral to the status, which was also associated with age and experience or tenure. Respondents in management positions were more likely to express intentions to stay. Fully half had moved into the role since they began their MSW education, direct evidence of growth opportunities.

The study's qualitative analysis suggests that respondents' intentions were indicative of more than just their career plans. Intentions to leave signaled not only respondents' dissatisfaction with the concrete circumstances of their work environment but a degree of personal disengagement in their work. Those who expressed intentions to leave recounted excessive stress, lack of recognition, insufficient autonomy, and few opportunities for growth. If they were able to practice what they had learned, they tended to do so individually, cautiously, and often felt that their work had little effect on broader system change. By contrast, respondents who expressed intentions to continue their careers in public child welfare presented as engaged and enthusiastic about their work, with manage-able levels of stress; they felt valued and recognized professionally and tended to have a broader systemic focus.

These distinctions carried into respective respondents' perceptions of their social work educational experiences. Those engaged and intent on staying were more effusive in their depictions of the relevance of their education to their work and career prospects, generally appreciated its child welfare focus and reaped benefits from their cohort relationships in terms of support, mentorship, and potential career advances. Those inclined towards leaving and less engaged were, by contrast, somewhat cooler in their assessment of their child welfare focused educational experience and tended to focus skill acquisition on its potential uses elsewhere.

The analysis reaches preliminary conclusions about the relationships between intention, work environment, and engagement. Yet, the results of this study capture impressions during a specific moment in time, albeit one that varied considerably, according to when the respondent graduated and when they completed the exit survey. The evolution of child welfare reforms in the state variably affected staffing shifts and promotional opportunities, during this period, as well as changes in case practice, which were implemented regionally (Deglau et al., 2015). The timing and roll-out of the changes likely influenced individual responses to the survey.

A shift in circumstances, whether it concerned a promotion, a change in the immediate work environment, or a growth opportunity, might concei-vably create a very different dynamic for individual respondents. Impressions, intentions, and even retrospective assessments of graduate social work experiences could change, as both personal and institutional circumstances changed.

The latter may very well have happened in ensuing years, to judge from actual retention rates for program participants at the 3-year post-service commitment mark for each cohort, which ranged from 90% to 95% (Akincigil, Ray, & Deglau, 2013; Department of Children and Families, n.d.).

Limitations

This study has several limitations. Passage of time was a significant limitation of the study. Staggered administration of the survey, because of the pattern of degree completion, presented challenges. This concerned both the evolving institutional context of a child welfare system in the midst of reform and variation in the intervals from graduation to survey, which may each have skewed respondents' perceptions of the work environment and affected retrospective interpretations of social work education, as already noted above. Anonymity of the survey also presented another challenge, as it prohibited matching respondents' future intentions to remain in the field with actual retention outcomes. While the context of the study and its design raise several questions as to the potential generalizability of its conclusions, the study itself provides an important object lesson about both the importance and challenges of conducting evaluative research during a formative period of program development and institutional change. If the findings of the study are far from conclusive and should be interpreted with caution, the questions raised are imperative to future study of intention, engagement, and workplace in similar contexts of program change.

Implications

This study has a number of implications for public child welfare agencies considering how to make the most productive use of limited training and workforce development dollars. The study demonstrates that investment in providing employee access to graduate social work education can produce tangible benefits for the workforce that extends well beyond individual employees. More than simply individual retention, which is apparent, professionalization from within builds on and adds value to the knowledge and expertise already present in the agency. It enhances social capital within the workforce (Boyas et al., 2013, 2015) and overall workplace morale. Offering even a limited number of employees the earned opportunity to pursue graduate education extends that knowledge out to others in the agency and reinforces an organizational culture of professionalism (Ellett, 2009). It also creates a cadre of future leadership that has both credibility and expertise.

For agencies seeking to reform their child welfare systems, credibility gained experientially combined with MSW knowledge, skills, and values is an important asset (Ahn et al., 2016; Deglau et al. 2009; McGuire et al., 2011). Welcoming new and credentialed social workers to public child welfare service at the onset of their careers is important to develop a competent workforce but cannot make up for seasoned experience and professional expertise committed to institutional and practice change.

This study has demonstrated that age, levels of stress, and opportunities for growth matter, with respect to respondents' future intentions and by implication, their engagement with their work. This was evident as much while students were in school as when they continued or moved into new responsibilities as MSWs. Cohorts played an important role for students across all age groups with respect to professional growth, mentorship, support, and the mitigation of stress. For many, similar to findings by Altman and Cohen (2016), involvement with a cohort has continued to play an important role, made evident in graduates' continuing communications with the program, and in participation at school-wide alumni and agency events. The supports, networking, and mentorship that developed organically through cohorts suggest that educational models directed to child welfare and other human service employees should consider providing opportunities for participants to find common ground, bond, and build networks of professional relationships.

In order to sustain engagement with the employees in whom it has invested, child welfare agencies need to recognize and nourish similar supports and implement others to help staff deal with stress and to enable them to continue professional development (Clark, Smith, & Uota, 2013; Fitch, Parker-Barua, & Watt, 2014). What this might look like may well differ by age and according to where employees are in their careers. It is clear, however, that opportunities for continued growth and a means to recognize and make full use of the expertise and potential contributions of MSWs are essential for their continued engagement.

Acknowledgments

We acknowledge the continuing service of the public child welfare employees who completed their MSW through this program and remember their colleague and our student, Leticia Zindell.

Funding

Data collection concerned graduates for whom MSW education was in full or in part supported by a grant from the Department of Children and Families, the State of New Jersey, from 2006 to 2010, although no grant funding supported the study.

References

Ahn, H., Keyser, D., & Hayward-Everson, R. (2016). A multi-level analysis of individual and agency effects on implementation of family-centered practice in child welfare. *Children and Youth Services Review, 69*, 11–18. doi:10.1016/j.childyouth.2016.07.014

Akincigil, A., Ray, A., & Deglau, E. (2013, November). *Career trajectories of public child welfare employees: Outcomes for MSW graduates.* Paper presented at the Council on Social Work Education 59th Annual Program Meeting, Dallas, Texas.

Altman, J. C., & Cohen, C. S. (2016). "I could not have made it without them": Examining trainee cohort perspectives on MSW education for public child welfare. *Journal of Public Child Welfare, 10*(5), 524.

Auerbach, C., McGowan, B., & Laporte, H. (2008). How does professional education impact the job outlook of public child welfare workers. *Journal of Public Child Welfare, 2*(3), 55–76.

Bagdasaryan, S. (2012). Social work education and title IV-E program participation as predictors of entry-level knowledge among public child welfare workers. *Children and Youth Services Review, 34*, 1590–1597. doi:10.1016/j.childyouth.2012.04.013

Bednar, S. G. (2003). Elements of satisfying organizational climates in child welfare agencies. *Families in Society: the Journal of Contemporary Human Services, 84*(1), 7–12.

Benton, A. D. (2016). Understanding the diverging paths of stayers and leavers: An examination of factors predicting worker retention. *Children and Youth Services Review, 65*, 70–77. doi:10.1016/j.childyouth.2016.04.006

Blome, W. W., & Steib, S. D. (2014). The organizational structure of child welfare: Staff are working hard, but it is hardly working. *Children and Youth Services Review, 44*, 181–188. doi:10.1016/j.childyouth.2014.06.018

Boyas, J., & Wind, L. H. (2010). Employment-based social capital, job stress, and employee burnout: A public child welfare employee structural model. *Children and Youth Services Review, 32*, 380–388. doi:10.1016/j.childyouth.2009.10.009

Boyas, J., Wind, L. H., & Kang, S. (2012). Exploring the relationship between employment-based social capital, job stress, burnout, and intent to leave among child protection workers: An age-based path analysis model. *Children and Youth Services Review, 34*, 50–62. doi:10.1016/j.childyouth.2011.08.033

Boyas, J. F., Wind, L. H., & Ruiz, E. (2013). Organizational tenure among child welfare workers, burnout, stress, and intent to leave: Does employment-based social capital make a difference? *Children and Youth Services Review, 35*, 1657–1669. doi:10.1016/j.childyouth.2013.07.008

Boyas, J. F., Wind, L. H., & Ruiz, E. (2015). Exploring patterns of employee psychosocial outcomes among child welfare workers. *Children and Youth Services Review, 52*, 174–183. doi:10.1016/j.childyouth.2014.11.002

Brimhall, K. C., Mor Barak, M. E., Hurlburt, M., McArdle, J. J., Palinkas, L., & Henwood, B. (2017). Increasing workplace inclusion: The promise of leader-member exchange. *Human Service Organizations: Management, Leadership & Governance, 41*(3), 222–239. doi:10.1080/23303131.2016.1251522

Cahalane, H., & Sites, E. W. (2008). The climate of child welfare employee retention. *Child Welfare, 87*(1), 114.

Clark, S. J., Smith, R. J., & Uota, K. (2013). Professional development opportunities as retention incentives in child welfare. *Children and Youth Services Review, 35*, 1687–1697. doi:10.1016/j.childyouth.2013.07.006

Collins-Camargo, C., & Royse, D. (2010). A study of the relationships among effective supervision, organizational culture promoting evidence-based practice, and worker self-efficacy in public child welfare. *Journal of Public Child Welfare, 4*(1), 1.

Deglau, E., Meyers, R., & Cho, M. (2009, November). *Evaluating MSW education for public child welfare employees: concepts, strategies, outcomes.* Panel presented at the Council on Social Work Education 55th Annual Program Meeting, San Antonio, Texas.

Deglau, E., Ray, A., Carre-Lee, N., Waldman, W., Conway, F., Cunningham, K., ... Powell, T. (2015). Practice change in child welfare: The interface of training and social work education. *Journal of Social Work Education, Special Edition: University-Child Welfare Agency Partnerships: Innovative Strategies to Advance Child Welfare Competency and Positive Workforce Outcomes, 51*(Supplement 2), S153–S172.

Deglau, E., Ray, A., Edwards, R. L., Carre-Lee, N., Harrison, T., & Cunningham, K. (2014). Transferring MSW education to practice: A qualitative study with public child welfare employees. *Journal of Public Child Welfare, 8*(3), 304–325.

Department of Children and Families, State of New Jersey. (n.d.). *PCWIW grads DCF Universe 2006-2016.* Human Resources Data Set (unpublished).

Dickinson, N., & Perry, R. (2002). Factors influencing the retention of specially educated public child welfare workers. In K. Briar-Lawson & J. Levy-Zlotnik (Eds.), *Evaluation research in child welfare: Improving outcomes through university-public agency partnerships* (pp. 89–103). New York, NY: The Haworth Press.

Ellett, A. J. (2009). Intentions to remain employed in child welfare: The role of human caring, self-efficacy, and professional organizational culture. *Children and Youth Services Review, 31*, 78–88.

Faller, K. C., Grabarek, M., & Ortega, R. M. (2010). Commitment to child welfare work: What predicts leaving and staying? *Children and Youth Services Review, 32*(6), 840–846.

Fernandes, G. M. (2016). Organizational climate and child welfare workers' degree of intent to leave the job: Evidence from New York. *Children and Youth Services Review, 60*, 80–87. doi:10.1016/j.childyouth.2015.11.010

Fitch, D., Parker-Barua, L., & Watt, J. W. (2014). Envisioning public child welfare agencies as learning organizations: Applying Beer's viable system model to title IV-E program evaluation. *Journal of Public Child Welfare, 8*(2), 119.

Gansle, K. A., & Ellett, A. J. (2002). Child welfare knowledge transmission, practitioner retention, and university-consortium impact: A study of title IV-E child welfare training. *Journal of Health and Social Policy, 15*, 69–88.

Griffiths, A., Royse, D., Culver, K., Piescher, K., & Zhang, Y. (2017). Who stays, who goes, who knows? A state-wide survey of child welfare workers. *Children and Youth Services Review, 77*, 110–117. doi:10.1016/j.childyouth.2017.04.012

Hartinger-Saunders, R., & Lyons, P. (2013). Social work education and public child welfare: A review of the peer-reviewed literature on title IV-E funded programs. *Journal of Public Child Welfare, 7*(3), 275.

Hopkins, K., Mudrick, N., & Rudolph, C. (1999). Impact of university agency partnership in child welfare on organizations, workers, and work activities. *Child Welfare, 78*(6), 749–773.

Johnco, C., Salloum, A., Olson, K. R., & Edwards, L. M. (2014). Child welfare workers' perspectives on contributing factors to retention and turnover: Recommendations for improvement. *Children and Youth Services Review, 47*, 397–407. doi:10.1016/j.childyouth.2014.10.016

Jones, L. P. (2002). A follow-up of title IV-E program's graduates retention rates in a public child welfare agency. In K. Briar-Lawson & J. Levy-Zlotnik (Eds.), *Evaluation research in child welfare: Improving outcomes through university-public agency partnerships* (pp. 39–52). New York, NY: The Haworth Press.

Jones, L. P., & Okamura, A. (2000). Reprofessionalizing child welfare services: An evaluation of a Title IV-E training program. *Research on Social Work Practice, 10*, 607–621.

Kim, A., & Mor Barak, M. E. (2015). The mediating roles of leader–Member exchange and perceived organizational support in the role stress–Turnover intention relationship among child welfare workers: A longitudinal analysis. *Children and Youth Services Review, 52*, 135–143. doi:10.1016/j.childyouth.2014.11.009

Kruzich, J. M., Mienko, J. A., & Courtney, M. E. (2014). Individual and work group influences on turnover intention among public child welfare workers: The effects of work group psychological safety. *Children and Youth Services Review, 42*, 20–27. doi:10.1016/j.childyouth.2014.03.005

Landsman, M. (2007). Supporting child welfare supervisors to improve worker retention. *Child Welfare, 86*(2), 105–124.

Lee, J., Forster, M., & Rehner, T. (2011). The retention of public child welfare workers: The roles of professional organizational culture and coping strategies. *Children and Youth Services Review, 33*, 102–109.

Lewandowski, C. (1998). Retention outcomes of a public child welfare long-term training program. *Professional Development; The International Journal of Continuing Social Work Education, 1*(2), 38–46.

Lizano, E. L., & Mor Barak, M. E. (2012). Workplace demands and resources as antecedents of job burnout among public child welfare workers: A longitudinal study. *Children and Youth Services Review, 34*, 1769–1776. doi:10.1016/j.childyouth.2012.02.006

Mason, S. E., LaPorte, H. H., Bronstein, L., & Auerbach, C. (2012). Child welfare workers' perceptions of the value of social work education. *Social Work Education, 34*(9), 1735–1741.

Mathias, C., Gilman, E., Shin, C., & Evans, W. T. (2015). California's title IV-E partnership: A statewide University–agency collaboration—characteristics and implications for replication. *Journal of Social Work Education, 51*, S270. doi:10.1080/10437797.2015.1073082

McCrae, J. S., Scannapieco, M., Leake, R., Potter, C. C., Menefee, D., Schudrich, W. Z., & McGowan, B. (2014). Who's on board? child welfare worker reports of buy-in and readiness for organizational change. *Children and Youth Services Review, 37*, 28–35.

McGuire, L. E., Howes, P., Murphy-Nugen, A., & George, K. (2011). Leadership as advocacy: The impact of a title IV-E supported MSW education on a public child welfare agency. *Journal of Public Child Welfare, 5*(2), 213.

Mor Barak, M. E., Levin, A., Nissly, J. A., & Lane, C. J. (2006). Why do they leave? Modeling child welfare workers' turnover intentions. *Children and Youth Services Review, 28*, 548–577. doi:10.1016/j.childyouth.2005.06.003

Mor Barak, M. E., Lizano, E. L., Kim, A., Duan, L., Rhee, M., Hsiao, H., & Brimhall, K. C. (2016). The promise of diversity management for climate of inclusion: A state-of-the-art review and meta-analysis. *Human Service Organizations: Management, Leadership & Governance, 40*(4), 305–333. doi:10.1080/23303131.2016.1138915

Nissly, J. A. (2004). Workforce survey (Appendix, pp. 235-242), in Prospective and retrospective examinations of factors related to intention to leave and turnover among public child welfare workers. *Dissertation Abstracts International.Section A: Humanities and Social Sciences, 65*(09), 3572.

Nissly, J. A., Barak, M. E. M., & Levin, A. (2005). Stress, social support, and workers' intentions to leave their jobs in public child welfare. *Administration in Social Work, 29*(1), 79–100.

Reed-Ashcraft, K., Westbrook, T. M., & Williams, E. (2012). North Carolina's child welfare education collaborative (NCCWEC): One state's long-term commitment toward an improved workforce. *Journal of Public Child Welfare, 6*(4), 425.

Scannapieco, M., & Connell-Carrick, K. (2003). Do collaborations with schools of social work make a difference for the field of child welfare? Practice, retention, and curriculum. *Journal of Human Behavior in the Social Environment, 7*(1/2), 35–51.

Scannapieco, M., & Connell-Carrick, K. (2007). Child welfare workplace: The state of the workforce and strategies to improve retention. *Child Welfare, 86*(6), 31–52.

Scannapieco, M., Hegar, R. L., & Connell-Carrick, K. (2012). Professionalization in public child welfare: Historical context and workplace outcomes for social workers and non-social workers. *Children and Youth Services Review, 34*(11), 2170–2178.

Shim, M. (2010). Factors influencing child welfare employees' turnover: Focusing on organizational culture and climate. *Children and Youth Services Review, 32*(6), 847–856.

Smith, B. D. (2005). Job retention in child welfare: Effects of perceived organizational support, supervisor support, and intrinsic job value. *Children and Youth Services Review, 27*(2), 153–169.

Thompson, H. M., Wojciak, A. S., & Cooley, M. E. (2017). Through their lens: Case managers' experiences of the child welfare system. *Qualitative Social Work, 16*(3), 411.

Travis, D. J., Gomez, R. J., & Mor Barak, M. E. (2011). Speaking up and stepping back: Examining the link between employee voice and job neglect. *Children and Youth Services Review, 33*, 1831-1841. doi:10.1016/j.childyouth.2011.05.008

Travis, D. J., Lizano, E. L., & Mor Barak, M. E. (2016). 'I'm so stressed!': A longitudinal model of stress, burnout and engagement among social workers in child welfare settings. *British Journal of Social Work, 46*(4), 1076–1095. doi:10.1093/bjsw/bct205

Travis, D. J., & Mor Barak, M. E. (2010). Fight or flight? Factors influencing child welfare workers' propensity to seek positive change or disengage from their jobs. *Journal of Social Service Research, 36*(3), 188–205.

Westbrook, T. M., Ellis, J., & Ellet, A. J. (2006). Improving retention among public child welfare workers: What can we learn from the insights and experiences of committed survivors? *Administration in Social Work, 30*(4), 37–62.

Whitaker, T., & Clark, E. (2006). Social workers in child welfare: Ready for duty. *Research on Social Work Practice, 16*(4), 406–411.

Williams, S. E., Nichols, Q. L., Kirk, A., & Wilson, T. (2011). A recent look at the factors influencing workforce retention in public child welfare. *Children and Youth Services Review, 33*, 157–160. doi:10.1016/j.childyouth.2010.08.028

Yankeelov, P., Barbee, A., Sullivan, D., & Antle, B. (2009). Individual and organizational factors in job retention in Kentucky's child welfare agency. *Child and Youth Services Review, 31*, 547–554.

Zeitlin, W., Augsberger, A., Auerbach, C., & McGowan, B. (2014). A mixed-methods study of the impact of organizational culture on workforce retention in child welfare. *Children and Youth Services Review, 38*, 36–43. doi:10.1016/j.childyouth.2014.01.004

Zlotnik, J. L., DePanfilis, D., Daining, C., & McDermott Lane, M. (2005). *Professional education for child welfare practice: Improving retention in public child welfare agencies (IASWR Research Brief 2)*. Washington, DC: Institute for the Advancement of Social Work Research.

"I was prepared for the worst I guess": S tayers'and leavers' perceptions of their Title IV-E education

Amy D. Benton and Michelle Iglesias

ABSTRACT

Child welfare workforces across the nation are experiencing high turnover and have for decades. The chronic cost of turnover makes efforts to increase retention crucial. The Title IV-E education stipend program is one way that many states employ to improve their child welfare worker tenure. Through qualitative interviews, this study examines Title IV-E graduates' experiences and perceptions of preparedness for working in child welfare agencies. Examining how the responses of stayers and leavers differ and assessing similarities collectively can inform educational and agency enhancements to improve services, as well as worker competence and retention.

Child welfare workforces across the nation are experiencing high turnover and have for decades (Faller et al., 2009; Strolin-Goltzman, Auerbach, McGowan, & McCarthy, 2007; Strolin-Goltzman et al., 2009). Struggles with staff retention may be inevitable given the stressful nature of child welfare work (Barth, Lloyd, Christ, Chapman, & Dickinson, 2008; Specht & Courtney, 1994). One of the three most reported issues by child welfare agencies is difficulties in recruiting and retaining caseworkers (Government Accountability Office, 2006). With an estimated cost of 110% of the caseworker's average salary to replace the lost worker (Nguyen, 2013), the chronic cost of turnover makes efforts to increase retention crucial. The Title IV-E education stipend program is one way that many states employ to improve their child welfare worker tenure (Social Work Policy Institute, 2012). The Department of Health and Human Services, Administration for Children and Families has requested 1.8 billion dollars over the next 10 years under the 2017 fiscal budget proposal for Title-IV education stipends (U.S. DHHS, 2017). Research that assists in identifying the best practices to retain these specially trained workers will maximize the Title IV-E investment.

Literature review

The needs of child welfare utilizers began outpacing the turnout of a qualified workforce, in part, due to changes in federal law during the 1960s that uncoupled social service provision from welfare financial supports (Briar-Lawson, 2014; Ellett, 2014). This divide grew further in the 1970s when new federal reporting mandates created an influx in child abuse and neglect reports (Ellett, 2014; McGuire, Howes, Murphy-Nugen, & George, 2011). Agencies were underprepared and short staffed for the number of cases being reported. Hiring requirements were reduced by agencies across the nation to address the staff shortage as it was thought that social work education requirements acted as a barrier to larger candidate pools (Ellett, 2009). The resulting impact on the child welfare workforce is often discussed in terms of the resulting de-professionalization of workers. Public agencies continue to struggle "with attracting and retaining qualified employees and this struggle has interfered greatly with the provision of quality services to clients" (Ellett, 2009, p. 78).

Title IV-E is the primary source of federal funding to strengthen the professionalism of the child welfare workforce (Briar-Lawson, 2014; NASW, 2003). A fundamental approach for provision and oversight of Title IV-E programs at the state level is through the formation of university–agency partnerships (Briar-Lawson, 2014; Vonk, Newsome, & Bronson, 2003; Zlotnik, 2002). Through these partnerships, Master of Social Work (MSW) students with and without current child welfare experience are educated and trained to provide competent, ethical services to children and families.

Title IV-E programs have shown promising results for reprofessionalizing child welfare. Social work degrees in professional child welfare overall are on the incline. The results of a 2008 survey found almost 50% of child welfare workers held social work degrees (Barth et al., 2008). This was an improvement on the estimates of the 1970s where only 28% of child welfare workers had social work degrees (Ellett, 2014). Efforts under the Title IV-E education partnership directly contribute to this improvement (Ellett, 2014).

Additionally, research indicates that Title IV-E programs are successful in preparing MSWs to work in public child welfare (Jones & Okamura, 2000; Vonk et al., 2003). Bagdasaryan (2012) found that Title IV-E MSWs significantly scored higher on knowledge tests than MSWs who did not participate in Title IV-E ($p < .01$). Studies further suggest that Title IV-E participants have longer tenures than non-Title IV-E participants (Jones, 2002; Madden, Scannapieco, & Painter, 2014; Rosenthal & Waters, 2006). Examining career trajectories over 3 years, Madden et al. (2014) discovered that Title IV-E participants were 1.28 times more likely to remain employed than non-Title IV-E recipients.

Exploring the experiences of stayers and leavers who graduated from Title IV-E programs is useful in furthering the efforts of funding partnerships meant to strengthen the knowledge base and professional preparedness for workers. This study examines select interview questions from a larger study assessing Title IV-E graduates' retention in child welfare. The questions analyzed here will improve the knowledge base by allowing for a better understanding of how the Title IV-E educational experiences of stayers and leavers differ or are similar; and collectively how their responses can inform educational and agency enhancements.

Method

This study is part of a larger ongoing mixed methods evaluation of the Title IV-E program in one state. Participants are invited to fill out a 12-page survey either paper or online 6 months to 1 year after they have completed their contractual work obligation; thus participants have been working in child welfare 2.5–3 years since receiving their MSW. At the survey's conclusion, participants are offered the opportunity to take part in a telephone interview. The telephone interview further explores their experiences in the Title IV-E program and public child welfare, as well as reasons for staying or leaving. Analyses of quantitative results are reported elsewhere (Benton, 2016). At this time, participant survey answers have not been linked to interview data, with the exception of participant demographics. This article focuses solely on qualitative analysis conducted on select questions from the larger study's interview instrument. The use of qualitative methods allows the participants themselves to identify what is important (Padgett, 2008). Interviews with stayers and leavers provide an insider perspective to working in public child welfare (Morazes, Benton, Clark, & Jacquet, 2010).

Participants

The study pulls a convenience sample from a larger sample of Title IV-E graduates from one state between 1995 and 2008 who had completed the quantitative survey. The qualitative sample, $n = 465$, reflects a 21% response rate from the population of all Title IV-E graduates for the 12-year period ($n = 2,242$); but a 41% of those who completed the survey ($n = 1,129$). Table 1 provides sample demographics.

The majority of participants were female and stayers. Almost 50% of the participants were white. The convenience sample is representative of the population except in regards to ethnicity and age. Black, Asian American, and Hispanic workers are underrepresented.

Table 1. Sample Demographics.

Employment status	n	%
Stayers	365	78
Leavers	100	28
Ethnicity		
Black	51	11
American Indian	9	2
Hispanic/Latino/a	100	22
Asian American	25	5
White	227	49
Pacific Islander/Filipino	10	2
Mixed/Other	41	9
Gender		
Female	378	82
Male	85	18
Age		
21–30	212	45.8
31–40	133	29
41–50	83	18
51–60	34	7
60+	1	0.2
Sample total	465	100

Research design

The interview instrument consisted of 18 open-ended questions, which explored the participants' thoughts, feelings, and experiences about being in the Title IV-E MSW program and about working in public child welfare. The interview instrument was developed by other researchers in the state based on relevant existing knowledge about the child welfare workforce. The question relevant for examining participant perceptions of the Title IV-E program is "did your education prepare you for your job in public child welfare?" The question includes two prompts or follow-up questions, asked of all participants:

(1) "In terms of clients, problems, the nature of the work, etc., what were you best prepared for?"
(2) "What were you not prepared for?"

Data collection

Participation in the interview was voluntary and participants could pass on any question or end the interview at any time. The phone interviews were conducted and transcribed in their entirety by trained graduate student researchers, with most interviews lasting about 30 minutes. All 465 interview transcripts were entered into NVivo 7 qualitative software (QSR International, 2010), which served to both organize the data and assist in analyzing the frequency of responses (Meadows & Dodendorf, 1999). The study was approved by the university's IRB.

Data analysis

Interview questions derived from existing knowledge about the field were used to form the broad categories for analysis. Thus, data were initially grouped by interview question and then analyzed. Subsequent themes were derived from gathered responses, combining both deductive and inductive approaches. A thematic framework was then created to re-organize participant responses into themes and subthemes, allowing for relevant observations (Attride-Sterling, 2001; Ritchie, Spencer, & O'Connor, 2003; Strauss & Corbin, 1990).

The transcribed responses to the interview question and related prompts were initially reviewed by the first author. Continuous readings enhanced understanding and configuration of relevant issues. Involvement of colleagues to assess and discuss evolving themes supported credibility and minimized bias. Finally, both authors conferred to discuss and interpret established themes for consistency. These steps enhance the trustworthiness of the findings.

Findings

Coding and analysis of the base question. Did your education prepare you? Was complex and mired by transcription format issues. Given the length of the study (12 years) a number of different graduate students transcribed the interviews. Some transcriptions identified the primary question answered and then the follow-up questions. Other transcriptions grouped all responses together as one. Additionally, all participants were asked to identify what they were not prepared for, even if they had answered, "yes I was prepared" to the base question. Likewise, those who answered the base question no, were still asked to identify what they were best prepared for. Given these issues, 100% yes or no responses were relatively rare. The researchers were initially interested in whether there would be a clear distinction between stayers and leavers (for example, would more leavers say no they were not prepared?). However, when asked the best and not prompts, almost everyone was able to provide responses. There were some participants who did report there was nothing they were not prepared for (a 100% yes) or there was nothing they were best prepared for (a 100% no). See Table 2 for breakdown of responses by leavers and stayers.

Table 2. Frequency of Responses to Question 14. Did Your Education Prepare You for Your Job in Public Child Welfare?

	100% Yes	100% No	Mixed response
Leavers (n = 100)	8 (8%)	9 (9%)	83 (83%)
Stayers (n = 365)	26 (7%)	19 (5%)	311 (85%)

There were 9 (3%) non-responders in Stayer sample.

Table 2 indicates no real difference in frequency of responses by leavers and stayers, with over three fourths of both groups giving a mixed response. Only 28 participants total provided a straight no answer (unable to provide any aspects they felt best prepared for).

Therefore, the findings that are more helpful for analysis are in what ways or for which aspects did each group feel more and less prepared. After reading and coding stayer and leaver responses for both best and not prepared prompts, the first author identified five themes or categories relevant for responses to both prompts: (a) university specific (comments specifically about school experience or coursework), (b) worker technical skills (range from writing skills to social work specific skills like "starting where the client is"), (c) worker psychological aspects (thoughts, feelings, and reactions to job), (d) job/agency aspects (such as bureaucracy or being on call), and (e) clients (specific problems or behaviors). Further analysis was conducted to explore frequency of responses per theme and per group. In other words, was a particular theme area more frequently mentioned when asked either the *best prepared* or *not prepared* prompts, and were these similar for stayers and leavers?

Best prepared

There are many similarities between leaver and stayer responses. Table 3 provides the themes and most frequent subthemes for best prepared for both leavers and stayers. The participant quotes that follow are identified as being from a Stayer or a Leaver.

Table 3. Best Prepared Themes and Subthemes for Leavers and Stayers.

	Leavers		Stayers
	University specific		**University specific**
1.	Internship/field	1.	Internship/field
2.	Theory	2.	Good foundation
3.	Generalist practice	3.	Coursework
	Worker technical skills		**Worker technical skills**
1.	Assessment/risk assessment	1.	Working with clients
2.	Working with clients	2.	Cultural diversity/competence
3.	Cultural diversity/competence	3.	Assessment/risk assessment skills
	Worker psychological aspects		**Worker psychological aspects**
1.	n/a[a]	1.	Reality, intensity & nature of job
2.	n/a	2.	Ability to be compassionate
3.	n/a	3.	Raised consciousness, know own issues
	Job/agency aspects		**Job/agency aspects**
1.	Court	1.	Court
2.	n/a	2.	Bureaucracy
3.	n/a	3.	Complexity of the system
	Clients		**Clients**
1.	n/a	1.	Family issues/systems/dynamics
2.	n/a	2.	Substance abuse
3.	n/a	3.	Mental health issues

[a] If there was only one participant coded per subtheme it was not included in ranking.

Worker technical skills

Both leavers and stayers described worker technical aspects the most when asked what they were best prepared for. Within this theme, both groups mention assessment/risk assessment skills, their abilities to work with clients such as building rapport, and cultural diversity/cultural competence.

> How to interact with people who are different from yourself and how to really listen to people rather than tell them what they need... (Leaver)

> Probably being a little more sensitive to people's culture, to their needs, to who they are as a person, just being open to people. (Stayer)

University specific

Stayers and leavers indicated the internship or fieldwork as the component of their Title IV-E MSW programs that best prepared them for working in public child welfare.

> The field placement definitely prepared me for my job at DCFS. It really opened my eyes more to having to look at all the issues that could be involved... (Leaver)

> I think that the most valuable part of my MSW program was my internships. Because there's the reality. (Stayer)

However, the groups differed in regards to other university specific themes, with leavers referencing theory and stayers describing having a good foundation for the work.

Job/agency aspects

Similarities continued under this theme with both groups reporting working with the courts as the aspect for which they felt most prepared.

> I would say understanding laws, understanding the welfare institution codes... how children and families go through the whole system. Understanding somewhat of the court aspects of it. (Leaver)

> I remember one session in the IV-E training where we were talked about how we have to sort of frame things so that you can tell the court what it needs to know without offending the parents. (Stayer)

Of note is the fact that court was the only subtheme mentioned by more than one leaver. Leavers did not provide any other job/agency aspects as best prepared for with any frequency or commonality.

Worker psychological aspects & clients

A stark contrast between stayers and leavers is offered in two theme areas. Leavers had no common responses in either the worker psychological or clients themes. For the worker psychological theme, there were only three leaver responses in total (each being cited by one person): being realistic, being flexible, and coping with stress. For the clients theme, there were only two leaver responses in total: substance abuse and child death.

Alternately, stayers frequently brought up components of both worker psychological and client issues as areas where they felt best prepared. The following stayer expresses being prepared with an understanding of the nature of the work:

> I think I went into it with a very realistic idea of what the client population was going to be... the fact that the clients are non-voluntary and kind of what that would mean for my ability to form relationships with them and where they are starting from in terms of being open to services. (Stayer)

> Another stayer reflects on learning how to keep boundaries and take care of self:

> I think that having the MSW-it helped me to focus on the individual, on them and on their problems and I'm able to keep myself out of it. I don't keep my heart out of it, but I keep everything else out of it. (Stayer)

For client issues, stayers often valued education about mental illness and/or substance use in their Title IV-E program.

> We learned a lot about substance abuse. I think that was very helpful because that is about 80% of what we deal with in this county. (Stayer)

Stayers were better prepared for the emotional impacts associated with the job, as well as the complexity of client problems, and could more easily identify those areas and issues. Leavers were limited in this aspect.

Not prepared

Participants were then asked the second prompt in regards to lack of preparedness. Stayers as well as leavers were able to identify areas for which they did not feel prepared. Furthermore, stayers and leavers again had very similar responses; this time across all the themes. Table 4 provides the themes and most frequent subthemes for what participants were not prepared for, within each theme for both leavers and stayers.

Worker technical skills

In regards to worker technical skills, both stayers and leavers noted they had to learn time management skills after beginning the job.

> [m]aking sure that [everything was] done on time and met deadlines. (Leaver)

> I was baffled by the number of task[s] I had to do, management of time became very critical. (Stayer)

Table 4. Not Prepared Themes and Subthemes for Leavers and Stayers.

Leavers		Stayers	
	University specific		**University specific**
1.	Theory/research vs. practice	1.	Theory/research vs. practice
2.	Courses lacked depth	2.	Internship/field was bad
3.	n/a	3.	Child welfare/development classes
	Worker technical Skills		**Worker technical Skills**
1.	Time management/prioritizing skills	1.	Time management/prioritizing skills
2.	Clinical skills	2.	Clinical skills
3.	Engaging clients, getting client buy in	3.	Understanding policies/laws/codes
	Worker psychological aspects		**Worker psychological Aspects**
1.	Stress	1.	Stress
2.	Reality, intensity & nature of job	2.	Reality, intensity & nature of job
3.	Dealing with children's emotional pain	3.	Own reaction to loss, feeling responsible
	Job/agency aspects		**Job/agency aspects**
1.	Court	1.	Court
2.	Bureaucracy/organizational culture	2.	Caseload/workload
3.	Caseload/workload	3.	Bureaucracy/organizational culture
	Clients		**Clients**
1.	Substance abuse	1.	Substance abuse
2.	Child death	2.	Mental health issues
3.	n/a	3.	Severity of abuse, extreme cases

University specific

Both groups indicated that their education focused too much on theory, research, or therapy skills and not enough on practical skills for working in child welfare. This finding is in contrast to other leavers who mentioned theory as a positive element of their preparation.

> I think they should spend more time on the legal aspects in child welfare. We have a lot of clinical work, and classes in theory that we discuss. When you go into child welfare, you really can't apply a lot of it. (Leaver)

> There is no training in that Masters program in how to case-manage. It's about being a clinician and the problem is that people go into child welfare expecting to do therapy. (Stayer)

Job/agency aspects

Under the job/agency theme, court was the number one response for both leavers and stayers.

> I probably wasn't prepared for the court part of testifying or having to speak up in front of the judge…when I did dependency investigation, I was in and out of court all the time. (Leaver)

> I did get some information on the court through my internship, but I could have used a lot more. (Stayer)

Thus, court is featured as both a best prepared and not prepared for element.

In addition, both groups frequently mentioned being unprepared for case-load size and paperwork.

> I wasn't informed about the amount of the paperwork in the job. (Leaver)

> I wasn't prepared for the amount of paperwork, even with the second year intern-ship and being in agency I think its different when you do the same job day after day and you're carrying a much higher caseload. (Stayer)

Finally, bureaucracy/organizational culture was also a major subtheme for both stayers and leavers. The organizational culture of child welfare agencies was highlighted in its contrast to social work values and competencies.

> The lack of ability to network with others and to be creative in looking for solutions that would provide the most benefit to those involved. The focus on regimentation and the punitive arena. Given what social work is about, that was hard for me. (Leaver)

> I was not prepared for how hard you have to work to be respected... They are waiting for people to leave as opposed to welcoming people, there is not an attitude of mentorship, its either you survive or you don't and that was surprising for social work. (Stayer)

Worker psychological aspects

Stayers and leavers shared common responses for worker psychological. Many participants did not feel prepared for the stress or the nature of the job.

> They don't tell you that morale is low and that people are unhappy or that social workers don't get treated very well and they are the first ones to get blamed if something goes wrong and that there aren't very many services to really help these kids and all these other kinds of problems. (Leaver)

> ...the thing I was least prepared for was probably taking care of myself, how to look out for myself, both from an emotional standpoint, psychological standpoint, to just a social standpoint... (Stayer)

Clients

While some stayers did indicate being prepared for a variety of client issues as noted earlier, other stayers remarked they were not prepared for what one stayer described as the "complexity of cases."

> I wasn't prepared for the mental health problems. I think it is critical for CPS workers to have more experience with mental health issues, because that's our clients, schizophrenia, depression, substance abuse, anxiety. (Stayer)

Similarly, leavers noted not being prepared for client mental health or substance abuse problems.

> I was not prepared for people who abuse drugs and alcohol, especially working frequently with people under the influence. (Leaver)

Discussion

The findings indicate that overall, stayers and leavers had comparable perceptions of preparedness and reactions to the job. For example, both groups reported being prepared for working with clients but not being prepared for high caseloads. Yet, an important difference is found in relation to worker psychological and client themes. There were both stayers and leavers who expressed lack of preparation for these themes. However, only stayers expressed feeling well prepared in these same areas, with leavers not reflecting preparation in these areas. This study's findings are important in part due to the sample involving Title IV-E graduates who had completed their work commitment. Therefore their status as stayer was not influenced by contractual obligation. Implications of these findings are addressed below.

Ironically, for both stayers and leavers, court was the agency/job aspect both *best prepared* for by some and *not prepared* for by others. For stayers only, the sub themes of clients within both best and not prepared are a close match; including substance abuse and mental health. The differences related to court and client issues could be due to the specific MSW program attended or participant cohort. For example, a school that did not have focused curriculum on substance abuse in early years may have added it for later cohorts.

Both stayers and leavers felt unprepared for technical aspects such as paperwork and time management. It is possible that stayers who felt not prepared for technical aspects, but prepared for the psychological aspects, may have found it easier to learn these on the job and thus been able to adjust or improve upon their initial experiences. Leavers who were not prepared for the psychological aspects of the job may have lacked coping skills that would allow them to adjust to those aspects, while also increasing comfort levels with paperwork and time management. They may not have had access to consistent, supportive supervision. Additionally, the organizational culture of the agency may have failed to support them in ways that provided for their on-the-job growth.

In regards to the role of the Title IV-E education in preparing workers for the job, many participants (both stayers and leavers) commented on the impossibility of being prepared for a job in public child welfare. Statements like "nothing can prepare you for this job" and "you have to do the job to know it" were common. This perception may account for why reality of the job was also a subtheme that showed up in both best and not prepared responses for stayers. So, a question may be is it realistic to think that universities could improve their preparation of Title IV-E MSWs in the areas of worker psychological and client issues? Ellett (2014) observed, "many students are attracted to IV-E programs because of the availability of stipend support provided rather than a broad understanding of the complexities of work in [child welfare]" (p. 76). Hence, indicating that perhaps economics are a key factor in participant selection of a Title IV-E program rather than desire or drive to work in child welfare. If this is the case then it may not be relevant to improve preparation for psychological issues.

However, one author of this current study previously found that it was not a matter of commitment to child welfare work that differentiated between leavers and stayers but, rather a disconnect between teaching what social work is and how to perform social work in practice (Morazes et al., 2010). Other research supports the idea of a disconnect between education and practice (Deglau et al., 2014; Strand, Dettlaff, & Counts-Spriggs, 2015). Social work graduates have complained that the realities of practice limitations under bureaucratic systems limit their skill sets and leave them feeling alienated (Briar-Lawson, 2014). Thus, it is recommended that schools and agencies explore how to improve the transfer of social work training into child welfare practices.

Workers in this study often did not get a sufficiently realistic preview of the scope of work or organizational culture of many child welfare agencies. As one participant in this study reflected the Title IV-E training "didn't prepare [them] for the pragmatic nature of the agencies and their parameters. The reality of constraints to helping people." This participant further distinguished the difference between organizational limitations and working with clients, declaring they "became disillusioned with the systemic functions of the agency, not the low functioning of the clients."

Implications for education

While Title IV-E programs do not have control over job factors, to the extent that the education can prepare participants for the extrinsic and intrinsic aspects of the job, retention may be improved. Research suggests that realistic job previews should improve worker retention in child welfare (Faller et al., 2009; Graef & Potter, 2002). Field placements provide an opportunity for realistic job preview but have mixed results. Some participants stated that the internship was what best prepared them for the work. However, other participants indicated that only having four cases or working only 2 days a week during field placements did not sufficiently reflect the work. Therefore schools may want to investigate how to structure field placements in a manner that would allow for a more realistic preview of actual caseload volumes, case management tools, and bureaucratic processes involved in casework.

Another specific area of child welfare work for exploration is worker interactions with and relation to the courts. While some leavers and stayers felt prepared for this, court was the top response for both leavers and stayers when asked for what they were least prepared. The lack of preparation and resulting stress reflected here in the participants' responses relate to other studies citing court work as one most stressful aspects of the job (Carnochan et al., 2007; Chenot, Boutakidis, & Benton, 2014; Vandervort, Gonzalez, & Faller, 2008). In order for Title IV-E MSWs to feel well prepared for court responsibilities, programs that do not currently offer preparation for court could add lessons to improve students' knowledge and skills for working with the legal system and how to cross potential barriers created by professional cultural differences (Madden, 2003; Taylor, 2006).

Can the degree of preparedness related to working in bureaucratic settings be influenced by MSW education and more specifically Title IV-E training? Often, social workers are not taught how to survive in bureaucracies (Kim & Stoner, 2008). Given the need for policies and regulations in the child welfare system it is unlikely that the bureaucracies will be dismantled. Thus it is proposed that schools of social work consider designing courses that increase students' awareness of bureaucratic conditions in child welfare and other social work organizations, as well as provide tools for how to balance professional and bureaucratic needs. Such courses, or enhancements to existing courses will inform front line workers as well as strengthen foundational administrative skills in future supervisors who remain with a child welfare agency. This recommendation reinforces similar suggestions that schools "take pains to feature in their educational programs supervision and supportive organizational administration as fundamental to effective worker coping" (Lee, Rehner, & Forster, 2010, p. 107).

Implications for child welfare agencies

Finally, while the focus is on Title IV-E education, there are some ways that agencies could consider reinforcing the education and improving the support and retention of Title IV-E MSWs. Organizational culture, working conditions, and support are often lacking for child welfare workers addressing some of the most challenging roles in social work (Briar-Lawson, 2014). The perceived lack of preparation for job, skills, clients, and psychological aspects of work, as identified, could be remedied by quality supervision. Although many stayers indicated being prepared for the psychological aspects, other stayers did not and none of the leavers did except one. Thus, supporting workers manage the psychological impacts of the job are vital. While it is not clarified in the interviews, it is possible that supervisors help stayers adjust and adapt in the areas in which they felt their education did not prepare them. Research has repeatedly shown a significant relationship between supervisor support and worker retention (Barbee et al., 2009; Benton, 2016; Dickinson & Painter, 2009).

Additionally, agencies may want to assess their organizational culture and climate for ways to improve worker experiences. Examining organizational culture in child welfare agencies can benefit not only the child welfare system, but our overall understanding of organizational culture. Social work organizations, particularly public agencies, are often described as stressful and bureaucratic, with norms inhibiting behaviors regardless of employee background (Glisson & Green, 2006). Thus it is an important arena to examine how organizational culture as well as individual characteristics influence outcomes. Research by Ellett and Millar (2004) indicated that perceived professional organizational culture was significantly correlated with intention to remain employed. Their definition described the shared norms, values and beliefs as "emanate[ing] from established professional ethics and standards" (Ellett & Millar, 2004, p. 31). This study highlights a continuing disconnect of social work from child welfare practices caused by the previous de-professionalization. If child welfare agencies want to reprofessionalize through an increase in workers with a MSW degree, they need to examine the setting they are asking social workers to enter into.

References

Attride-Sterling, J. (2001). Thematic networks: An analytic tool for qualitative research. *Qualitative Research*, 1(3), 385–405.

Bagdasaryan, S. (2012). Social work education and Title IV-E program participation as predictors of entry-level knowledge among public child welfare workers. *Children and Youth Services Review*, 34, 1590–1597. doi:10.1016/j.childyouth.2012.04.013

Barbee, A., Antle, B., Sullivan, D., Huebner, R., Fox, S., & Hall, J. (2009). Recruiting and retaining child welfare workers: Is preparing social work students enough for sustained commitment to the field? *Child Welfare*, 88(5), 69–86.

Barth, R. P., Lloyd, E. C., Christ, S. L., Chapman, M. V., & Dickinson, N. S. (2008). Child welfare worker characteristics and job satisfaction: A National Study. *Social Work*, 53(3), 199–209.

Benton, A. (2016). Understanding the diverging paths of stayers and leavers: An examination of factors predicting worker retention. *Children and Youth Services Review, 65,* 70–77. doi:10.1016/j.childyouth.2016.04.006

Briar-Lawson, K. (2014). Building the social work workforce: Saving lives and families. *Advances in Social Work, 15*(1), 21–33.

Carnochan, S., Taylor, S., Abramson-Madden, A., Han, M., Rashid, S., Maney, J., ... Austin, M. (2007). Child welfare and the courts: An exploratory study of the relationship between two complex systems. *Journal of Public Child Welfare, 1*(1), 117–136.

Chenot, D., Boutakidis, I., & Benton, A. (2014). Equity and fairness perceptions in the child welfare workforce. *Children and Youth Services Review, 44,* 400–406. doi:10.1016/j.childyouth.2014.07.006

Deglau, E., Ray, A., Edwards, R., Carre-Lee, N., Harrison, T., & Cunningham, K. (2014). Transferring MSW education to practice: A qualitative study with public child welfare employees. *Journal of Public Child Welfare, 8*(3), 304–325.

Dickinson, N., & Painter, J. (2009). Predictors of undesired turnover for child welfare workers. *Child Welfare, 88*(5), 187–208.

Ellett, A. (2009). Intentions to remain employed in child welfare: The role of human caring, self-efficacy beliefs, and professional organizational culture. *Children and Youth Services Review, 31*(1), 78–88. doi:10.1016/j.childyouth.2008.07.002

Ellett, A. (2014). A first-hand account of Title IV-E child welfare initiatives in social work education and practice. *Advances in Social Work, 15*(1), 63–79.

Ellett, A., & Millar, K. (2004). Professional organizational culture and retention in child welfare: Implications for continuing education for supervision and professional development. *Professional Development: the International Journal of Continuing Social Work Education, 7*(3), 30–38.

Faller, K., Masternak, M., Grinnell-Davis, C., Grabarek, M., Sieffert, J., & Bernatovicz, F. (2009). Realistic job previews in child welfare: State of innovation and practice. *Child Welfare, 88*(5), 23–47.

Glisson, C., & Green, P. (2006). The effects of the organizational culture and climate on the access to mental health care in child welfare and juvenile justice systems. *Administration and Policy in Mental Health and Mental Health Services Research, 33*(4), 433–448.

Government Accountability Office. (2006). *Improving social service program, training, and technical assistance information would help address long-standing service-level and workforce challenges. (GAO-07-75).* Washington, D.C.: U.S. Government Printing Office.

Graef, M., & Potter, M. (2002). Alternative solutions to the child protective services staffing crisis: Innovations from industrial/organizational psychology. *Protecting Children, 17*(3), 18–31.

Jones, L. (2002). A follow-up of a Title IV-E program's graduates' retention rates in a public child welfare agency. *Journal of Health & Social Policy, 15*(3), 39–51.

Jones, L., & Okamura, A. (2000). Reprofessionalizing child welfare services: An evaluation of a Title IVE training program. *Research on Social Work Practice, 10*(5), 607–621.

Kim, H., & Stoner, M. (2008). Burnout and turnover intention among social workers: Effects of role stress, job autonomy and social support. *Administration in Social Work, 32*(3), 5–25. doi:10.1080/03643100801922357

Lee, J., Rehner, T., & Forster, M. (2010). Employees' intentions to remain employed in child welfare: Testing a conceptual model. *Journal of Public Child Welfare, 4*(2), 174–197. doi:10.1080/15548731003799613

Madden, E., Scannapieco, M., & Painter, K. (2014). An examination of retention and length of employment among public child welfare workers. *Children and Youth Services Review, 41,* 37–44.

Madden, R. (2003). Legal content in social work education: Preparing students for inter-professional practice. *Journal of Teaching in Social Work, 20*(1/2), 3–17.

McGuire, L. E., Howes, P., Murphy-Nugen, A., & George, K. (2011). Leadership as advocacy: The impact of a Title IV-E supported MSW education on a public child welfare agency. *Journal of Public Child Welfare, 5*, 213–233.

Meadows, L., & Dodendorf, D. (1999). Data management and interpretation: Using computers to assist. In B. Crabtree & W. Miller (Eds.), *Doing qualitative research.* Thousand Oaks, CA: SAGE.

Morazes, J., Benton, A., Clark, S., & Jacquet, S. (2010). Views of specially-trained child welfare social workers: A qualitative study of their motivations, perceptions, and retention. *Qualitative Social Work, 9*(2), 227–247.

NASW. (2003).*Fact Sheet: Title IV-E child welfare training program.* Retrieved from http://www.socialworkers.org/advocacy/updates/2003/081204a.asp

Nguyen, L. H. (2013). Using return on investment to evaluate child welfare training programs. *Social Work, 58*(1), 75–79.

Padgett, D. (2008). *Qualitative methods in social work research* (2nd ed.). Los Angeles, CA: Sage.

QSR International. (2010). *NVivo 7.* Retrieved from https://www.qsrinternational.com/nvivo/home

Ritchie, J., Spencer, L., & O'Connor, W. (2003). Carrying out qualitative analysis. In J. Ritchie & J. Lewis (Eds.), *Qualitative research practice: A guide for social science students and researchers* (pp. 219–262). London, UK: Sage Publications.

Rosenthal, J., & Waters, E. (2006). Predictors of child welfare worker retention and performance: Focus on Title IV-E-funded social work education. *Journal of Social Service Research, 32*(3), 67–85.

Social Work Policy Institute. (2012). Educating social workers for child welfare practice: The status of using Title IV-E funding to support BSW & MSW education. *National Association of Social Workers.* September, 2012. Retrieved from https://www.socialworkers.org/Practice/Child-Welfare/Child-Welfare-Related-Resources

Specht, H., & Courtney, M. (1994). *Unfaithful angels: How social work has abandoned its mission.* New York, NY: The Free Press.

Strand, V. C., Dettlaff, A. J., & Counts-Spriggs, M. (2015). Promising innovations in child welfare education: Findings from a national initiative. *Journal of Social Work Education, 51* (Suppl 2), S195–S208.

Strauss, A., & Corbin, J. (1990). *Basics of qualitative research: Grounded theory procedures and techniques* (pp. 15–32). Newbury Park, CA: Sage Publications.

Strolin-Goltzman, J., Auerbach, C., McGowan, B., & McCarthy, M. (2007). The relationship between organizational characteristics and workforce turnover among rural, urban, and suburban public child welfare systems. *Administration in Social Work, 32*(1), 77–91.

Strolin-Goltzman, J., McCarthy, M., Smith, B., Caringi, J., Bronstein, L., & Lawson, H. (2009). Correction: 'Should I stay or should I go? A comparison study of intention to leave among public child welfare systems with high and low turnover rates.'. *Child Welfare: Journal of Policy, Practice, and Program, 88*(2), 125–143.

Taylor, S. (2006). Educating future practitioners of social work and law: Exploring the origins of inter-professional misunderstanding. *Children and Youth Services Review, 28*, 638–653.

U.S. Department of Health and Human Services. (2017). *HHS FY 2017 budget in brief – ACF – Mandatory – Foster care and permanency.* Retrieved from https://www.hhs.gov/about/budget/fy2017/budget-in-brief/acf/mandatory/index.html#foster-care

Vandervort, F., Gonzalez, R. P., & Faller, K. C. (2008). Legal ethics and high child welfare worker turnover: An unexplored connection. *Children and Youth Services Review, 30*(5), 546–563.

Vonk, M., Newsome, W., & Bronson, D. (2003). An outcome evaluation of competency based training for child welfare. *Advances in Social Work, 4*(2), 82–93.

Zlotnik, J. (2002). Preparing social workers for child welfare practice: Lessons from an historical review of the literature. *Journal of Health and Social Policy, 15*(3/4), 5–21.

Preparing Child Welfare Practitioners: Implications for Title IV-E Education and Training Partnerships

Austin Griffiths ⊚, David Royse, Kristine Piescher ⊚, and Traci LaLiberte ⊚

ABSTRACT

High rates of child welfare practitioner turnover remain a national problem with significant consequences. Title IV-E education and training programs prepare child welfare practitioners for this line of work with the intent that they will create long term careers. This study analyzed qualitative data from a 2016 statewide electronic survey launched to obtain frontline child welfare practitioner feedback about workforce turnover and assist the agency in retention efforts.

Practitioner insight resulted in 189 responses specifically related to improving the state's Title IV-E supported education and training program–the "Academy." A qualitative thematic analysis identified three main themes: making it more realistic and hands on (n = 104), needing additional training and specific content (n = 45), and feeling overwhelmed with the experience (n = 40). Practitioner feedback illustrated the existing tensions with using a blended model to educate and train the workforce. Implications for Title IV-E education and training partnerships are discussed.

Child welfare and social work education

In the United States, social work education and the child welfare system share an important and historical relationship. Largely built through the utilization of federal financial support, the primary funding for the social work education of the public child welfare workforce is Title IV-E of the Social Security Act (Zlotnik & Pryce, 2013). The Children's Bureau has also provided financial support to undergraduate and graduate students specializing in child welfare through a variety of initiatives (e.g., 426 grants) for more than 25 years (Barbee, Antle, Sullivan, Dryden, & Henry, 2012). Guided by the belief that social work education is the ideal preparation for future child welfare practitioners (Folaron & Hostetter, 2007; Zlotnik, 2003), this vested and chronicled relationship between public child welfare agencies and social work education programs has been well established.

Research has suggested that having a social work education background better prepares individuals for their positions. For instance, Dhooper, Royse, and Wolfe (1990) found that Department of Social Services welfare practitioners with a degree in social work outperformed their peers on child welfare quality assurance measures and state merit examinations. Additionally, having a social work educational background has been shown to improve the entry level knowledge of child welfare practitioners (Bagdasaryan, 2012). Further, a number of studies have indicated that having a social work education is a significant factor in predicting child welfare practitioners' retention (Madden, Scannapieco, & Painter, 2014; Mason, LaPorte, Bronstein, & Auerbach, 2012; Rosenthal & Waters, 2006). However, at least one study found the opposite—that child welfare practitioners with a Master of Social Work degree were more likely to leave the agency than those without (Yankeelov, Barbee, Sullivan, & Antle, 2009). Given that this study was focused on the experiences of new employees over a four-year span and only 5% of the entire sample (n = 723) had an MSW, these results must be interpreted with caution.

Despite research suggesting that a social work education may be the optimal preparation for child welfare practitioners, it cannot be ascertained that having this particular background means the profession has figured out the best way to prepare child welfare practitioners for the long haul. Child welfare practitioners continue to leave their positions at alarming rates, creating a national problem (Cahalane & Sites, 2008) with tremendous costs in both human and economic terms. Compared with social workers in other settings, public child welfare practitioners experience higher workloads, have greater role conflict, and experience feelings of lower personal accomplishment (Kim, 2011). As a result, high rates of turnover have been an issue for decades in child welfare. Turnover rates have been estimated to range from 30–40% nationwide (Government Accounting Office, 2003), yet rates vary substantially by region. For example, turnover rates in some jurisdictions have been documented to be as high as 90% (Child Welfare Information Gateway, 2014).

Child welfare professionals who leave their positions increase the workload on remaining staff; which leads to increased stress and challenges in meeting casework performance standards (Scannapieco & Connell-Carrick, 2007). Replacing experienced practitioners with newer ones negatively affects productivity levels (Ellet, Ellis, Westbrook, & Dews, 2007), and results in significant financial costs for the agency. According to the National Child Welfare Workforce Institute, the estimated cost for each child welfare practitioner leaving the agency is approximately $54,000 (NCWWI). Yet, these costs do not take into consideration the extraordinary burden placed on remaining workers or the effect on families as a result of turnover (Cahalane & Sites, 2008; GAO, 2003; Strolin-Goltzman, Kollar, & Trinkle, 2010).

Practitioners leave their positions for a myriad of reasons. Researchers have examined the issues associated with retention for decades and have identified important personal and organizational factors that influence whether child welfare practitioners will leave their positions. For example, concerns about safety (Kim & Kao, 2014), feeling undervalued (Ellett, Ellis, Westbrook, & Dews, 2007), high levels of emotional exhaustion (Williams, Nichols, Kirk, & Wilson, 2011), and loss of professional commitment (Ellett, Ellett, & Rugutt, 2003) are personal factors that influence practitioner retention. The lack of organizational support (Kim & Kao, 2014), organizational stress (Nissly, Barak, & Levin, 2005), and unreasonable workloads (Zlotnik, DePanfilis, Daining, & Lane, 2005) have also been identified as important organizational factors that affect practitioner turnover. With the challenging nature of child welfare work and the high costs associated with practitioner turnover, it is important to implement effective strategies to prepare the workforce for the challenges they will face.

Approaches to child welfare education

An exploration of the peer-reviewed literature illustrates the importance of both the training of child welfare practitioners (Collins, Kim, & Amodeo, 2010) and of the collaborative Title IV-E partnerships between universities and public child welfare agencies in preparing practitioners for work in child welfare (Barbee et al., 2009; Hartinger-Saunders & Lyons, 2013; Rheaume, Collins, & Amodeo, 2011; Scannapieco & Connell-Corrick, 2007; Zlotnik & Pryce, 2013). While the number of studies on how the profession should prepare child welfare practitioners is very limited, innovative practices for preparing child welfare practitioners have begun to be implemented and tested across the United States. Pecukonis et al. (2016) used a rigorous controlled design to integrate live supervision and standardized clients while teaching motivational interviewing to MSW students placed in a child welfare setting. Lery, Putnam-Hornstein, Wiegmann, and King (2015) used aggregate data from California's child welfare system to develop analytic capacity and statistical literacy among Title IV-E MSW students. Providing students with exposure to "real world" scenarios, Burry, Shdaimah, Richardson, & Rice, K. (2011) used an interdisciplinary approach to allow social work students a simulated court experience with faculty and students from the law program. Whipple, Solomon-Jozwiak, Williams-Hecksel, Abrams, and Bates (2006) modelled the 'Grand Rounds' hospital teaching concept to prepare BSW and MSW students for child welfare practice.

Although the literature contributes some important notions, one cannot help but wonder what valuable ideas would arise to help social work educators and Title IV-E trainers better prepare the next generation of child welfare practitioners, if it were possible to solicit suggestions from frontline practitioners working in "the trenches." This technique has been used to elicit valuable feedback about factors contributing to retention and turnover (Ellett et al., 2007; Johnco, Salloum, Olson, & Edwards, 2014), yet limited literature drawing upon child welfare practitioners' perceptions and suggestions for improving education and training exists. Accordingly, this study was developed to address this gap in knowledge and solicit information and ideas from practitioners who have completed their foundation child welfare training and are currently working in the field.

Methodology

Design and data collection

A descriptive, mixed methods research design was implemented to obtain practitioner feedback about child welfare turnover and to assist the state child welfare agency in its retention efforts. In January 2016, the new Commissioner of the state's child welfare system sent a preliminary email to her workforce and encouraged her child welfare practitioners to share their feedback by participating in an upcoming electronic survey. This preliminary email identified the research team's affiliation with a major university and not with the state's child welfare system. One week later, an administrator at the agency distributed an email to the statewide child welfare workforce that began with a cover letter to outline the voluntary and anonymous nature of participation in this survey. Access to the electronic Qualtrics survey was provided through an embedded hyperlink, and a reminder email was sent to the entire listserv two weeks later as a reminder to those who had not visibly responded.

Overall, the survey included 14 demographic questions and 25 Likert style questions that were designed to capture feedback about levels of satisfaction on a variety of important domains found to influence the practitioner's experience (e.g. peer support, salary, recognition, professional development, accomplishment, supervision, and workload). Although some of the results from that quantitative study have been published (Griffiths, Royse, Culver, Piescher, & Zhang, 2017), the current article provides findings from qualitative responses related to training when practitioners were asked to provide ideas that may help the agency retain employees. The study was approved by the appropriate Institutional Review Boards at both the university and the agency.

Sampling

The subject population for the current study was comprised of frontline child welfare practitioners (as defined as having direct client contact and not working in any supervisory role) who received the survey through the state agency's email distribution. A total of 511 frontline child welfare practitioners voluntarily and anonymously participated in the study, a response rate of 38%. The response rate in this study was in keeping with other similar studies (e.g., Augsberger, Schudrich, McGowan, & Auerbach, 2012). Of the 511 practitioners who responded to the survey, 490 (96%) provided qualitative feedback for the agency to consider in improving the retention of its workforce.

The sample was primarily female (86.0%), had worked at the agency for an average of 8.2 years (SD 7.5), and had a mean age of 37.62 years (SD 9.8). There was limited diversity, as 88% reported being White and 39 individuals identified being Black or African American (8.0%). Educationally, almost half of the sample (47.7%) had a background in social work education. Forty percent (195) reported having a Bachelor of Social Work degree and 60% had an undergraduate degree in a related field. While the majority of practitioners (67.9%) did not have a graduate degree, 110 (22.4%) reported having an MSW and 44 had a graduate degree in another field. The majority of the sample (72.6%) identified this as their first job in child welfare. Practitioners in this statewide study primarily worked in a rural area (64.7%), with 35.3% reporting that they primarily worked in an urban area.

Kentucky's title IV-E education & training program

Kentucky's Credit for Learning initiative (hereafter, the "Academy") was established in 2002 to prepare professionals for work in Kentucky's child welfare program. This innovative consortium-based model merged social work education and training, as practitioners receive graduate level social work credits for the completion of their child welfare agency training (Sar et al., 2008). The Title IV-E Funded State-University partnership is designed for new child welfare practitioners to undergo up to six months of training while being assigned a reduced caseload. The Academy is a consortium offered at the state's largest three universities (University of Kentucky, University of Louisville, & Western Kentucky University) and participants alternate between weeks in the classroom and weeks in the field. In total, the Academy provides education and training over four primary areas (foundations, assessment, case management, and child sexual abuse) allowing the newly hired child welfare practitioner to earn up to 12 hours of graduate education credit. Because of the unique structure of the Academy, child welfare training in this state can be described as a blend of education and training. Given the length of employment reported by the practitioners, it can be assumed that most (77.6%) of the sample received their child welfare foundation training through the current Academy structure.

Qualitative data analysis

Qualitative thematic content analysis was utilized to examine child welfare practitioners' open-ended text responses to the following item "Provide any ideas you have that might help [the agency] retain employees in terms of benefits, training, workload, supervision, support, and recognition." Response by response, line by line, the first author used qualitative data analysis software (MaxQDAPlus 12) for open coding. Following the guidelines of Braun and Clarke (2006), the first author engaged in the six-phase process of becoming familiar with the data, initial coding, searching for themes, re-evaluating the themes, defining and naming of the themes, and finalizing a formal report. These themes were confirmed by all co-authors who read practitioner responses, examined their collective contributions and categorization into themes, and looked for errors in coding or bias. Investigator triangulation was used to check the validity of the first author's coding (Carter, Bryant-Lukosius, DiCenso, Blythe, & Neville, 2014).

Results

Regarding frontline practitioner suggestions for improving retention, 189 responses were specifically related to improving the state's Title IV-E supported education and training system–the "Academy." Practitioners provided suggestions for improvement in three main categories. These categories included making the training more realistic and/or hands-on (n = 104), the addition of training in specific content areas (n = 45), and feeling overwhelmed by the information presented and caseloads carried (n = 40).

The theme of make it realistic and hands on

A total of 104 responses established the most common theme in the content analysis, with practitioners recommending that the preparation and training they receive through the Academy become more realistic. Practitioners stated that if they were better prepared, they would be more likely to remain employed at the agency. One practitioner suggested, "the Academy does not truly prepare any practitioner for this job. There needs to be more hands-on type of training, as what is in textbooks is typically not the real world." Another stated that, "if training was not so focused on the Academy, and more focused on the actual field work, it would be much more beneficial to new workers. I do not feel that I learned valuable information while in the Academy." Several practitioners noted that "the training that we currently receive does not really teach you how to do the job," and they desired "training that is realistic and applicable." A typical response was illustrated by a practitioner who said "the training required in this profession should accurately reflect the duties of this job. There have been so many things I have learned after training that were never formally discussed. What is taught in training is not as valuable as what you learn in the field."

Comments about dramatically refocusing the Academy to reflect the realities of frontline child welfare work became saturated quickly. Practitioners noted that the agency should "provide more in-the-field training rather than in the classroom" and they desired "training that actually teaches us how to do our jobs rather than talking about the philosophy behind the job." Practitioners provided specific suggestions for improvement, stating that the Academy should "include real-life scenarios and cases instead of having workers read from a textbook and write a chapter summary" or instead of "working on imaginary cases."

Practitioners also spoke about their concerns related to the qualifications and experience of those teaching the courses. A respondent described frustration stemming from the instructors' lack of experience: "most of the teachers have never worked for [the agency.]" Another respondent supported this idea by stating "it helps if the trainer has actually done the job." A third added that practitioners should be "trained by people who directly are doing the job."

Over one hundred comments were made by practitioners wanting a more realistic and hands-on education and training experience. Though their statements were similar in nature, the most poignant quote was made by a practitioner who stated "there is a disconnect between training and the field. Practice should influence research and research should influence practice." Overall, practitioners' responses suggested that considerable effort must be made to improve the applicability of the state's Title IV-E education and training program by utilizing the expertise and wisdom of those who have done the job and by using pedagogical approaches that promote applied learning.

Theme of needing additional training (specific content)

Through a total of 45 responses, practitioners indicated that additional content and specialized training would have better prepared them for child welfare work. Practitioners not only requested additional training to improve their interaction with clients, but also requested support in caring for themselves while working in this important capacity.

With respect to practitioner involvement with clients, some of the responses centered on concrete tasks or processes required for child welfare work. For instance, one practitioner suggested that a "required training about time management skills to teach staff to multi-task and prioritize" would be helpful. Another requested preparation on "how to fill out OOHC paperwork, court paperwork, maybe how to install a car seat." Several practitioners felt that further education on how to effectively complete paperwork would be beneficial. These individuals asked for "paperwork training," "examples on how to complete petitions," and "training to focus on the different forms and paperwork we're required to use."

Additionally, practitioners recommended including specialized content areas focused on the current issues encountered in child welfare practice. In particular, practitioners reported needing additional preparation to work effectively with parents struggling with chemical dependency issues. One practitioner noted that "workers have no training on different types of street drugs, what they look like, etc. and a vast majority of cases are related to drug use." Another asked for "more training done regarding the medical field–specifically regarding drugs and reading medical records (or at least what to try and look for)." One practitioner's comment appeared to capture the sentiment of several other respondents' statements; this practitioner requested that the agency "provide training on mental health, substance abuse, and community services."

Practitioners also sought to improve their professional selves, requesting additional training that might improve their health and well-being. One respondent stated that, "supervisors need extensive training on how stress and trauma affect the brain and effectively shut down the part of our brain responsible for learning new material and sometimes just functioning nor-mally." Another mentioned that the Academy would benefit practitioners by integrating "a specific training about caring for your own mental health [and] ways to help detach yourself from the job when you're not working." Safety was also important, as one practitioner stated that participants would benefit from "more training about safety and how to protect ourselves from aggres-sive clients."

In summary, practitioners noted that additional and specialized content was needed in the state's Title IV-E education and training program to promote workforce retention. Practitioner comments suggested that relating training to issues specific to their geographical region (e.g. training on the effects of heroin in the Midwest) may present a better opportunity for practitioners to feel that they are prepared to do this job. Practitioners also reiterated the fact that learning how to properly conduct self-care in this line of work cannot be underestimated.

Theme of being overwhelmed

The third and final theme of this content analysis included a total of 40 responses, as practitioners described being overwhelmed. Practitioners described having an onslaught of cases assigned when they first started their positions; this contributed to feeling overwhelmed when the education and training protocol was added to practitioners' workload. One practitioner shared concerns about this trajectory by stating that "our new workers need to be transitioned a bit slower. It seems as though they start out with six cases or so and then a couple of weeks later they are up to 20 or more and this is very overwhelming to a brand-new worker." Another proclaimed a clear sense of urgency, pleading "don't slam workers who are still in the Academy with 15 cases and expect them to stay." Several practitioners continued to drive this point home by noting "all employees should be required to complete all training before having a caseload" and to "stop throwing 15–20 cases at new employees during their trainings." In addition to reduced caseloads, some called for the training to be shortened. One practitioner stated "the Academy should be for a shorter period of time. I would have loved for it to have been crammed into 8–10 weeks straight, going home on the weekends, and then be done."

Several practitioners articulated the dilemmas caused by attending the state's six-month long Title IV-E education and training program while trying to manage their new positions and caseloads. One respondent said that "training in the 'Academy' takes workers out of the field for weeks, while attempting to maintain a caseload is unmanageable, and compromises the ability to effectively perform job tasks and maintain integrity as a social worker." Another practitioner similarly explained "the training program is way too long and the amount of time it takes to complete assignments takes me away from what I need to do for my clients." A practitioner shed additional light, stating that "people are punished for missing classes when they have to attend court for a case." Finally, another respondent mentioned that "it's very overwhelming to have a full case load while still in training, it makes it difficult to prioritize what's more important."

Overall, practitioners shared a number of relevant concerns about how they felt the Academy was overwhelming, and how it was a significant barrier toward keeping practitioners employed at the agency. Practitioners who were able to provide additional insight into the dilemmas caused by concurrently completing the Academy and carrying a child welfare caseload noted that the Academy and child welfare field work impose different, and sometimes, conflicting requirements for practitioners. They noted that not only were these requirements overwhelming, but they presented ethical issues as well.

Discussion

Kentucky's Title IV-E education and training program - the Credit for Learning initiative (aka the "Academy")–operates as a unique consortium-based approach of integrating education and training via federal Title IV-E funding. Despite this innovative and integrated model put in place to support and prepare its child welfare workforce, high turnover in the system con-tinues (Griffiths et al., 2017). This study was developed to elicit feedback from practitioners to develop strategies for improving employee retention – those practitioners who have experienced years of challenges of working in the state's child welfare system. Given the recent change in leadership, the responses of practitioners are not a reflection on the current administration. Practitioners recognized the need to improve the way in which the workforce is educated and trained, by reporting a disconnect between the pedagogy of the Academy and what practitioners felt they needed to know to effectively work in the field. Practitioners wanted their education and training experience to be more realistic of the type of cases and/or scenarios they will encounter and facilitated by professionals with direct, front-line experience. Second, they recognized some of their own knowledge inadequacies and requested specific content areas to be included in the Academy. Third, practitioners felt overwhelmed with balancing time commitments required for training, while carrying full caseloads and the length of time required to complete the Academy. Taken together, these recommendations provide the Academy (and other Title IV-E education and training systems) with an opportunity to enhance the adult learning experience, the knowledge base of newly hired child welfare practitioners, and ultimately to improve workforce retention.

Implications for title IV-E education & training programs

Education and training are often thought about and implemented as two separate processes. Whereas education can be viewed as foundation and context for professional preparation, training is often viewed as the conduit for skill development and processes for accomplishing day-to-day tasks. Title IV-E partnerships can serve as a mechanism to blend these two approaches, harnessing the unique strengths of each approach to promote effective strategies for workforce preparation and retention. Kentucky's Title IV-E education and training program is one example of this blend of education and training. While blending education and training approaches may be beneficial for preparing new child welfare practitioners, a natural tension between the two approaches exists due to differing viewpoints of the practice and academic communities (Rheume, Collins & Amodeo, 2011). These tensions will be discussed relative to each of the three main themes found in the current study.

Make it realistic and/or hands on
Practitioners in this study identified the natural tension that exists in a blended Title IV-E education and training system with respect to providing a theoretical and foundational knowledge base in a University setting and the desire for application-based learning. In response, practitioners suggested ways in which Title IV-E education and training systems may be improved.

These changes may serve to increase the effectiveness of Title IV-E education and training systems while also reducing the inherent tension practitioners identified, thus promoting workforce retention.

Recommendations from participants in this study dovetail with several innovative approaches to educating and training social work practitioners being used in the U.S.—particularly variations in the use of simulation in teaching and learning. The use of simulation for workforce education and training has been implemented widely in fields outside of child welfare for decades (Damewood, 2016; Daupin et al., 2016; Moorthy, Vincent, & Darzi, 2005; Munangatire & Naidoo, 2017; Nyström, Dahlberg, Hult, & Dahlgren, 2016). Recently, Title IV-E education and training programs across the U.S. have begun implementing simulations as part of their curriculum. Whether coupled with live supervision (Pecukonis et al., 2016) or focused on unique aspects of the work, such as attending court hearings (Burry, Shdaimah, Richardson, & Rice, 2011) or practicing home visits (Blackwell-Pittman, 2016), simulations offer learners with opportunities to try new and different approaches that they otherwise may be hesitant to use with the children and families they serve. These experiences offer learners opportunities to test out strategies for building rapport, conducting assessments, and engaging in realistic communication in uncomfortable and unfamiliar places. Although the long-term impact and generalizability of these strategies is not yet clear in child welfare, research in other fields supports the use of simulations for skill development (Negrão Baptista, Amado Martins, Carneiro Ribeiro Pereira, & Mazzo, 2014; Richardson & Claman, 2014; Stocker et al., 2012). While simulations are most often utilized in new worker training, their use in ongoing training with seasoned workers also offers opportunity for learning and skill refinement as innovations are introduced into practice and agencies want to offer ongoing professional development to their longer-term employees.

In this theme practitioners also suggested that instructors facilitating the Academy need to have the capacity to contextualize their instruction via real-world child welfare experience. Implied is the notion that some faculty, although academically prepared with appropriate credentials, may have conducted research on child abuse, domestic violence and so forth without having direct practice experience as child welfare practitioners. This is a tension that is difficult to resolve as some faculty could have had practice experience years ago qualifying them as "experts" yet lack familiarity with the current procedures involved in this line of work. One possible solution is to implement a team-teaching approach, utilizing a combination of instructors from academic and workforce backgrounds. Another solution is to utilize the strength of the relationship between the State-University partnership to provide academic faculty with recurrent opportunities to engage in field work through ride-along and participation in case consultations, group supervision, etc. These solutions promote a more nuanced and contextualized approach for blending the education and training needs of practitioners, thus enhancing the more realistic experience requested by practitioners.

Need for additional training about specific content

In this theme practitioners expressed a desire for additional training and education that focused on specific circumstances they encounter and tasks they must complete when working with children and families involved in the child welfare system. For example, practitioners indicated they wanted additional opportunities to learn about how to work with families struggling with mental health and chemical dependency issues as well as concrete tasks such as completing case plans. They also noted that they needed additional support and education to better manage the stress of working in their positions. While these requests may further support the knowledge base of practitioners, incorporating additional content within the current Academy may also exacerbate current tensions described by respondents which included time away from their caseloads to attend extended trainings. In particular, adding content to the Academy may serve to lengthen the amount of time required for completion and therefore add to the feelings of being overwhelmed expressed by respondents. This isn't to say that these requests for additional information be ignored. Rather, incorporating this information in a purposeful and strategic approach is warranted.

Because specific aspects of the Academy that lead to breakdowns in learning cannot be ascertained from practitioner responses, a thorough review of content composition, instructional design, and instruction delivery models is necessary. While the responses of practitioners in this study were specific to ways in which Kentucky's Title IV-E training and education system could be improved to increase retention, Title IV-E education and training programs across the U.S. could benefit from this type of review. In such a review, consistency and quality of instruction, content and its applicability to real-time practice (e.g., current/geographically-specific drug crises), and the process for connecting learning in the field with that occurring in the classroom must be attended to. As a result, enhanced training of instructors and/or quality assessments of instruction might be put into place. Additionally, new structures used to connect classroom and field learning, such as an iterative learning structure (which also could be used to address the tension between education and training), could be adopted. A timely review of the Academy as suggested, inclusive of feedback from instructors and frontline workers serving as core members on the review team could result in the identification of key areas of concern as well as strategies for systematically improving the effectiveness of training and education provided by the Academy.

For example, if the area of concern uncovered during the review is that of simply incorporating additional opportunities for hands-on approaches within particular content areas, the Academy (and other training and education programs) may seek to partner with the valuable resources offered within the University structure. Mirroring the work of Swift and Stosberg (2015), training and education programs can partner with the University's drama or theatre department to prepare simulated clients to enhance practice assessment skills and treatment planning. When there is a law school affiliated with the University, faculty can partner to plan moot courts that could involve newly hired practitioners having a role with prepared child welfare cases. Similarly, training and education programs can reach out to faculty in other areas of the University for expertise on such topics as assessing drug dependence and deliver them to learners via guest lectures or videos. Hosting expert videos on publicly available websites would also provide practitioners an opportunity to access additional areas of content on an as-needed basis–even after completion of training.

If, during the review, it appears as though transfer of learning activities are lacking, practical guidance for and curriculum that requires the completion of caseload-relevant paperwork and effective system navigation could be incorporated (Parton, 2009). Today's child welfare practitioners are functioning in a fast-paced, high-pressure environment where immediate decisions need to be made, timely documentation is expected, and tasks are greater than one can reasonably complete. Title IV-E training and education programs may assist new practitioners develop their time management and prioritization skills by emulating some of the strategies used in business and in management. Specifically, using in-basket training exercises (Dessler, 2016) where the practitioner is presented with a list of activities s/he must complete and then asked to prioritize and respond to them within the specified time limit or using Eisenhower's method of arranging tasks by urgency and importance (Krogerus & Tschappeler, 2011) to test out various strategies for decision-making in the field.

Conducting a critical review and implementing strategies to improve Title IV-E education and training programs is not a one-time activity. Rather, Title IV-E programs must continually assess the necessity of integrating and/or removing content based upon prevailing circumstances associated with this line of work. Presenting problems, family challenges, and even regional/geographical problems in one part of a state should be consistently assessed and guide decision making for improvements to Title IV-E education and training.

The theme of feeling overwhelmed
Child welfare practitioners consistently described their experience in the Academy as overwhelming. Attempting to learn copious amounts of information to effectively work in this environment, while being a full-time

student and assigned a caseload may be unreasonable. This common theme has significant policy and practice implications. An option that agencies must consider is the use of *induction units* where a cohort of new hires would share the same supervisor who would fulfill a role as their liaison with the Title IV-E education and training program and child welfare casework. The induction unit would serve to protect practitioner caseloads and effectively support the application of knowledge learned in Title IV-E education and training. This may be easier to do in larger counties and metropolitan areas.

Regardless of whether an induction unit exists, agencies must restrict the maximum number of cases that practitioners are assigned to support the balance between training and practice. According to the Child Welfare League of America (2012), practitioners providing family-centered casework should be assigned no more than 12 families; practitioners making initial CPS assessments should have no more than 12 active reports per month. A recommendation for newly hired practitioners in these Title IV-E training and education programs would be to limit the cases to 60% of this capacity— or about seven cases each, depending on specific job duty. This is a tension that neither trainers nor educators can resolve. Regardless, immediate efforts must be made to address this issue as unmanageable caseloads not only influence workers leaving their positions (Ellett et al., 2007; Griffiths et al., 2017; Zlotnik et al., 2005) and hinder service provisions to families (Cahalane & Sites, 2008; GAO, 2003) but also surely must affect the amount of learning that new workers can absorb from their education and training experience.

Limitations

While this study was benefitted by feedback from a large number of respondents, the generalizability of this study may be limited by the fact that the thoughts and suggestions from this workforce come from a single agency. In addition, the way in which questions were asked in relation to suggestions to reduce turnover did not allow for practitioners to provide insight into what was working well about the Credit for Learning initiative. Although not all survey respondents received their training through Kentucky's current Academy structure, 78% of respondents did complete the current education and training program. Despite a range of changes to the education and training program over time, core content and training processes have remained similar.

Conclusion

Authors of the federal Title IV-E policy had the foresight to recognize that not only can education and training coexist but their integration is essential for elevating the knowledge and professionalism of the child welfare workforce while providing the essential elements practitioners need in their day-to-day practice. Education is integral for providing child welfare practitioners with foundational knowledge and credentials to do child welfare work while training is essential for job preparation and skill enhancement. These two facets cannot be taken in isolation but rather must be presented as a coordinated, seamless process. While many jurisdictions have found a way to implement the two side by side (i.e., State-University partnerships), a truly effective integrated model recognizes and responds to the challenges of instilling an educational foundation, balancing the need for concrete skill development, and concurrently carrying caseloads in fast-paced, high-pressure environment. The results of this study speak to the challenges and issues associated with using a blended Title IV-E education and training model to prepare child welfare practitioners. Recognizing the differing perspectives of the academic and practice communities, this structure provides a natural bridge that must capitalize on the associated strengths to better prepare and retain child welfare practitioners. Universities have resources, nimbleness and the flexibility necessary to deliver content based on both established and cutting-edge research. They are also well-equipped to evaluate the effectiveness of teaching and learning strategies (e.g., prior to students' first field placement, after the field placement, after an elective or required course on child abuse & neglect). However, agency trainers must supply the critical base for practice on the front lines. The alignment of education and training is beneficial for the retention of child welfare practitioners (Rheaume et al., 2011), and the results of this statewide study suggest that we have just begun exploring the best combination. However, it is clear that one opportunity for future research concerns the examination of benefits associated with bringing child protection trainers and supervisors together with university faculty on a regular basis to address concerns identified in this paper. Perhaps with increased opportunities for conversation and planning, child welfare practitioners will be even better prepared and higher retention rates will follow.

Acknowledgement

The authors would like to acknowledge the support of Adria Johnson, Commissioner of Kentucky's Department for Community Based Services. Commissioner Johnson's leadership is currently using the voices of her workforce to revamp and improve Kentucky's Title IV-E training and education program. Further, the authors would like to acknowledge the Western Kentucky University College of Health and Human Services for their support in this statewide study.

ORCID

Austin Griffiths ⓘ http://orcid.org/0000-0002-6670-3150
Kristine Piescher ⓘ http://orcid.org/0000-0002-9784-1919
Traci LaLiberte ⓘ http://orcid.org/0000-0002-2812-3032

References

Augsberger, A., Schudrich, W., McGowan, B. G., & Auerbach, C. (2012). Respect in the workplace: A mixed methods study of retention and turnover in the voluntary child welfare sector. *Children and Youth Services Review, 34*(7), 1222–1229.

Bagdasaryan, S. (2012). Social work education and Title IV-E program participation as predictors of entry-level knowledge among public child welfare workers. *Children & Youth Services Review, 34*(9), 1590–1597. doi:10.1016/j.childyouth.2012.04.013

Barbee, A., Sullivan, D., Borders, K., Antle, B., Hall, C. J., & Fox, S. (2009). Evaluation of an innovative social work education model: The Kentucky public child welfare certification program (PCWCP). *Journal of Social Work Education, 45*(3), 427–444.

Barbee, A. P., Antle, B. F., Sullivan, D. J., Dryden, A. A. A., & Henry, K. (2012). Twenty-five years of the Children's bureau investment in social work education. *Journal of Public Child Welfare, 6*(4), 376–389. doi:10.1080/15548732.2012.705237

Blackwell-Pittman, A. (2016). *Building student competence and confidence in child welfare field placements*. Oral Presentation at the National Title IV-E Roundtable Conference in Salt Lake City, UT.

Braun, V., & Clarke, V. (2006). Using thematic analysis in psychology. *Qualitative Research in Psychology, 3*(2), 77–101. doi:10.1191/1478088706qp063oa

Burry, C. L., Shdaimah, C. S., Richardson, L., & Rice, K. (2011). Child welfare in the court: A collaboration between social work and law faculty to prepare social work students for work with the courts. *Journal of Public Child Welfare, 5*(4), 426–444. doi:10.1080/15548732.2011.599769

Cahalane, H., & Sites, E. W. (2008). The climate of child welfare employee retention. *Child Welfare, 87*(1), 91–114.

Carter, N., Bryant-Lukosius, D., DiCenso, A., Blythe, J., & Neville, A. J. (2014). The use of triangulation in qualitative research. *Oncology Nursing Forum, 41*(5), 545–547. doi:10.1188/14.ONF.545-547

Child Welfare Information Gateway. (2014). *Child maltreatment 2012: Summary of key findings*. Washington, DC: U.S. Department of Health and Human Services, Children's Bureau.

Child Welfare League of America. (2012). *Direct service workers' recommendations for child welfare financing and system reform*. Washington, DC: Author.

Collins, M., Kim, S., & Amodeo, M. (2010). Empirical studies of child welfare training effectiveness: Methods and outcomes. *Child & Adolescent Social Work Journal, 27*(1), 41–62. doi:10.1007/s10560-009-0190-0

Damewood, A. (2016). Current trends in higher education technology: Simulation. *TechTrends: Linking Research & Practice to Improve Learning, 60*(3), 268–271. doi:10.1007/s11528-016-0048-1

Daupin, J., Atkinson, S., Bédard, P., Pelchat, V., Lebel, D., & Bussières, J.-F. (2016). Medication errors room: A simulation to assess the medical, nursing and pharmacy staffs' ability to identify errors related to the medication-use system. *Journal of Evaluation in Clinical Practice, 22*(6), 907–916. doi:10.1111/jep.12558

Dessler, G. (2016). *Fundamentals of human resource management*. Boston, Massachusetts: Pearson.

Dhooper, S. S., Royse, D. D., & Wolfe, L. C. (1990). Does social work education make a difference? *Social Work, 35*(1), 57–61.

Ellett, A. J., Ellett, C. D., & Rugutt, J. K. (2003). *Executive summary: A study of personal and organizational factors contributing to employee retention and turnover in child welfare in Georgia*. Athens, GA: University of Georgia, School of Social Work.

Ellett, A. J., Ellis, J. I., Westbrook, T. M., & Dews, D. (2007). A qualitative study of 369 child welfare professionals' perspectives about factors contributing to employee retention and turnover. *Children and Youth Services Review, 29*(2), 264–281. doi:10.1016/j.childyouth.2006.07.005

Folaron, G., & Hostetter, C. (2007). Is social work the best educational degree for child welfare practitioners? *Journal of Public Child Welfare, 1*(1), 65–83. doi:10.1300/J479v01n01_04

Government Accountability Office. (2003). *Child welfare: HHS could play a greater role in helping child welfare agencies recruit and retain staff (GAO Publication No. 03-357)*. Washington, DC: U.S. Government Printing Office.

Griffiths, A., Royse, D., Culver, K. Piescher, K., & Zhang, Y. (2017). Who stays, who goes, who knows? A state-wide survey of child welfare workers. *Children and Youth Services Review, 77*, 110–117.

Hartinger-Saunders, R. M., & Lyons, P. (2013). Social work education and public child welfare: A review of the peer-reviewed literature on Title IV-E funded programs. *Journal of Public Child Welfare, 7*(3), 275–297. doi:10.1080/15548732.2013.798246

Johnco, C., Salloum, A., Olson, K. R., & Edwards, L. M. (2014). Child welfare workers' perspectives on contributing factors to retention and turnover: Recommendations for improvement. *Children and Youth Services Review, 47 Part*(3(0)), 397–407. doi:10.1016/j.childyouth.2014.10.016

Kim, H. (2011). Job conditions, unmet expectations, and burnout in public child welfare workers: How different from other social workers? *Children and Youth Services Review, 33*(2), 358–367. doi:10.1016/j.childyouth.2010.10.001

Kim, H., & Kao, D. (2014). A meta-analysis of turnover intention predictors among US child welfare workers. *Children and Youth Services Review, 47*, 214–223. doi:10.1016/j.childyouth.2014.09.015

Krogerus, M. & Tschappeler, R. (2011). *The decision book: 50 models for strategic thinking*. London, UK: Profile Books.

Lery, B., Putnam-Hornstein, E., Wiegmann, W., & King, B. (2015). Building analytic capacity and statistical literacy among Title IV-E MSW students. *Journal of Public Child Welfare, 9*(3), 256–276. doi:10.1080/15548732.2015.1043421

Madden, E. E., Scannapieco, M., & Painter, K. (2014). An examination of retention and length of employment among public child welfare workers. *Children and Youth Services Review, 41*, 37–44. doi:10.1016/j.childyouth.2014.02.015

Mason, S. E., LaPorte, H. H., Bronstein, L., & Auerbach, C. (2012). Child welfare workers' perceptions of the value of social work education. *Children and Youth Services Review, 34*(9), 1735–1741. doi:10.1016/j.childyouth.2012.05.005

MAXQDA, software for qualitative data analysis. (1989-2016). Berlin, Germany: VERBI Software – Consult – Sozialforschung GmbH.

Moorthy, K., Vincent, C., & Darzi, A. (2005). Simulation based training. BMJ. *British Medical Journal (International Edition)*, 493–494. doi:10.1136/bmj.330.7490.493

Munangatire, T., & Naidoo, N. (2017). Exploration of high-fidelity simulation: Nurse educators' perceptions and experiences at a school of nursing in a resource-limited setting.

African Journal of Health Professions Education, 9(1), 44–46. doi:10.7196/AJHPE.2017. v9i1.739

National Child Welfare Workforce Institute. *Why the workforce matters.* Retrieved from https://ncwwi.org/files/Why_the_Workforce_Matters.pdf

Negrão Baptista, R. C., Amado Martins, J. C., Carneiro Ribeiro Pereira, M. F., & Mazzo, A. (2014). High-fidelity simulation in the nursing degree: Gains perceived by students. *Simulação De Alta-Fidelidade No Curso De Enfermagem: Ganhos Percebidos Pelos Estudantes, 4*(1), 131–140.

Nissly, J. A., Barak, M. E. M., & Levin, A. (2005). Stress, social support, and workers' intentions to leave their jobs in public child welfare. *Administration in Social Work, 29* (1), 79. doi:10.1300/J147v29n01_06

Nyström, S., Dahlberg, J., Hult, H., & Dahlgren, M. A. (2016). Enacting simulation: A sociomaterial perspective on students' interprofessional collaboration. *Journal of Interprofessional Care, 30*(4), 441–447. doi:10.3109/13561820.2016.1152234

Parton, N. (2009). Challenges to practice and knowledge in child welfare social work: From the 'social' to the 'informational'? *Children and Youth Services Review, 31*(7), 715–721. doi:10.1016/j.childyouth.2009.01.008

Pecukonis, E., Greeno, E., Hodorowicz, M., Park, H., Ting, L., Moyers, T., & Wirt, C. (2016). Teaching motivational interviewing to child welfare social work students using live supervision and standardized clients: A randomized controlled trial. *Journal of the Society for Social Work and Research, 7*(3), 479–505. doi:10.1086/688064

Rheaume, H., Collins, M. E., & Amodeo, M. (2011). University/agency IV-E partnerships for professional education and training: Perspectives from the states. *Journal of Public Child Welfare, 5*(5), 481–500. doi:10.1080/15548732.2011.617261

Richardson, K. J., & Claman, F. (2014). High-fidelity simulation in nursing education: A change in clinical practice. *Nursing Education Perspectives (National League for Nursing), 35*(2), 125–127. doi:10.5480/1536-5026-35.2.125

Rosenthal, J. A., & Waters, E. (2006). Predictors of child welfare worker retention and performance: Focus on title IV-E-funded social work education. *Journal of Social Service Research, 32*(3), 67–85. doi:10.1300/J079v32n03_04

Sar, B. K., Bledsoe, L. K., Sullivan, D. J., Weeks, P. L., Fox, S., Barrett, L. H., & Cashwell, S. T. (2008). Professionalizing the child welfare workforce: Kentucky's Credit for Learning (CFL) Initiative. *Journal of Public Child Welfare, 2*(4), 471–494.

Scannapieco, M., & Connell-Carrick, K. (2007). Child welfare workplace: The state of the workforce and strategies to improve retention. *Child Welfare, 86*(6), 31–52.

Stocker, M., Allen, M., Pool, N., Costa, K., Combes, J., West, N., & Burmester, M. (2012). Impact of an embedded simulation team training programme in a paediatric intensive care unit: A prospective, single-centre, longitudinal study. *Intensive Care Medicine, 38*(1), 99–104. doi:10.1007/s00134-011-2371-5

Strolin-Goltzman, J., Kollar, S., & Trinkle, J. (2010). Listening to the voices of children in foster care: Youths speak out about child welfare workforce turnover and selection. *Social Work, 55*(1), 47–53. doi:10.1093/sw/55.1.47

Swift, M. C., & Stosberg, T. (2015). Interprofessional simulation and education: Physical therapy, nursing, and theatre faculty work together to develop a standardized patient program. *Nursing Education Perspectives (National League for Nursing), 36*(6), 412–413. doi:10.5480/15-1652

Whipple, E. E., Solomon-Jozwiak, S., Williams-Hecksel, C., Abrams, L. A., & Bates, L. (2006). Preparing social workers for child welfare practice: An innovative university-agency learning collaborative. *Social Work Education, 25*(1), 92–107. doi:10.1080/ 02615470500477979

Williams, S. E., Nichols, Q. L., Kirk, A., & Wilson, T. (2011). A recent look at the factors influencing workforce retention in public child welfare. *Children and Youth Services Review, 33*(1), 157–160. doi:10.1016/j.childyouth.2010.08.028

Yankeelov, P. A., Barbee, A. P., Sullivan, D., & Antle, B. F. (2009). Individual and organizational factors in job retention in Kentucky's child welfare agency. *Children and Youth Services Review, 31*(5), 547–554. doi:10.1016/j.childyouth.2008.10.014

Zlotnik, J. L. (2003). The use of Title IV-E training funds for social work education. A historical perspective. *Journal of Human Behavior in the Social Environment, 7*(1/2), 35–51. doi:10.1300/J137v07n01_02

Zlotnik, J. L., DePanfilis, D., Daining, C., & Lane, M. (2005). *Factors influencing retention of child welfare staff: A systematic review of research.* Washington, DC: Institute for the Advancement of Social Work Research.

Zlotnik, J. L., & Pryce, J. A. (2013). Status of the ese of title IV-E funding in BSW and MSW programs. *Journal of Public Child Welfare, 7*(4), 430–446. doi:10.1080/15548732.2013.806278

The role of Title IV-E education and training in child protection workforce diversification

Kristine N. Piescher ⓞ, Traci LaLiberte, and Mihwa Lee

ABSTRACT

Educating, training, and diversifying the workforce are strategies that may help reduce racial/ethnic disparities that plague child protection system (CPS). Title IV-E education and training programs support the development of a specially trained, highly skilled workforce; yet, little research examining their impact on workforce diversification exists. The current study assessed the relationship between Title IV-E education and training and workforce diversity and leadership in a state system that is plagued with racial disparities using data from a statewide child welfare survey ($n = 679$) and existing population-level sources. Findings revealed that while children of color were disproportionately overrepresented in the CPS, professionals of color were disproportionately underrepresented (as compared to the state's overall population and the population of children served within CPS). Title IV-E education and training programs were associated with both child protection workforce diversity and CPS leadership roles. Implications for recruitment, retention, education, and partnership are discussed.

Racial/ethnic disproportionality and disparity plague the United States (U.S.) child protection system (CPS); in particular, Black and American Indian children have been and continue to be overrepresented throughout CPS (Ards, Myers, Malkis, Sugrue, & Zhou, 2003; Font, 2013; Summers, 2015; U.S. Department of Health and Human Services, 2016, 2017). In 2014, Black children comprised 13.8% of the children in the U.S. but 22.6% of alleged victims within CPS while American Indian children comprised 0.9% of the children in the U.S. but 1.3% of alleged victims (USDHHS, 2016). Racial disparities within CPS become even more prominent when children enter out-of-home care. In 2014, Black children were represented in foster care at a rate 1.8 times greater than their representation in the general population and American Indian children were represented in foster care at a rate 2.8 times greater than their representation in the general population (USDHHS, 2016).

However, racial disparities that exist within CPS vary dramatically by geographic region (Summers, 2015; USDHHS, 2016). Minnesota has one of the highest disproportional representation and disparity rates of children by race and ethnicity in the CPS in the U.S. (USDHHS, 2017). In 2015, children who identified as Black, American Indian, and those who identified with two or more races were significantly overrepresented in accepted maltreatment reports as compared to White children. In particular, American Indian children were 5.5 times more likely to be involved in accepted maltreatment reports than White children, while children who identified with two or more races and Black children were both three times more likely (Minnesota Department of Human Services, 2016). These disproportionalities continued and grew larger as children of color proceeded deeper into Minnesota's CPS. Compared to White children, American Indian, Black, and children who identified with two or more races were 16.9, 3.4, and 4.7 times more likely to experience out-of-home care, respectively (Minnesota Department of Human Services, 2017b).

Racial/ethnic disproportionality and disparity in CPS remains a major concern in the field, and possible causes of the disproportionality and disparity have been explored within the professional literature (Enosh & Bayer-Topilsky, 2014; Fluke, Harden, Jenkins, & Ruehrdanz, 2011; Font, Berger, & Slack, 2012; Hill, 2004; Putnam-Hornstein, Needell, King, & Johnson-Motoyama, 2013; Webb, Maddocks, & Bongilli, 2002). Biases exhibited by individuals including child protection professionals, mandated reporters, and other non-mandated reporters may significantly influence disproportionality and disparity rates, as personal biases affect decision-making for children at risk of maltreatment or abuse (Dettlaff & Rycraft, 2010; Lewis, 2010). For example, Ards and colleagues (2012) examined racialized attitudes, perceptions, and beliefs in child protective services workers using vignettes that included variations of child victims by race. Their research revealed that scenarios that included a picture of an Black baby were more likely to be substantiated as child maltreatment than scenarios in which the picture either did not contain a baby or contained a White baby (Ards et al., 2012). Further, research by Dettlaff et al. (2011) and Rivaux et al. (2008) revealed that race, risk, and family income can affect case decisions. For example, Black families were more likely to be involved in a substantiated case of maltreatment, have their children removed, and receive family-based safety services than White families even though they received lower risk scores than White families (Dettlaff et al., 2011; Rivaux et al., 2008). Researchers suggest training, educating, and diversifying the workforce as ways to mitigate personal worker bias and therefore their impacts on decision-making and CPS case outcomes (Dettlaff, 2014; Lancaster & Fong, 2015).

Historically, the majority of child protection social workers have tended to be White. While increased racial/ethnic diversity is evident in more recent years, the workforce remains largely non-Hispanic White and unrepresentative of the race/ethnicities of children and families served in CPS. According to data from the National Survey of Child Adolescent Well-Being II, approximately 58% of child welfare caseworkers identified themselves as non-Hispanic White; 24% identified as Black, 15% identified as Hispanic, and 4% identified as another other race and/or ethnicity (Dolan, Smith, Casanueva, & Ringeisen, 2011).

Having a racially and ethnically diverse child protection workforce allows for the potential for more critical analysis and the identification of bias that exists or could exist (Leung, Cheung, & Stevenson, 1994). In addition, child protection workers who share or understand the culture or language of families from diverse backgrounds may have a better understanding of the family's background and needs (Dettlaff & Rycraft, 2010; Gelman, 2004; Weaver, 1999). Taken together, having a racially and ethnically diverse child protection workforce enhances their collective ability to be receptive to different traditions and ideas, resulting in better serving and protecting people across a variety of cultures and communities (Leung et al., 1994).

Title IV-E education and training programs may serve as one way to help diversify the child protection workforce. Title IV-E education and training programs began in the early 1990s as funding sources to stabilize the child protection workforce while enhancing qualifications and competencies of the workforce (Zlotnik, 2003). Most programs operate in public universities in partnership with state human service agencies. Benefits of these partnerships include enhanced child protection curriculum, public and tribal child protection field placements, enhanced learning opportunities, and funding mechanisms designed to attract and encourage students to select careers in child protection (Barbee, Antle, Sullivan, Dryden, & Henry, 2012; Pierce, McGuire, & Howes, 2015; Zlotnik & Pryce, 2013). These partnerships are bolstered by dedicated attention to pressing issues in the social work field and alignment with the values and ethics of the National Association of Social Work, including social justice and inclusiveness. Following completion of the Title IV-E education and training program, Title IV-E alumni enter into a work obligation in which they are required to find employment at a public or tribal child protection agency for a period of time at least equal to that for which they received Title IV-E support. Title IV-E education and training programs currently exist in most U.S. states (Cheung, 2017).

Title IV-E University-agency partnerships have been deemed "promising practices for addressing the staffing crisis in child welfare, in part by improving both recruitment and retention" (U.S. General Accounting Office, 2003,

p. 4), and there is correlational evidence to support this position (e.g., Madden, Scannapieco, & Painter, 2014; Rheaume, Collins, & Amodeo, 2011). In addition to these benefits, Title IV-E education and training programs have been associated with improved service delivery and outcomes for children and families in CPS. Research has shown that Title IV-E alumni are more confident in their abilities (Barbee et al., 2009; Gansle & Ellett, 2002; O'Donnel & Kirkner, 2009), are more competent in terms of their knowledge and skills (Bagdasaryan, 2012; Gansle & Ellett, 2002), make better prepared caseworkers than non-IV-E trained professionals (Barbee et al., 2009), and are associated with better child and family outcomes, namely those related to permanency (Leung & Willis, 2012) than their peers without the educational background that Title IV-E provides. Although much of the research aimed at understanding the effects of Title IV-E education and training programs is correlational in nature, the evidence suggests that these programs are associated with positive outcomes for the workforce as well as for children and families.

Purpose of this study

While Title IV-E education and training programs are poised to assist in the development of a competent workforce required to ameliorate the racial/ethnic disproportionalities that currently exist in many state CPSs, there is a dearth of research literature examining the impact of Title IV-E education and training on workforce diversity and opportunities to create lasting practice change through leadership roles within the agency. The current study assessed the relationship between Title IV-E education and training and the diversity and leadership opportunities associated with it in a state system that is plagued with racial disparities (Minnesota Department of Human Services, Children and Family Services, 2016, 2017b). Using data from a statewide child welfare survey coupled with secondary population level data, this study aimed to:

(1) describe the regional and statewide racial/ethnic composition of Minnesota's population, its child protection workforce, and the children served by CPS.
(2) compare racial/ethnic characteristics of the population of Minnesota, its child protection workforce (both alumni of IV-E programs and alumni of other programs), and children served by CPS to quantify the magnitude of child protection workforce diversity needs.
(3) assess the associations between Title IV-E education and training programs and child protection workforce diversity and leadership roles.

Methods

Participants

All frontline professionals working in public child welfare in Minnesota and their direct supervisors were invited to participate in the Workforce Stabilization Study. Because Minnesota's child welfare system is a state-supervised and county-administered system, study researchers invited child welfare professionals to participate in an online survey through an email sent by each agency's director in February 2016. Agency directors agreed to distribute the invitation as a means of reaching the full contingency of the workforce while also encouraging participation. Following the distribution of the survey invitation, agency directors reported that they invited 1,948 professionals working as frontline staff or supervisors in child welfare (including child protection services, children's mental health, foster care, adoption and permanency, prevention and early intervention services, and other related children's services). A total of 862 child welfare professionals from 81 (of 87) counties responded to the survey, a 44% statewide response rate. Of the responses, 823 included complete information for most items contained within the survey. For the purposes of this study, the sample was restricted to case-carrying professionals and their direct supervisors working in child protection, involuntary foster care, and/or adoption/permanency ($n = 679$; see Table 1).

Table 1. Workforce characteristics by Title IV-E alumni status ($N = 679$).

	IV-E alumni ($n = 108$)		Non-IV-E alumni ($n = 571$)		Total	
	N	%	N	%	N	%
Gender*						
Female	90	84.1	495	86.8	585	86.4
Male	17	15.9	75	13.2	92	13.6
Race						
White	89	82.4	524	91.8	613	90.3
Black/Black	5	4.6	10	1.8	15	2.2
Asian/Pacific Islander	3	2.8	8	1.4	11	1.6
American Indian	3	2.8	9	1.6	12	1.8
Two or more races	4	3.7	15	2.6	19	2.8
Decline/Missing	4	3.7	5	0.9	9	1.3
Age						
20–30	23	21.3	141	24.7	164	24.1
31–40	43	39.8	168	29.4	211	31.1
41–50	17	15.7	153	26.8	170	25.0
51+	25	23.1	109	19.1	134	19.7
Highest degree attained						
MSW	72	66.7	97	17.0	169	24.9
Other master degree	2	1.9	83	14.5	85	12.5
BSW	27	25.0	189	33.1	216	31.8
Other bachelor degree	7	6.5	202	35.4	209	30.8
CP/IFC/A/P Tenure (mean, sd)**	5.31 years		5.10 years		5.13 years	
	(2.83)		(3.17)		(3.11)	

Note. *Gender was missing in the case of two participants. **CP/IFC/A/P Tenure = Years worked in child protection, involuntary foster care, adoption, and/or permanency.

Instrumentation

The Minnesota Child Welfare Workforce Stabilization Study was designed to inform the development of strategies to stabilize the child welfare workforce and ensure employee retention in a time of CPS reform. The online survey on which the current study is based was developed by a team of researchers at the University of Minnesota and informed by a comprehensive review of existing literature, including previous research conducted by Ellett, Ellett, and Rugutt (2003). The survey was presented to an association of Minnesota county human service directors (Minnesota Association of County Social Service Administrators [MACSSA]) and representatives of the Children and Families Division of the Minnesota Department of Human Services for review, modification, and adoption prior to implementation. The workforce survey consisted of 67 items of which 10 measured demographic characteristics of the workforce, eight focused on current agency role, 20 were about current job satisfaction (including satisfaction with organizational issues, policy and program development, experiences with secondary traumatic stress, and supervision), 21 were related to intent to remain employed, seven items assessed child protection reform, and one item was available for respondents to offer additional feedback or to clarify any responses deemed necessary.

Other data sources

Two sources of existing data were also utilized in the current study to allow for comparisons among Minnesota's child protection workforce, its population, and the children served by CPS. First, U.S. Census data were used as the source of information about Minnesota's total population and the population of those who identified as people of color in 2015 (U.S. Census Bureau, 2016). Second, existing data from the Minnesota Department of Human Services were used to identify the population of children who were alleged victims of maltreatment in 2015 and the proportion of those who were identified as children of color (Minnesota Department of Human Services, 2017a). Further description of these data elements and calculations applied to these data for the current study are described below.

Measures

A regional framework, developed and utilized by MACSSA, served as the organizational framework for many of the measures used in the current study. MACSSA's framework divides the state's 87 counties into 11 regions (Figure 1). This framework was selected due to its current use in the provision of social services in the state as well as for its ability to

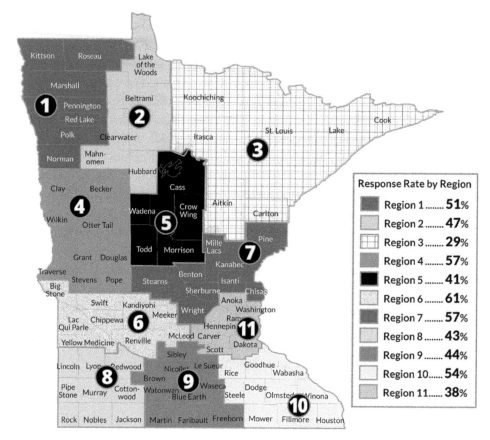

Figure 1. Minnesota Association of County Social Service Administrators regions and response rates.

promote the protection of confidentiality for study participants. This is particularly true for smaller counties where few individuals of color reside.

Title IV-E alumni status. Information about a child protection professional's Title IV-E alumni status was gathered via the Minnesota Child Welfare Workforce Stabilization Survey. In the survey, professionals self-identified as Title IV-E alumni by responding to the question, "Are you currently, or have you ever been, a student or graduate of a Title IV-E child welfare education program?" A binary alumni status code (1) alumni or (0) not alumni was used in the current study.

Role within the agency. In the Minnesota Child Welfare Workforce Stabilization Survey, child protection professionals were asked to identify their current position from the following response options: caseworker\social worker, supervisor (no caseload responsibilities), supervisor (with caseload responsibilities), case aide, and other (please specify). For the current study, responses were recoded into two mutually exclusive categories— caseworker/ social worker (1) and supervisor (2). (Case aides and professionals working in other capacities were excluded from the study, as described in the participants section.)

Racial/ethnic diversity. For the current study, several measures of racial/ ethnic diversity were calculated for the population of the state, its child protection workforce, and the children served by CPS. To protect the confidentiality of individuals residing within the state (where some racial/ethnic groups are small in number), racial/ethnic data were aggregated into a binary code that indicated whether the individual identified as a person of color. Further description of these aggregates and any derivative measure(s) are presented below.

General population diversity. Minnesota population estimates for 2015 based on the 2010 Census were used to calculate each region's population of color (U. S. Census Bureau, Population Division, 2016). Using county-level data, the number of individuals identified as Black or African-American, American Indian or Alaskan Native, Asian, Native Hawaiian or Other Pacific Islander and those identified as two or more races were summed within each MACSSA region; the total was then divided by the total population for all counties within that region to calculate regional population diversity. Statewide population diversity measures were similarly calculated.

Workforce diversity. Information about the racial/ethnic diversity of Minnesota's child protection workforce was gathered via the Minnesota Child Welfare Workforce Stabilization Survey. In the survey, professionals working in Minnesota's county child protection agencies self-identified their race and ethnicity by responding to two questions, "With which race(s) do you identify? Check all that apply." and "With which ethnicity or cultural community do you identify? Check all that apply." Responses to these questions were aggregated to create a binary variable that indicated whether an individual self-identified as a person of color. The number of individuals those identified as people of color (including those who identified as Black/African-American, Asian/Pacific Islander, or American Indian, and those who identified as Hispanic/Latino/ Latina, Hmong, Somali, Karen, Vietnamese, Kenyan, Nigerian, or another ethnicity [e.g., wrote in "Cherokee"] indicating identity as a person of color) were summed within each MACSSA region; the total was then divided by the total number of professionals who responded to the survey within that region to calculate regional workforce diversity. Statewide population diversity measures were similarly calculated.

Alleged victim diversity. Information about the racial/ethnic diversity of children served in Minnesota's CPS in 2015 (i.e., alleged victims in an accepted child maltreatment case) was provided by the Minnesota Department of

Human Services (2017a). Using county-level data, the number of children identified as African-American/Black, American Indian, Asian or Pacific Islander and those identified as two or more races were summed within each MACSSA region; the total was then divided by the total number of children served in the CPS within that region to calculate regional population diversity. Statewide population diversity measures were similarly calculated. It is important to note that there was one consortium of counties that crossed two MACSSA regions (regions 9 and 10). In this case, the numerators and denominators used to calculate the regions' alleged victim diversity were prorated according to the size of each county's population. It is also important to note that data on alleged child victims were derived from county administrative data; therefore, children served by the two tribes that receive Title IV-E funding were not included in the victim counts. Thus, a more conservative estimate of alleged victim diversity for Minnesota is presented in this study. However, the majority of children in CPS who identify as American Indian (82%) were served by Minnesota counties (Minnesota Department of Human Services, 2017a) and therefore included in this study.

Disparity indices (DIs) were also calculated for each MACSSA region and for the state as a whole. The DI provides an unbiased comparison of the level of representation for one group (in this study, children of color) versus all others (in this study, all White children; Shaw, Putnam-Hornstein, Magruder, & Needell, 2008). Using other calculations may be misleading in situations where the group of interest comprises a relatively small or large proportion of the population; the DI corrects for this potential bias by comparing the relative rates of the two groups. DIs were calculated as follows:

$$DI = \frac{(\#\text{ children of color in CPS}/\#\text{ all children in CPS})/(\#\text{ children of color in population}/\#\text{ all children in population})}{(\#\text{ White children in CPS}/\#\text{ all children in CPS})/(\#\text{ White children in population}/\#\text{ all children in population})}$$

Racial/ethnic diversity comparisons. For this study, the three aforementioned racial/ethnic diversity measures were used to make comparisons among the state's population, its child protection workforce, and the children served by CPS. Comparisons were made at the regional and statewide levels. *Workforce disproportionality by state population.* Differences between the proportion of professional of color (POC) in the workforce and that of the population were calculated by subtracting the proportion of POC in the workforce from the proportion of POC in the population for each region and for the state. This number was then multiplied by the estimated workforce size to calculate the number of workers of color needed to make the proportion of POC equal in the workforce and the population.

Workforce disproportionality by child victim population. Differences between the proportion of POC in the workforce and that of the children of color served in CPS were calculated by subtracting the proportion of POC in the workforce from the proportion of children of color in CPS for each region and for the state. This number was then multiplied by the estimated workforce size to calculate the number of workers of color needed to make the proportion of POC equal in the workforce and the population.

Analytic plan

Descriptive analysis was used to assess the 1) racial/ethnic composition of Minnesota's population, its child protection workforce, and the children served by CPS, 2) geographic variations of Minnesota's racial/ethnic populations, 3) disproportionalities evident for children of color within Minnesota's CPS (via disproportionality indices), and 4) differences in the racial/ethnic composition of Minnesota's child protection workforce as compared to the State's population and children served by CPS. Chi-square analysis was used to examine associations among Title IV-E alumni status and both the racial/ethnic diversity and attainment of leadership roles within Minnesota's child protection workforce.

Results

Descriptive findings revealed that only a small proportion of Minnesota's population identified as people of color. Across the state approximately 15% of Minnesota's population identified as people of color, but regional variation was evident (see Table 2). In particular, regions with large metropolitan areas and those that included multiple American Indian reservations had higher proportions of individuals identifying as people of color than other regions. For example, the populations of region 11 (a metropolitan region) and region 2 (a region including multiple American Indian reservations) were each comprised of 21% of people of color.

While similarly low levels of diversity were evident in Minnesota's CPS workforce, the same was not true of the children served by the CPS. Over 40% of all alleged victims in Minnesota's CPS were identified as children of color, resulting in disproportionate representation of children of color within the system (see Table 2). Regional comparisons revealed that alleged victims of color were represented in the CPS at rates nearly three to six times greater than victims identified as White.

The CPS workforce was the least diverse of any of the populations compared in this study, with less than 10% of the workforce identifying as professionals of color overall. In fact, the proportion of the CPS workforce identifying as people of color equaled that of the population in only four of Minnesota's 11 regions (including regions 3, 4, 5, and 10; see Table 2). The difference between the proportion of individuals identifying as people of color in the child protection workforce as compared to that of the general population ranged from 4% to 8% across regions. However, the disproportionality

Table 2. Racial/ethnic diversity in Minnesota and resultant disproportionalities.

	Population		Alleged victims		Workforce			Population comparisons		Alleged victim comparisons	
Region	N	POC (%)	N	POC (%)*	N*	POC (%)	DI	Workforce POC deficit (%)	Workforce POC deficit (N)	Workforce POC deficit (%)	Workforce POC deficit (N)
1	86,102	5.75	559	18.60	27	0.00	3.75	5.75	2	18.60	5
2	84,510	20.41	739	47.77	45	14.29	3.57	6.12	3	33.48	15
3	325,803	7.53	2,977	33.25	193	10.71	6.12	-3.19	-6	22.54	44
4	227,038	5.95	1,981	24.99	91	5.77	5.26	0.18	0	19.22	18
5	163,041	5.54	1,021	20.08	73	6.67	4.29	-1.13	-1	13.41	10
6	159,688	4.17	1,094	14.53	75	0.00	3.91	4.17	3	14.53	11
7	580,850	6.27	3,054	22.76	168	6.25	4.41	0.02	0	16.51	28
8	117,597	7.91	816	21.32	35	0.00	3.16	7.91	3	21.32	7
9	261,611	5.01	1,482	14.74	75	0.00	3.28	5.01	4	14.74	11
10	471,237	8.59	2,604	20.99	189	9.80	2.83	-1.21	-2	11.18	21
11	3,012,117	20.88	15,221	57.83	563	16.82	5.20	4.06	23	41.01	231
Total	5,489,594	14.65	31,548	40.39	1,535	9.72	3.95	4.93	76	30.67	471

Note: * This is an estimated workforce N, provided by each county's child welfare director.
DI, Disparity index; POC, professional of color.

evident in the CPS workforce in comparison to the population of alleged victims was much greater. The proportion of the CPS workforce identifying as people of color was substantially less than that of alleged victims in every Minnesota region; these workforce race/ethnicity deficits in comparison to the population of alleged victims ranged from 11% to 41% across regions.

In order to diversify the CPS workforce to reflect the racial and ethnic diversity of the people of Minnesota and/or the population of children served within the system, substantial numbers of professionals of color must be hired. Given the estimated CPS workforce population of Minnesota ($n = 1,535$), 76 professionals of color would need to be hired to reflect the racial/ethnic diversity of Minnesota's people (see Table 2). This is equivalent to replacing 5% of the White professionals within Minnesota's CPS workforce with professionals of color. On the other hand, Minnesota would need to hire 471 professionals of color to reflect the racial and ethnic diversity of the children within the CPS system—equivalent to replacing approximately one out of every three White CPS professionals with a POC (30%).

Chi-square analysis was used to determine the extent to which Title IV-E education and training programs were associated with opportunities for diversifying the workforce (based on race/ethnicity) and creating leadership roles within child protection agencies. Results revealed a significant relationship between Title IV-E alumni status and identification as a POC in Minnesota's CPS (see Table 3). A larger proportion of Title IV-E alumni identified as professionals of color (16.7%) than professionals who did not graduate from a Title IV-E education and training program (8.4%). Chi-square analysis also revealed a significant relationship between Title IV-E alumni status and role within the child protection agency (see Table 3). A significantly larger proportion of Title IV-E alumni in Minnesota's CPS were supervisors (22.2%) as compared to professionals who did not graduate from a Title IV-E education and training program (14.4%).

To test whether the relationship between Title IV-E alumni status and agency role was a function of professionals' identification as a person of color, a layer (i.e., identification as POC) was added to the chi-square analysis. The results revealed that the relationship between being a Title IV-E alumni and one's role within the agency did not differ by whether one identifies as a person of color (see Table 4). In other words, leadership positions related to IV-E alumni status are similar for professionals of color and White professionals working in child protection.

Discussion

This study was developed to understand and critically examine Minnesota's child protection workforce needs with a focus on the role of Title IV-E education and training programs in supporting workforce diversity and

Table 3. Chi-square analysis of associations among identification as POC, agency role, and Title IV-E alumni status.

	IV-E alumni		Non-IV-E alumni		Total			
	N	%	N	%	N	χ^2	df	p
Race						7.062	1,679	0.008
Non-POC	90	83.3	523	91.6	613			
POC	18	16.7	48	8.4	66			
Agency role						4.261	1,679	0.039
Supervisor	24	22.2	82	14.4	110			
Frontline	84	77.8	489	85.6	604			

Note. POC, professional of color.

Table 4. Chi-square analysis of the association between agency role and Title IV-E alumni status, with POC identification.

	Frontline		Supervisor		Total			
	N	%	N	%	N	χ^2	df	p
White						3.439	1,679	0.064
IV-E alumni	70	13.5	20	20.8	90			
Non-IV-E	447	86.5	76	79.2	523			
POC						0.963	1,679	0.327
IV-E alumni	14	25.0	4	40.0	28			
Non-IV-E	42	75.0	6	60.0	48			

Note. POC, professional of color.

leadership opportunities within CPS. Overall, this study revealed that the racial/ethnic diversity of the state's child protection workforce did not reflect that of the general population of the state and that it dramatically differed from that of the children served by CPS. Problematic is the fact that while children of color are disproportionately *over*represented in Minnesota's CPS, professionals of color are disproportionately *under*represented in Minnesota's CPS, contradicting what best practice tells us about mitigating bias and reducing disparities in child protection (Dettlaff, 2014; Lancaster & Fong, 2015). While this study was based on Minnesota's CPS, the challenges uncovered herein are not unique to Minnesota (Ards et al., 2003; Summers, 2015; USDHHS, 2016).

Researchers have asserted that biases and their impacts on decision-making and case outcomes in CPS may be mitigated through education, training, and diversifying the workforce (Dettlaff, 2014; Hill, 2004; Lancaster & Fong, 2015; Webb et al., 2002). Fortunately, most states in the U.S. have operating Title IV-E education and training programs. Currently, these programs exist in at least 34 of 50 U.S. states, a conservative estimate given the voluntary nature of data collection (Cheung, 2017). While each program is tailored to the unique strengths and needs of its community and child protection practice, the goals are shared across programs. These include preparing a highly skilled, specially trained group of practitioners and stabilizing the child protection workforce so that families experience positive outcomes. Over and above the research that supports the effectiveness of these programs in meeting their goals (Barbee et al., 2012; Pierce et al., 2015; Zlotnik & Pryce, 2013), the current study revealed that Title IV-E programs were associated with increased workforce diversity and roles in CPS leadership (which were found *not* to be a function of the professionals' racial/ethnic identification). While existing (though correlational) evidence suggests that these programs are beneficial to the workforce and to children and families served in child protection, opportunities for continued improvement remain.

Implications for policy and practice

With over 30 years of history and demonstrated successes across numerous areas of workforce development, Title IV-E education and training programs in the U.S. are poised to harness their strengths to continue to modify their programming and operation in order to maximize their outcomes. Opportunities for continued improvement that build upon on the unique and shared strengths of each Title IV-E education and training program exist along the continuum of programmatic efforts—from recruitment and retention to employment partnerships and effective service delivery. Title IV-E education and training programs must 1) be attractive and desirable places for workforce preparation and advancement to support recruiting and retaining a diverse student body, 2) educate the workforce in the current context of practice and findings of cutting-edge research, and 3) provide a strong path for postgraduation employment and advancement in order to both diversify the child protection workforce and to provide that evolving and increasingly diverse workforce with the knowledge and skills needed to effectively address the disparities that persist.

Recruitment and retention of a diverse student body. In order to attract a diverse and well-qualified student body, Title IV-E education and training programs must first and foremost have a solid reputation within the community and the CPS. These programs must be rigorous in their curriculum, be engaged with and responsive to the current context of the community, and provide opportunities for applied learning and skill demonstration. With a foundation of strong reputation and curriculum, social work admissions departments, at both the baccalaureate and Master's levels, are positioned to attract a diverse group of students from a variety of communities into their programs. This is critical to diversifying the child protection workforce, as admitted students within social work programs are the applicant pool from which Title IV-E programs recruit and select their scholars. Without a diverse social work student body, recruitment of students of color into Title IV-E programs, and therefore into the child protection workforce, is compromised.

Given the fact that many Title IV-E education and training programs operate out of public-university partnerships and are located in large metropolitan areas where a variety of communities reside, there are huge pools of prospective students from which schools of social work may recruit in their efforts to increase the diversity of their student bodies. In fact, the websites of most Title IV-E education and training programs boast of recruiting and retaining students of color and students from diverse backgrounds. Despite their assertions, the use of traditional recruiting methods is limiting and challenges remain. There is a perception about the child protection field that may deter prospective students from applying. Research has demonstrated that there is a perception that the CPS is often isolated from the communities that it is mandated to serve (Dettlaff & Rycraft, 2010). While it has been recommended that CPSs ally themselves with communities and draw on the strengths of communities to address this problem of negative perception (Dettlaff & Rycraft, 2010), the authors of the current study would argue that similar challenges exist in recruiting students of color. Therefore, authors assert that schools of social work and the Title IV-E education and training programs operating within must also increase alliances and community partnerships across local communities of color.

Recruitment is only part of the solution; it is imperative that schools of social work and the Title IV-E education and training programs within be prepared to support a diverse student body once admitted. Research suggests that individual and institutional approaches to support students of color are necessary, including (a) recognizing and engaging issues of race, (b) incorporating effective and race-sensitive mentorship, (c) creating and sustaining multitiered and multipurpose support networks, and (d) establishing formal and informal support structures (Young & Brooks, 2008). The Council on Social Work Education (CSWE) Council on Racial, Ethnic, and Cultural Diversity (CRECD) (n.d.) has developed a list of resources to support best practices in recruiting and retaining students from oppressed and historically underrepresented groups. Taken together over time, the incorporation of practices to increase the diversity of the applicant recruitment and support a student body that is representative of communities served within CPS could have the potential to dramatically transform the child protection workforce.

Workforce education in context and through cutting-edge research. Simultaneously with addressing the need to diversify the student body, schools of social work and the Title IV-E education and training programs within must continue to provide an educational foundation that is built upon best practices and knowledge generated through cutting-edge research. To effectively address issues of racial/ethnic disparity in practice, Title IV-E education and training programs must prepare the workforce to address biases exhibited by the individuals themselves (Dettlaff & Rycraft, 2010;

Lewis, 2010) as well as the structural racism that exists within the CPS (Ards et al., 2003; Hill, 2004). These curricular areas of focus cannot simply be taught at the abstract/theoretical level; rather, this content should be taught within the current context of the local CPS and with attention to the direct application of these issues to practice. For example, using a combination of methods to identify and address biases that exist for individuals and the CPSs in which they will work may include integration of a tool to assess inter-cultural competence (e.g., the Intercultural Development Inventory Hammer, Bennett, & Wiseman, 2003), an experiential learning opportunity held within and led by a community that is disproportionately represented in the local CPS (e.g., Johnston-Goodstar et al., 2016), and simulation lab scenarios designed to allow students to apply their learning outside of the classroom to a practice scenario (e.g., Sunarich & Rowan, 2017).

Paths for postgraduation employment and advancement. The goal of increasing the diversity of the child protection workforce lies with successful hiring, retention, and advancement of professionals of color into positions of leadership within the field. Agencies have an opportunity to look within their current workforce to invest in and create pathways for professionals of color who do not yet meet the educational requirements of CPS frontline work (i.e., have a bachelor or Master's degree), but who desire to work in the field (e.g., case assistants, cultural navigators, etc.). For instance, hiring cultural navigators to bridge cultural divides within agencies is currently occurring across the country. However, this solves a short-term issue. Investing in these individuals and supporting them in IV-E education and training programs is a longer-term solution—one which provides an already dedicated and moti-vated pool of candidates with opportunities for further growth and development.

Title IV-E education and training programs are uniquely positioned to serve as the bridge to public and tribal child protection employment due to the postgraduation employment obligation that is required by this unique funding mechanism. Reasonably, if Title IV-E education and training programs admit, educate, and train an increased number of professionals of color, the workforce will subsequently expand in the desired direction of diversification. Retention within the field, however, then becomes critical. While the current study did not focus on retention, one of its implications is surely that maintaining the employment of effective professionals of color and previous research has revealed that this may be a challenge (Griffiths, Royse, Culver, Piescher, & Zhang, 2017). Creating spaces that value and make room for the voices of a diverse workforce is integral in serving and protecting people across a variety of cultures and communities in CPS (Leung et al., 1994), and will likely support the retention of professionals of color within CPS.

Limitations

Several limitations should be considered while contemplating this study's results and the generalizability of such results. First, associations between the characteristics of Title IV-E alumni, their educational preparation, and their representation in the workforce are correlational rather than causal. The paths by which these associations have come to be were not a focus of this research and are not yet well understood. While this study contributed to a greater understanding of the role that Title IV-E education and training programs may play in workforce preparation, the existing body of research is limited by its reliance on correlational findings (this study not withstanding). In addition, we did not study how increased diversity within the workforce and/or leadership affects child and family outcomes. Second, a binary representation of race/ethnicity was used in this study to protect the confidentiality of study participants; critical thought about how to diversify the workforce beyond this rudimentary definition is crucial, especially in light of Detlaff & Rycraft's (2010) findings that suggest the workforce not be simply representative of a variety of racial and/or ethnic identities but rather representative of the *communities* that are served within the CPS. It is important to consider the variety of ethnicities that are represented within the community (e.g., Somali, Hmong, etc.) and how their representation changes over time in the workforce as the composition of communities change in the population. Finally, this study relied on county-level data stemming from surveys and administrative records; thus, the study did not include children served directly by the two tribes in Minnesota with Title IV-E funding or their workforce. In all, 82% of American Indian children in Minnesota was served by county-based CPS systems (Minnesota Department of Human Services, 2017a) and therefore included in this study, leaving 18% of American Indian children in Minnesota's CPS unaccounted within this study.

Conclusion

This is, to our knowledge, one of the first studies to assess the association between Title IV-E education and training programs and the representation of professionals of color within the workforce. This research is timely in that Minnesota, like many other jurisdictions, is challenged with confronting the racial disparities that exist within the CPS (Minnesota Department of Human Services, Children and Family Services, 2016, 2017b). In their introduction to the *Child Welfare* special issue on strengthening the child welfare workforce, Zlotnik, Strand, and Anderson (2009) stated:

> The child welfare workforce is the backbone of child welfare service delivery. Without
> committed, qualified, culturally competent, and caring frontline staff and supervisors,

agencies are hard-pressed to implement the array of service delivery strategies needed to meet the needs of our most vulnerable children and families. (p. 7)

Title IV-E education and training programs may be uniquely positioned to assist agencies in meeting those service needs, with particular attention to addressing the racial disparities that exist in the CPS through increased efforts in recruiting and supporting students of color. Title IV-E education and training programs must continue to enhance the programmatic elements that have positioned them as a "promising practice" for employment and retention and extend that to encompass positive outcomes for children and families served within the CPS. Taken together, Title IV-E education and training programs may be a critical element in a multipronged, comprehensive approach to serving racially and ethnically diverse children and families within child protection.

ORCID

Kristine N. Piescher http://orcid.org/0000-0002-9784-1919

References

Ards, S. D., Myers, S. L., Malkis, A., Sugrue, E., & Zhou, L. (2003). Racial disproportionality in reported and sustained child abuse and neglect: An examination of systematic bias [Special issue]. *Children and Youth Services Review, 25*(5–6), 375–392. doi:10.1016/S0190-7409(03)00027-6

Ards, S. D., Myers, S. L., Ray, P., Kim, H. E., Monroe, K., & Arteaga, I. (2012). Racialized perceptions and child neglect. *Children and Youth Services Review, 34*(8), 1480–1491. doi:10.1016/j.childyouth.2012.03.018

Bagdasaryan, S. (2012). Social work education and Title IV-E program participation as predictors of entry-level knowledge among public child welfare workers. *Children and Youth Services Review, 34,* 1590–1597. doi:10.1016/j.childyouth.2012.04.013

Barbee, A. P., Antle, B., Sullivan, D., Huebner, R., Fox, S., & Hall, J. C. (2009). Recruiting and retaining child welfare workers: Is preparing social work students enough for sustained commitment to the field? *Child Welfare, 88,* 69–86.

Barbee, A. P., Antle, B. F., Sullivan, D. J., Dryden, A. A., & Henry, K. (2012). Twenty-five years of the children's bureau investment in social work education. *Journal of Public Child Welfare, 6*(4), 376–389. doi:10.1080/15548732.2012.705237

Barbee, A. P., Sullivan, D. J., Antle, B. F., Moran, E. B., Hall, J. C., & Fox, S. (2009). The public child welfare certification program: Worker retention and impact on practice. *Journal of Social Work Education, 45,* 427–444.

Cheung, M. (Ed.). (2017). *National survey of IV-E stipends and paybacks.* Houston, TX: University of Houston. Retrieved from http://www.uh.edu/socialwork/New_research/cwep/title-iv-e/Stipends-Paybacks/

Council on Social Work Education, Council on Racial, Ethnic and Cultural Diversity. (n.d.). *Toolkit on recruitment & retention of historically underrepresented faculty and doctoral students in social work education.* Alexandria, VA: Council on Social Work Education. Retrieved from www.cswe.org/About-CSWE/Governance/Commissions-and-Councils/Commission-for-Diversity-and-Social-and-Economic-J/Council-on-Racial,-Ethical-and-Cultural-Diversity/CRECD-Toolkit-on-Recruitment-and-Retention

Dettlaff, A. J. (2014). The evolving understanding of disproportionality and disparities in child welfare. In *Handbook of child maltreatment* (pp. 149–168). New York, NY: Springer.

Dettlaff, A. J., Rivaux, S. L., Baumann, D. J., Fluke, J. D., Rycraft, J. R., & James, J. (2011). Disentangling substantiation: The influence of race, income, and risk on the substantiation decision in child welfare. *Children and Youth Services Review, 33*(9), 1630–1637. doi:10.1016/j.childyouth.2011.04.005

Dettlaff, A. J., & Rycraft, J. R. (2010). Factors contributing to disproportionality in the child welfare system: Views from the legal community. *Social Work, 55*(3), 213–224. doi:10.1093/sw/55.3.213

Dolan, M., Smith, K., Casanueva, C., & Ringeisen, H. (2011). *NSCAW II baseline report: Introduction to NSCAW II.* Washington, DC: Office of Planning, Research and Evaluation, Administration for Children and Families, US Department of Health and Human Services. Retrieved from https://www.acf.hhs.gov/sites/default/files/opre/nscaw2_intro.pdf

Ellett, A. J., Ellett, C. D., & Rugutt, J. K. (2003). *A study of personal and organizational factors contributing to employee retention and turnover in child welfare in Georgia: Final project report.* Athens, GA: University of Georgia.

Enosh, G., & Bayer-Topilsky, T. (2014). Reasoning and bias: Heuristics in safety assessment and placement decisions for children at risk. *The British Journal of Social Work, 45*(6), 1771–1787. doi:10.1093/bjsw/bct213

Fluke, J., Harden, B. J., Jenkins, M., & Ruehrdanz, A. (2011). Research synthesis on child welfare: Disproportionality and disparities. *Disparities and disproportionality in child welfare: Analysis of the research, 1.* Retrieved from https://repositories.lib.utexas.edu/bitstream/handle/2152/15376/Casey_Disparities_ChildWelfare.pdf?sequence=5

Font, S. A. (2013). Service referral patterns among Black and White families involved with child protective services. *Journal of Public Child Welfare, 7*(4), 370–391. doi:10.1080/15548732.2013.818087

Font, S. A., Berger, L. M., & Slack, K. S. (2012). Examining racial disproportionality in child protective services case decisions. *Children and Youth Services Review, 34*(11), 2188–2200. doi:10.1016/j.childyouth.2012.07.012

Gansle, K., & Ellett, A. (2002). Child welfare knowledge transmission, practitioner retention, and university-community impact: A study of Title IV-E child welfare training. *Journal of Health and Social Policy*, *15*(3/4), 69–88. doi:10.1300/J045v15n03_06

Gelman, C. R. (2004). Empirically-based principles for culturally competent practice with Latinos. *Journal of Ethnic and Cultural Diversity in Social Work*, *13*(1), 83–108. doi:10.1300/J051v13n01_05

Griffiths, A. G., Royse, D., Culver, K., Piescher, K., & Zhang, Y. (2017). Who stays, who goes, who knows? A state-wide survey of child welfare workers. *Children and Youth Services Review*, *77*, 110–117. doi:10.1016/j.childyouth.2017.04.012

Hammer, M. R., Bennett, M. J., & Wiseman, R. (2003). The Intercultural Development Inventory: A measure of intercultural sensitivity. *International Journal of Intercultural Relations*, *27*, 421–443.

Hill, R. B. (2004). Institutional racism in child welfare. *Race and Society*, *7*(1), 17–33. doi:10.1016/j.racsoc.2004.11.004

Johnston-Goodstar, K., Piescher, K., & LaLiberte, T. (2016). Critical experiential learning in the native American community for Title IV-E students: A pilot evaluation. *Journal of Public Child Welfare*, *10*, 310–326. doi:10.1080/15548732.2016.1181021

Lancaster, L., & Fong, R. (2015). Disproportionality and disparities in the public child welfare system. In R. Fong, A. Dettlaff, J. James, & C. Rodriguez (Eds.), *Addressing racial disproportionality and disparities in human services* (pp. 169–207). New York, NY: Columbia University Press.

Leung, P., Cheung, K. F. M., & Stevenson, K. M. (1994). A strengths approach to ethnically sensitive practice for child protective service workers. *Child Welfare*, *73*, 707–721.

Leung, P., & Willis, N. (2012). The impact of Title IV-E training on case outcomes for children serviced by CPS. *Journal of Family Strengths*, *12*(1), 1–16. Retrieved from http://digitalcommons.library.tmc.edu/jfs/vol12/iss1/9/

Lewis, N. N. (2010). *How cultural competency of social workers affects their decisions to remove children from their parents* (MSW thesis). Retrieved from Sacramento State ScholarWorks: http://hdl.handle.net/10211.9/491

Madden, E. E., Scannapieco, M., & Painter, K. (2014). An examination of retention and length of employment among public child welfare workers. *Children and Youth Services Review*, *41*, 37–44. doi:10.1016/j.childyouth.2014.02.015

Minnesota Department of Human Services. (2017a). *2015 Minnesota child victim race by county*. Unpublished raw data. St. Paul, MN: Author.

Minnesota Department of Human Services. (2017b). *Minnesota's out-of-home care and permanency report 2015*. Retrieved from https://www.leg.state.mn.us/docs/2017/mandated/170067.pdf

Minnesota Department of Human Services, Children and Family Services. (2016). *Minnesota's child maltreatment report 2015: Report to the 2016 Minnesota Legislature.* Retrieved from https://www.leg.state.mn.us/docs/2016/mandated/161102.pdf

O'Donnel, J., & Kirkner, S. (2009). Title IV-E programs: Preparing MSW students for public child welfare practice. *Journal of Teaching in Social Work*, *29*, 241–257. doi:10.1080/08841230903022050

Pierce, B., McGuire, L. E., & Howes, P. (2015). Ready, set, go…again: Renewing an academy–Agency child welfare partnership. *Journal of Social Work Education*, *51*(sup2), 239–251.

Putnam-Hornstein, E., Needell, B., King, B., & Johnson-Motoyama, M. (2013). Racial and ethnic disparities: A population-based examination of risk factors for involvement with child protective services. *Child Abuse & Neglect*, *37*(1), 33–46. doi:10.1016/j.chiabu.2012.08.005

Rheaume, H., Collins, M. E., & Amodeo, M. (2011). University/Agency IV-E partnerships for professional education and training: Perspectives from the states. *Journal of Public Child Welfare, 5*, 481–500. doi:10.1080/15548732.2011.617261

Rivaux, S. L., James, J., Wittenstrom, K., Baumann, D., Sheets, J., Henry, J., & Jeffries, V. (2008). The intersection of race, poverty, and risk: Understanding the decision to provide services to clients and to remove children. *Child Welfare, 87*, 151.

Shaw, T., Putnam-Hornstein, E., Magruder, J., & Needell, B. (2008). Measuring racial disparity in child welfare. *Child Welfare, 87*, 23–36.

Summers, A. (2015). *Disproportionality rates for children of color in foster care (fiscal year 2013)*. Retrieved from http://www.ncjfcj.org/Dispro-TAB-2013

Sunarich, N., & Rowan, S. (2017, May). Social work simulation education in the field. *Field Educator (Vol 7.1)*. Retrieved from: http://www2.simmons.edu/ssw/fe/i/16-130.pdf

U.S. Census Bureau, Population Division. (2016). *Annual Estimates of the resident population by sex, race, and Hispanic origin for the United States, states, and counties: April 1, 2010 to July 1, 2015*. Retrieved from https://factfinder.census.gov

U.S. Department of Health & Human Services, Children's Bureau. (2016). *Racial disproportionality and disparity in child welfare*. Retrieved from https://www.childwelfare.gov/pubPDFs/racial_disproportionality.pdf

U.S. Department of Health & Human Services, Children's Bureau. (2017). *Child maltreatment 2015*. Retrieved from http://www.acf.hhs.gov/programs/cb/research-data-technology/statistics-research/child-maltreatment

U.S. General Accounting Office. (2003, March). *HHS could play a greater role in helping child welfare agencies recruit and retain staff (GAO-03-357)*. Washington, DC: Author.

Weaver, H. N. (1999). Indigenous people and the social work profession: Defining culturally competent services. *Social Work, 44*, 217–225. doi:10.1093/sw/44.3.217

Webb, E., Maddocks, A., & Bongilli, J. (2002). Effectively protecting black and minority ethnic children from harm: Overcoming barriers to the child protection process. *Child Abuse Review, 11*, 394–410. doi:10.1002/car.760

Young, M. D., & Brooks, J. S. (2008). Supporting graduate students of color in educational administration preparation programs: Faculty perspectives on best practices, possibilities, and problems. *Educational Administration Quarterly, 44*, 391–423. doi:10.1177/0013161X08315270

Zlotnik, J. L. (2003). The use of Title IV-E training funds for social work education: An historical perspective. *Journal of Human Behavior in the Social Environment, 7*(1–2), 5–20. doi:10.1300/J137v07n01_02

Zlotnik, J. L., & Pryce, J. A. (2013). Status of the use of Title IV-E funding in BSW and MSW programs. *Journal of Public Child Welfare, 7*, 430–446. doi:10.1080/15548732.2013.806278

Zlotnik, J. L., Strand, V. C., & Anderson, G. R. (2009). Introduction: Achieving positive outcomes for children and families: Recruiting and retaining a competent child welfare workforce. *Child Welfare, 88*, 7.

IV-E or not IV-E, that is the question: Comparisons of BSW Child Welfare Scholars and matched trainee confidence and retention

Greta Yoder Slater ⓘ, Marissa O'Neill ⓘ, Lisa E. McGuire ⓘ, and Elizabeth Dickerson

ABSTRACT

Our longitudinal study examined the effectiveness of BSW IVE Scholar training ($n = 52$) compared with a matched cohort ($n = 57$) of traditionally trained employees. The BSW IV-E Scholars felt significantly more prepared than their traditionally-trained coworkers. BSW IV-E Scholars were significantly more likely to be retained in the first five years of employment than the matched cohort trainees. The study lends strong support for the retention and preparation advantages of BSW Title IV-E training over traditional employee training. This is important given the significant investment of training dollars for IV-E at the Federal, state, and local levels.

Introduction

Turnover in public child welfare agencies is expensive and associated with poor outcomes for children and families. Some national studies have estimated the rate of turnover between 40% and 57%, depending on the setting (US General Accounting Office [GAO], 2003; Wilson, Nichols, Kirk, & Wilson, 2010). When workers leave, they take their expertise with them and it takes a significant amount of time to have similarly well-trained employees ready to take over the case. Two estimates place the cost per vacancy at between $10,000 for posting and training a new worker (Graef & Hill, 2000) and $16,000 (Cowperthwaite, 2006). There are emotional costs as

Lisa McGuire, at Indiana University at the time of the BSW IV-E study, is now at the Department Chair at James Madison University, Harrisonburg, VA.

This research was not supported by grant funding. Previous description of the BSW IV-E study partnership between Indiana University and the Department of Child Services has been published in the *Journal of Social Work Education*.

well for the workers left behind and the supervisors who are working hard to cover their units. Caseworker turnover has some damaging outcomes for children and families too. Ryan and colleagues (2006) found children had longer stays in care and decreased chances for reunification due to turnover. Decreased retention also has negative effects on meeting Federal timelines (Benton, 2016; US GAO, 2003). Clearly, turnover is a challenge that needs even more attention.

One bright spot in the effort to retain child welfare workers is the Title IV-E Program and the university/public child welfare agency partnerships (Mathias, Gilman, Shin, & Evans, 2015; Pierce, McGuire, & Howes, 2015). Specialized training, tuition support, and stipends have demonstrated positive effects for the retention of workers in public child welfare settings even after the pay-back periods have passed (Barbee et al., 2009; Rosenthal & Waters, 2006). MSW IV-E Scholars who receive training and educational opportunities report feeling more competent and prepared for the work (Ellett, Ellett, & Rugutt, 2003; Hartinger-Saunders & Lyons, 2013; Hopkins, Mudrick, & Rudolph, 1999).

Although the IV-E Partnerships have been funded for 40 years, there are not as many evaluation studies of the funding's efficacy as we might expect and fewer have focused on undergraduate training for child welfare practice. Very few studies have compared child welfare worker participants of Title IV-E program with non-IV-E participants regarding retention and child welfare competency. The current study compared perception of preparation of key child welfare competencies and retention of workers who had completed a BSW Title IV-E program and matched Trainees who did not.

Literature review

Child welfare worker retention

Worker retention is an ongoing issue for many child welfare agencies. Turnover can include workers who leave the agency, but also workers who move positions within the agency. Turnover rates vary depending on the source. The Child Welfare Information Gateway reports rates can be as high as 90% (n.d.), while a study by the California Social Work Education Center (CALSWEC, 2012) found only 6.1% external turnover. One-third of the staff surveyed had some change in their position within the agency, making the number closer to 36%. A 2008 study of child welfare workers who left their positions in Texas reported between 32% and 42% turnover rate (Burstain, 2009). High turnover rates are important because of the expense to the agencies and effects on clients (Flower, McDonald, & Sumski, 2005). A study by the Maine Department of Health and Human Services estimated that it cost over $16,000 to replace a child welfare worker in separation, replacement. and training costs (Cowperthwaite, 2006). In addition to agency costs, foster children have reported experiencing a lack of stability and trust when case workers continually turnover (Stolin-Goltzman, Kollar, & Trinkle, 2010). Flowers et al. (2005) found that turnover affects the rate that foster children achieved permanency. Reducing worker turnover and increasing retention are important challenges in child welfare.

Previous research has examined many aspects of worker turnover. Mor Barak, Nissly, and Levin (2001) analyzed 25 published articles in their meta-analysis of the demographic, personal, and organizational factors affecting retention and turnover of child welfare employees. They found that stress (i.e., role ambiguity, role conflict, fear factors, task factors, job-related tension, need for clarity, role stress, case factors, helplessness, and role overload), social support (coworker, supervisor, and team cohesiveness), and fair management practices (income, leadership considerations, and perceived inequity) were significant organizational predictors of worker intention to quit—the most significant predictor of actual turnover (Mor Barak et al., 2001). This study supports the organizational factors found elsewhere in the literature. For example, good stress management (Middleton & Potter, 2015), financial rewards/salary (Benton, 2016; Scannapieco & Connell-Carrick, 2003), support from supervisors and coworkers (Benton, 2016; Dickinson & Perry, 2002), and reasonable workloads (Benton, 2016; Cyphers, 2001) have been found to reduce worker turnover. In a meta-analysis of IV-E-specific studies, Hartinger-Saunders and Lyons (2013) found that supervisor support, coworker support, office politics, lack of promotions, and stress were predictive of the intent to leave.

Mor Barak and colleagues (2001) found the following personal factors to be significant predictors of the intention to quit in their meta-analysis of 25 studies of child welfare workers: experience, burnout, value conflicts, job satisfaction, organizational, and professional commitment. Personal factors that affect retention found elsewhere in the literature include commitment to families and children, job satisfaction (Ellett et al., 2003), work-life balance, social support (Nissly, Mor Barak, & Levin, 2005), and organization and time management skills (Westbrook, Ellis, & Ellett, 2006). Although they did not directly link self-care and turnover, Bloomquist and colleagues (2015) found that professional, emotional, and spiritual self-care were predictive of lower levels of burnout in MSW-level practitioners and Nissly and colleagues (2005) found that burnout was predictive of turnover.

There are many studies focusing on Title-IV-E participants or programs broadly (Bagdasaryan, 2012; Barbee et al., 2009; Cahalane & Sites, 2008; DeHart, 2013; Franke, Bagdasaryan, & Furman, 2009; Hartinger-Saunders & Lyons, 2013; Madden, Scannapieco, & Painter, 2014; O'Donnell & Kirkner, 2009a; Pierce et al., 2015; Zlotnik & Corneilius, 2000), but only a few examined the retention question. For an excellent review of Title IV-E studies, see Hartinger-Saunders and Lyons (2013). Of the IV-E retention studies, only some report the retention rate for IV-E program participants and compare those rates with non-program workers (Dickinson & Perry, 2002; Gansle & Ellett, 2002). Of the few who do have a comparison group, participation in the Title-IV-E program is shown to be effective for retention and reduction in turnover (Madden et al., 2014; Rosenthal & Waters, 2006; Yankeelov, Barbee, Sullivan, & Antle, 2009). Madden and colleagues (2014) conducted a rigorous longitudinal study of retention over a 10-year period in Texas (N = 9,195). They found that IV-E participants were disproportionately more likely to stay at the agency than non IV-E Trainees. Having a social work degree also increased the odds that they would work longer at the Agency too. They noted that only one other published study (Rosenthal & Waters, 2006) had examined length of employment among child welfare caseworkers (Madden et al., 2014).

Yankeelov and colleagues (2009) in a study of case workers in Kentucky found that MSW workers were more likely to leave than those with an undergraduate degree, and those who graduated from the Title IV-E program were significantly more likely to stay than non-participants through the fourth year. Jones (2002) also found caseworkers in a California county stayed longer if they had participated in the Title IV-E. Contradicting findings by Yankeelov et al. (2009), workers with an MSW were retained longer. Both Madden et al. (2014) in a study in Texas and Rosenthal and Waters (2006) in Oklahoma in a study including both BSW and MSW degrees and found similar results after the third year of employment.

Child welfare competencies

If one of the goals of the Title IV-E program is to prepare students for work in child welfare (Zlotnik, 2003), it is logical to examine knowledge and skills of traditional trainees and to compare them to IV-E Scholar trainees. Several researchers have found that former IV-E program participants rate themselves as highly prepared for work in child welfare (Barbee et al., 2009; O'Donnell & Kirkner, 2009b); however, few studies include a comparison group. In a study by Gansle and Ellett (2002) of child welfare knowledge on the topics of child protection, family preservation, and adoption, both MSW and BSW students were given a pretest one year before graduation and a posttest at graduation. The sample included 72 MSW and 102 BSW graduates in Louisiana. Both MSW and BSW students had a significant gain in knowledge; however, only BSW students showed a difference between students who received a Title IV-E stipend and non-stipend students. Students who received the financial support had significantly better results.

It is important to know if the significant investment of Federal, state, and local funds in the training of workers is having the intended effect on competency. To this end, Bagdasaryan (2012) tested new caseworkers in LA County on general knowledge, permanency planning, and case management before attending new hire training. New workers with MSW degrees scored higher than workers with BSW or other MA/MS degrees. When comparing workers with an MSW, those who participated in a Title IV-E program scored higher than non-participants. Jones and Okumura (2000) also studied new caseworker ($N = 266$) knowledge in San Diego. New workers took a test of knowledge needed for child welfare work before the training. They were asked to rate their confidence level to perform 19 competencies. Title IV-E graduates scored higher on child welfare knowledge and rated themselves more confident on competence than non-Title IV-E workers. This is similar to findings in another study by Franke and colleagues (2009) who found that Title IV-E participants scored significantly higher on pretest/posttest comparisons. The evidence is beginning to show that effectiveness of Title IV-E programs, but few studies have examined the longitudinal impact of IV-E training on retention and competency with a comparison group. The purpose of this study was to expand the knowledge of how Title IV-E programs improve retention and competency when compared with matched cohorts of new employee Trainees who were not BSW Scholars. The hypotheses were as follows: (1). *BSW Title IV-E students will report being more prepared for child welfare practice than workers who did not participate in a BSW Title IV-E program*; (2). *BSW Title IV-E students will maintain child welfare employment longer than workers who did not participate in a BSW Title IV-E program.*

Methods

The BSW Child Welfare Scholars Partnership model is based on the Kentucky Model for Title IV-E Training (Barbee et al., 2009) and an in-depth discussion of the model is outlined elsewhere (Pierce et al., 2015). In a nutshell, the training program is a collaboration involving all public state universities offering BSW degrees (including nine different sites) in a Midwestern state. BSW Scholars were selected with a rigorous application process that mirrored the hiring of new family case managers. University faculty members and the statewide public child welfare agency supervisors jointly interviewed the student applicants and used the same interview guide at each university and the same interview guide used by the statewide public child welfare agency in hiring new employees. BSW Scholars completed five full days of training and a two-course sequence during their training program. In addition, they each completed a practicum at a county office. Both the BSW Scholars and the Trainee comparison group were required to complete the same series of computer-assisted trainings and transfer of learning activities. The University Partnership provided all the trainings for both the IV-E Scholars and the new employee Trainee cohorts. This consistency across groups helps strengthen the research because the program is the same for both groups and the training program is manualized, consistent, and replicable.

Participants

The pilot study invited two cohorts of successive year BSW Scholar graduates ($N = 54$) who were employed as child welfare case managers who were compared with two cohorts of new employee Trainees ($N = 57$) who completed their pre-service training at about the same time that the BSW Scholars graduated. All of the participants were surveyed between 4 and 10 months of employment as the approximate 6-month anniversary on the job is regarded as critical for retention (Dickinson and & Perry, 2002). The Scholars tended to be younger than the Trainee comparison group with a mean age of 26.65 years for graduates (range 21–48) and 31.24 years for the comparison group of Trainees (range 23–46). The full sample ($N = 107$) was 12.15% male ($n = 13$) and 87.85% female ($n = 94$).

Measurement

Participants in this study were asked to complete a 36-item questionnaire regarding their perceived competence for public child welfare practice. This survey was created from a list of child welfare competencies developed by the New Jersey Consortium for Child Welfare (personal communication, D. Stockon). The competencies were grouped into the subcategories of *Workplace Management, Human Behavior and the Social Environment, Ethnic and Multicultural Practice,* and *Core Child Welfare.* An additional item targeted competence in using the state practice model of family teaming. Respondents were asked to self-rate their preparation for competency on a scale of 1 to 5 with 1 as "inadequately prepared" to 5 as "extremely well-prepared." Basic competency was considered a 3 ("adequately prepared"). The agency also reported continued employment as of a specific cutoff date, and the number of months was included in the analysis for retention. The survey response rate for Scholars was 68.5% ($n = 37$) and the response rate for traditional trainees was 40% ($n = 21$). The overall response rate of 54.2% is well above the published average for organizational research of 35.7% and near the 52.7% average response rate for studies of individuals (Baruch & Holtom, 2008). We also collected data from the statewide public child welfare agency about each of the Scholars and traditional trainees who were invited to participate. Those data included the group membership (Scholar or traditional trainee), gender, age, start and end hire date, number of months employed, and if the employee was retained. Reliability analysis of the instrument showed a highly reliable scale ($\alpha = 0.969$) with seven factors that explained 75.90% of the variance. The Kaiser–Meyer–Olkin measure supported the sampling adequacy (KMO = .793) and Bartlett's test of sphericity also supported the factor analysis (χ^2 = 1951.55, df = 630, p < .000).

Retention data continued to be collected each year for six years using the statewide public child welfare agency employee personnel database. Employment in months was calculated for each employee in the IV-E and traditional trainee cohorts. For employees no longer working at the Agency each year, social media and publicly available sources were used to determine approximately when the employees left during the previous year. Facebook and Linked-In were used to find the date that employees left the county agency and started new positions. Google searches were also used to find publicly available information about court filings, news stories, or job announcements indicating what month the employee left the county agency. In cases where the date could not be estimated, we assumed the most conservative estimate possible–that the employee had left the month we last collected data from statewide public child welfare agency in that year. Group averages were compared for IV-E and Trainee cohorts for each year.

Data analysis

The BSW Scholars and Trainee comparison group data were analyzed using SPSS 24.0 and Excel. Individual descriptive statistics, frequency distributions, correlations, skewness, and kurtosis properties were examined for all variables. Underlying assumptions of each statistical test were examined and the observations were independent, although not randomly assigned. Reliability analysis was conducted on the 36-item scale and factor analysis was used to check the subscale factor structure and collinearity. Principal components factor analysis with varimax rotation was used to examine the psychometric properties of the scale. The group differences were analyzed using ANOVA, Chi-square, and logistic regression. We did not include gender or race in our analysis, because the numbers of men and employees of color were too limited.

Results

Although the BSW Scholars were significantly younger than the new employee trainees and had less time on the job, they rated themselves significantly more prepared than their traditional trainee coworkers. BSW Scholars' average age in our study was 26.65 years old and the Trainees was 31.24 ($F_{1,56}$ = 6.265, p = .015). The Trainees had been working, on average, 8.76 months and the BSW Scholars had been working, on average, 6.52 months ($F_{1,56}$ = 46.91, p < .001). BSW Scholars rated themselves more prepared on every one of the 36 items. Fourteen of the items did not have significant differences between the BSW Scholars and traditional trainees, but 22 items did have differences. In the area of workplace differences, traditional trainees rated themselves as being significantly less prepared in their knowledge of the basic structure of the agency, awareness of community resources, and working productively with team members on case planning. Table 1 shows the BSW Scholars and Trainee means, standard deviations, F-ratios, and significance levels. A rating of 3.0 or higher is considered "adequately prepared" and the BSW Scholars averages were above 3.0 for all the workplace items. Trainees, on the other hand, felt inadequately prepared on all the workplace items except working productively with agency staff and clients and understanding the vision, values, and mission of the county agency. The biggest difference in means between BSW Scholars and Trainees was in the knowledge of community resources ($F_{1, 57} = 21.16$, $p < .001$).

BSW Scholars and Trainees rated themselves much differently in the area of theoretical understanding of human behavior in the social environment (HBSE) and areas of cultural competence. Tables 2 and 3 summarize these differences. Both Trainees and BSW Scholars felt similarly well prepared in the area of understanding the impact of child maltreatment, which is good. Both groups

Table 1. Descriptive and Mean Differences on Workplace and Professional Items.

Work place		Non-IV-E mean	sd	BSW IV-E Mean	sd	$F_{1,58}$
1	Demonstrate knowledge of basic structure of Agency	2.62	.92	3.35	.72	11.37***
2	Understand the vision, values, and mission	3.62	1.02	3.84	.80	NS
3	Work productively with agency staff and clients	3.38	1.12	3.73	1.10	NS
4	Demonstrate awareness of community resources	2.00	1.14	3.24	.90	21.16***
5	Work productively with team members on case plan	2.24	1.09	3.22	.85	14.33***
6	Plan, prioritize, and complete activities on time	2.67	1.20	3.19	1.22	NS
7	Be aware of stress and develop self-care strategies	2.62	1.02	3.16	1.19	NS
	Total	2.74	1.07	3.39	.97	

NS = Not Significant, *$p < .05$, **$p < .01$, ***$p < .001$.

Table 2. Descriptive and Mean Differences on HBSE Items.

HBSE		Non-IV-E mean	sd	BSW IV-E mean	sd	$F_{1,58}$
1	Demonstrate understanding of child development	2.76	1.04	3.41	.99	5.48*
2	Understand impact of child maltreatment	3.62	.81	4.03	.80	NS
3	Understand adult development and family life	2.81	1.08	3.49	.65	8.93**
4	Demonstrate understanding of effects of poverty and oppression	2.90	.89	3.92	.64	25.24***
5	Understand influence of culture on behavior	3.19	.75	3.89	.57	16.81***
6	Demonstrate understanding of strengths perspective	3.19	1.03	4.00	.75	11.92***
	Total	3.08	.93	3.79	.733	

NS = Not Significant, *$p < .05$, **$p < .01$, ***$p < .001$.

Table 3. Descriptive and Mean Differences on Cultural Competence Items.

Culture		Non-IV-E mean	sd	BSW IV-E mean	sd	$F_{1,58}$
1	Sensitivity to clients' differences in culture	3.48	.81	4.03	.73	7.07**
2	Demonstrate ability to conduct culturally sensitive assessment	3.24	.90	3.76	.72	NS
3	Understand importance of client's primary language	3.29	.78	3.65	.75	NS
4	Understand culturally based childrearing practices	3.14	1.01	3.62	.79	3.97*
5	Demonstrate ability to collaborate and advocate	2.71	1.23	3.54	.84	9.23**
	Total	3.17	.95	3.72	.77	

NS = Not Significant, *$p < .05$, **$p < .01$, ***$p < .001$.

Table 4. Descriptive and Mean Differences on Core Child Welfare Knowledge Items.

CORE		Non-IV-E mean	sd	BSW IV-E mean	sd	$F_{1,58}$
1	Demonstrate ability to identify family dynamics	3.14	.96	3.68	.82	4.99*
2	Demonstrate understanding of person in environment	3.24	1.04	3.84	.87	5.53*
3	Understand emotional and behavioral indicators of abuse	2.76	1.04	3.62	.79	12.46**
4	Understand forms of oppression and discrimination	2.90	1.04	3.65	.86	8.61**
5	Understand dual responsibilities of child protection and providing family services	3.29	.90	3.68	.94	NS
6	Understand dynamics of family violence	2.86	1.01	3.57	.90	7.63**
7	Recognize the need to monitor child safety and risk	3.10	1.04	3.70	.78	6.36*
8	Demonstrate understanding of legal process and roles	2.67	1.02	2.78	1.13	NS
9	Understand attachment and separation effects on children	3.00	.89	3.54	.90	4.85*
10	Understand evidence-based practice and research	2.62	1.02	3.24	.98	5.24*
11	Understand concurrent and permanency planning	2.67	1.07	3.19	1.13	NS
12	Demonstrate case management skills in working with teams	2.86	.96	3.24	.98	6.49*
13	Demonstrate professional values and ethics	3.33	.91	3.89	.84	5.54*
14	Understand power in professional relationships and the dynamics of working with involuntary clients	3.24	1.09	3.54	1.04	NS
15	Demonstrate ability to assess own emotional response	3.33	.73	3.68	.94	NS
16	Understanding of termination process	2.48	1.03	3.16	1.04	5.86*
17	Understanding of documentation	3.19	1.03	3.57	1.19	NS
18	Capacity for using Teaming, Engaging, Assessing, Planning and Intervening Practice Model (TEAPI)	3.19	1.03	3.57	.96	NS
	Total	2.99	.99	3.51	.95	

NS = Not Significant, *$p < .05$, **$p < .01$, ***$p < .001$.

rated themselves adequately prepared with the Trainee average of 3.62 (sd = .81) and the BSW Scholars rating of 4.03 (sd = .80). Trainees felt significantly less prepared than BSW Scholars in the understanding of child development ($F_{1, 57} = 5.48$, $p = .023$), adult development and family life ($F_{1, 57} = 8.93$, $p = .004$), the effects of poverty and oppression ($F_{1, 57} = 25.24$, $p < .001$), and the strengths perspective ($F_{1, 57} = 11.92$, $p = .001$). Regarding cultural competence, the differences were not as large between the two groups because both Trainees and BSW Scholars rated themselves fairly high in this category. There were significant differences in feeling prepared to be sensitive to client differences in culture, ethnicity, and sexual orientation ($F_{1,\ 57} = 7.07$, $p = .01$) and their ability to collaborate and advocate ($F_{1,57} = 9.23$, $p = .004$).

Some of the differences between BSW IV-E Scholars and matched traditional trainees were less marked than for the other areas. Table 4 includes the differences between these groups on core child welfare competencies. There were significant differences in 11/18 items on this scale. The biggest differences were found between the mean scores on items related to identifying the emotional and behavioral indicators of abuse ($F_{1,58} = 12.46$, $p = .01$), understanding the forms of oppression and discrimination ($F_{1,58} = 8.61$, $p = .01$), and understanding the dynamics of family violence ($F_{1,58} = 7.63$, $p = .01$). There were no differences in seven areas including dual responsibilities, concurrent and permanency planning, and the dynamics of working with involuntary clients.

When comparing categorical retention data (retained or not), the picture is interesting. In the first year, only four Scholars left (out of 54) and 22 Trainees left (out of 53). Of the original 107 employees, 81 were still working at the agency at the one-year mark (75.70% retention). After the legal commitment to the Agency was complete, a total of 23 employees had left the agency. A large majority (70.37%) of Scholars continued employment ($n = 38$) and 20 Trainees were still employed (37.73%). At the three-year mark, 42.59% of the Scholars were still working ($n = 23$), but this was still higher than the 16 Trainees who were left (30.19%). Only two Scholars left between years 3 and 4, and somewhat surprisingly to us, no Trainees left between years 3 and 6. In year 5, five Scholars left and all of those workers were still working at the Agency in year 6. By the end of the study period, the number of Scholars and Trainees from the original cohorts was exactly the same—16 employees were retained from the original 54 Scholars and 53 Trainees. The retention rate overall was just under 30% (32 were left of the original 107 hired) over the six-year study period. When looking at these data in terms of turnover from year to year, instead of comparing to the initial numbers, the percentage of Scholars who were retained in years 1–6 are as follows: 92.59% (year 1), 76.00% (year 2), 60.53% (year 3), 91.30% (year 4), and 76.19% (years 5 and 6).

When looking more deeply at the average number of months employed by each cohort, the IV-E Scholars stayed significantly longer than the matched traditional trainees in every year except the sixth; by that point, the differences between IV-E Scholar and Trainee retention numbers were minimal. Table 5 shows the mean number of months, standard deviations, minimum, maximum, 95% CI, and F-ratios for group differences between IV-E and non-IVE Trainees over the six-year study period. The average number of months employed by the IV-E Scholars at the first year was 11.71 and for Trainees it was 9.19 ($F_{1,\ 106} = 20.320$, $p < .001$). IV-E Scholars average number of months was significantly longer than Trainees in

Table 5. Descriptive and Group Differences between Non-BSW IV-E and BSW IV-E Scholars for Years 1–6.

| | | N | Mean (in months) | sd | 95% confidence interval for mean | | Min | Max | F |
					Lower bound	Upper bound			
Year 1	Non IV-E Scholar	53	9.19	3.95	8.10	10.28	.25	12.00	20.320***
	IV-E Scholar	54	11.71	1.12	11.40	12.01	6.25	12.00	
	Total	107	10.46	3.14	9.86	11.06	.25	12.00	
Year 2	Non IV-E Scholar	53	14.32	8.72	11.91	16.72	.25	24.00	19.412***
	IV-E Scholar	54	20.54	5.57	19.02	22.06	6.25	24.00	
	Total	107	17.46	7.91	15.94	18.97	.25	24.00	
Year 3	Non IV-E Scholar	53	18.23	13.52	14.49	21.94	.25	36.00	13.126***
	IV-E Scholar	54	26.63	10.32	23.82	29.45	6.25	36.00	
	Total	107	22.47	12.68	20.03	24.90	.25	36.00	
Year 4	Non IV-E Scholar	53	21.84	18.58	16.72	26.96	.25	48.00	8.718**
	IV-E Scholar	54	31.56	15.35	27.37	35.75	6.25	48.00	
	Total	107	26.75	17.64	23.37	30.13	.25	48.00	
Year 5	Non IV-E Scholar	53	25.46	23.86	18.89	32.04	.25	60.00	5.939*
	IV-E Scholar	54	35.88	20.22	30.36	41.39	6.25	60.00	
	Total	107	30.72	22.61	26.38	35.05	.25	60.00	
Year 6	Non IV-E Scholar	53	32.86	35.14	23.17	42.55	.25	92.00	2.320
	IV-E Scholar	54	42.32	28.86	34.44	50.20	6.25	86.00	(NS)
	Total	107	37.63	32.33	31.44	43.83	.25	92.00	

NS = Not Significant, *p < .05, **p < .01, ***p < .001.

year 2 also with means of 20.54 and 14.32, respectively ($F_{1, 106} = 19.412, p < .001$). In year 3, the average number of months the county agency retained IV-E Scholars was 26.63 and Trainees was 18.23. This difference of nearly 8.5 months was significant ($F_{1, 106} = 13.126, p = .001$). The differences were still marked at the four-year point, with average number of months for IV-E Scholars at 31.56 and Trainees at 21.84 ($F_{1, 106} = 8.718, p = .004$). The last year of significant differences was in year 5. The IV-E Scholars average months retained that year was 35.88 and the Trainees average was 25.46 ($F_{1, 106} = 5.39, p = .016$). The differences between average months worked were not significant at year 6. IV-E Scholars were retained an average of 42.32 months and Trainees were retained 32.86 months. Although Scholars stayed almost 10 months longer, those differences were not significant ($F_{1,106} = 2.320, p = .131$).

Discussion

The present study lends strong support for the retention and competency advantages of BSW-level Title IV-E training over traditional employee train-ing. This is important given the significant investment of training dollars for

IV-E at the Federal, state, and local levels. We need to know that the money invested is translating into workers who stay longer and are prepared to practice. Undergraduate IV-E Scholars in our study rated their preparation for practice significantly higher, despite being younger and on the job for less time than the Trainees. Awareness of community resources, knowledge of agency structure, case planning, understanding child development, the effects of poverty, understanding culture, strengths perspective, understanding emotional and behavioral indicators of abuse, family violence dynamics, knowledge of professional ethics, and evidence-based practices were much higher for the IV-E Scholars than the comparison group. Our findings are consistent with previous studies of worker competency and preparation (Bagdasarayan, 2012; Franke et al., 2009; Gansle & Ellett, 2002; Jones & Okamura, 2000). BSW IV-E Scholars in those studies performed much better than non-Scholar Trainees on knowledge tests. Other areas where BSW Scholars reported significantly more prepared were knowledge of community resources, child and adult development, family life, effects of poverty and oppression, and sensitivity to cultural differences.

We were somewhat surprised by the similar (nonsignificant) scores between groups regarding culturally sensitive assessments, understanding power differentials in professional relationships, self-care practices, and the worker's ability to assess their own emotional response. In social work programs, significant attention is usually paid to these topics—above and beyond what might be covered in the employee training program. Students in the CSWE-accredited programs in the Partnership have multiple units in multiple courses that cover cultural competence, power and oppression, and emotional self-awareness and self-care. We expected the IV-E Scholars to score much higher in their knowledge of these areas. It would be interesting to investigate this further with in-depth interviews with IV-E and non-IV-E Trainees. It would also have been interesting to have the degree information for non-IV-E Trainees to see what their educational background included and if issues of cultural competence, power dynamics, emotional regulation, and self-care were covered.

The results of this study also support the second hypothesis: BSW Title IV-E students maintained child welfare employment longer than workers who did not participate in a BSW Title IV-E program. IV-E Scholar employment retention rates were much higher than the published retention rates in the literature: 92.59% (year 1), 76.00% (year 2), 60.53% (year 3), 91.30% (year 4), and 76.19% (years 5 and 6). Year 3 appears to be an important time of discernment for the Scholars. By the fourth year of employment, those who stayed past year 3 stayed for another three (many of whom are still working there at the time of publication). These findings are consistent with the findings from Scannapieco and Painter (2014) and Rosenthal and Waters (2006). Our data supported the longevity question through year 5, which is similar to Yankeelov et al. (2009) in Kentucky who found that graduates of the Title IV-E program were significantly more likely to stay through the fourth year than non-IV-E Trainees.

The retention question is a complex one, but it is clear from our study and others that IV-E Scholars tend to stay past the legal commitment period and they stay significantly longer than those without agency–university partnership training programs. In the only other longitudinal study of IV-E training with a comparison group, Madden et al. (2014) found that IV-E Scholars were significantly more likely to stay over the 10-year study period than the comparison group. This is similar to Rosenthal and Waters (2006) and Scannapieco and Connell-Carrick (2007) who found 39% reduction in termination risk and 46.61% retention rates, respectively. Dickinson and Perry (2002) found that a BSW caseworker was 75% less likely than someone with a MSW to leave or be fired. Many different factors affect retention, including organizational commitment, professional commitment, burnout, job satisfaction, stress, and lack of social support, fairness management practices, and intention to leave (Mor Barak et al., 2001). Professional commitment and organizational commitment had the largest effects on intentions to quit (Mor Barak et al., 2001).

Limitations

There are several limitations for the present study. Self-report data were used to assess competency and observations of actual skills would have been more robust. Small sample size and low response rates were also a concern. If identified early, training could focus on developing specific competencies and identifying which ones are more likely to lead to the worker exiting or staying in the organization. Another shortcoming was not asking the Trainees about their educational background. Some of the Trainee comparison group could have earned BSW degrees from a non-partnership university or from other states' IV-E programs. It would have strengthened the study to use standardized instruments and to have some qualitative exploration of reasons for staying and leaving. Despite these limitations, this study contributes to the knowledge on Title IV-E education, and retention by suggesting promising results in the preparation of BSW social workers with regard to perceived competency and retention. Furthermore, it provides additional evidence that Title IV-E programs are effective in professionalizing the workforce and preparing students for child welfare work.

Implications

Future research could explore retention and competency with stayers and leavers. It might be helpful to identify self-care practices used by workers who stay and those who leave to identify areas that might be targets for intervention. Retention is a complex area of research and how workers care for themselves could be a vital link in the workforce development process. As recommended by many researchers, future studies should also examine Title IV-E programs impact on client outcomes. These could include caseload size, number of caseworker changes per case and placement rates, time in care, and meeting Federal timeline mandates. Although our study did not examine cost, this would be a logical next step for administrators to consider. For every dollar invested in BSW IV-E training, how much is returned in longevity and how much is saved in training new workers? Future research could expand on the question of undergraduate versus graduate investment costs too. For example, are investments in BSW training more cost effective than MSW? When the pilot results of the results of this study were first shared with the Agency, the Agency Director increased annual funding for BSW student education from 36 slots to 50 slots per year. This step provided financial support for 50 new BSW social workers each year to enter the child welfare workforce as professional social workers and the workforce was incrementally more professionalized. The study is useful for strengthening the argument for the professionalization of child welfare workers. Our study found that Title IV-E supported social work education and structured IV-E training made a significant difference in the preparation of child welfare workers in our state. Child welfare workforce development, retention, and turnover are complex issues. This study is a useful step in measuring longer-term effects of IV-E Partnership training, retention, and competency.

ORCID

Greta Yoder Slater ◎ http://orcid.org/0000-0001-6851-468X
Marissa O'Neill ◎ http://orcid.org/0000-0003-1477-566X
Lisa E. McGuire ◎ http://orcid.org/0000-0003-0699-5144

References

Bagdasaryan, S. (2012). Social work education and Title IV-E program participation as predictors of entry-level knowledge among public child welfare workers. *Children and Youth Services Review, 34*, 1590–1597. doi:10.1016/j.childyouth.2012.04.013

Barbee, A., Antle, B., Sullivan, D., Hall, C., Borders, K., & Fox, S. (2009). Evaluation of an innovative social work education model: The Kentucky Public Child Welfare Certification Program (PCWCP). *Journal of Social Work Education, 45*(3), 427–444.

Baruch, Y., & Holtom, B. C. (2008). Survey response rate levels and trends in organizational research. *Human Relations, 61*(8), 1139–1160. doi:10.1177/0018726708094863

Benton, A. D. (2016). Understanding the diverging paths of stayers and leavers: An examination of factors predicting worker retention. *Children and Youth Services Review, 65*, 70–77. doi:10.1016/j.childyouth.2016.04.006

Bloomquist, K. L., Wood, L., Friedmeyer-Trainor, K., & Kim, H. W. (2015). Self-care and professional quality of life: Predictive factors among MSW practitioners. *Advances in Social Work, 16*(2), 292–311. doi:10.18060/18760

Burstain, J. (2009). A better understanding of caseworker turnover within Child Protective Services. http://library.cppp.org/files/4/364%20DFPS%20workforce.pdf

Cahalane, H., & Sites, E. W. (2008). The climate of child welfare employee retention. *Child Welfare, 87*, 91–114.

California Social Work Education Center. (2012). *Turnover & service assignment changes among social workers & supervisors in California's public child welfare agencies.* Retrieved from http://calswec.berkeley.edu/sites/default/files/uploads/pdf/CalSWEC/CalSWEC/turnover_2011.pdf

Cowperthwaite, A. (2006). Cost of child welfare worker turnover. *Child Welfare Training Institute.* Retrieved from http://www.cwti.org/RR/Ann%20C/Turnover%20costs%20report%206-06%20formatted.pdf

Cyphers, G. (2001). Report from the child welfare workforce survey: State and county data findings. Washington, DC: American Public Human Services Association.

DeHart, D. (2013). Perfecting the craft: Formative assessment of a university-agency partnership for social work education. *Social Work Education, 32*(6), 748–761. doi:10.1080/02615479.2012.701280

Dickinson, N. S., & Perry, R. E. (2002). Factors influencing the retention of specially educated public child welfare workers. *Evaluation Research in Child Welfare, 15*, 89–103.

Ellett, A. J., Ellett, C. D., & Rugutt, J. K. (2003). *Final report: A study of personal and organizational factors contributing to employee retention and turnover in child welfare in Georgia* (330 pp.). Athens, GA: University of Georgia, School of Social Work.

Flower, C., McDonald, J., & Sumski, M. (2005). *Review of turnover in Milwaukee County private agency child welfare ongoing case management staff.* Retrieved June 30, 2017, from http://www.uky.edu/SocialWork/cswe/

Franke, T., Bagdasaryan, S., & Furman, W. (2009). A multivariate analysis of training, education, and readiness for public child welfare practice. *Children and Youth Services Review, 31*(12), 1330–1336.

Gansle, K. A., & Ellett, A. J. (2002). Child welfare knowledge transmission, practitioner retention, and university-community impact: A study of child welfare training. *Journal of Health & Social Policy, 15*, 69–88.

Graef, M. L., & Hill, E. L. (2000). Costing child protective services staff turnover. *Child Welfare, 79*(5), 517–533.

Hartinger-Saunders, R., & Lyons, P. (2013). Social work education and public child welfare: A review of the peer-reviewed literature on title IV-E funded programs. *Journal of Public Child Welfare, 7*, 275–297.

Hopkins, K. M., Mudrick, N. R., & Rudolph, C. S. (1999). Impact of university/agency partnerships in child welfare on organizations, workers, and work activities. *Child Welfare, 78*(6), 749–773.

Jones, L. (2002). A follow-up of a Title IV-E program's graduates' retention rates in a public child welfare agency. *Journal of Health & Social Policy, 15*, 39–51.

Jones, L., & Okamura, A. (2000). Re-professionalizing child welfare services: An evaluation of a Title IV-E Training Program. *Research on Social Work Practice, 22*(5), 355–371.

Madden, E. E., Scannapieco, M., & Painter, K. (2014). An examination of retention and length of employment among public child welfare workers. *Children and Youth Services Review, 41*, 37–44. doi:10.1016/j.childyouth.2014.02.015

Mathias, C., Gilman, E., Shin, C., & Evans, W. T. (2015). California's Title IV-E partnership: A statewide university-agency collaboration—Characteristics and implications for replication. *Journal of Social Work Education, 51*(Supp. 2), S252–S270. doi:10.1080/10437797.2015.1073082

Middleton, S. J., & Potter, C. C. (2015). Relationship between vicarious traumatization and turnover among child welfare professionals. *Journal of Public Child Welfare, 9*, 195–216. doi:10.1080/15548732.2015.1021987

Mor Barak, M. E., Nissly, J. A., & Levin, A. (2001). Antecedents to retention and turnover among child welfare, social work, and other human service employees: What can we learn from past research? A review and meta-analysis. *Social Service Review, 75*(4), 625–661. doi:10.1086/323166

National Association of Social Workers. (2004). *Fact sheet: Title IV-E child welfare training program.* Retrieved from http://www.socialworkers.org/advocacy/updates/2003/081204a.asp

Nissly, J. A., Mor Barak, M. E., & Levin, A. (2005). Stress, social support, and workers' intentions to leave their jobs in public child welfare. *Administration in Social Work, 29*, 79–100. doi:10.1300/J147v29n01_06

O'Donnell, J., & Kirkner, S. L. (2009a). A longitudinal study of factors influencing the retention of title IV-E Master's of social work graduates in public child welfare. *Journal of Public Child Welfare, 3*(64–86). doi:10.1080/15548730802690841

O'Donnell, J., & Kirkner, S. L. (2009b). Title IV-E programs: Preparing MSW students for public child welfare practice. *Journal of Teaching in Social Work, 29,* 241–257. doi:10.1080/08841230903022050

Pierce, B., McGuire, L., & Howes, P. (2015). Ready, set, go… again: Renewing an academy-agency child welfare partnership. *Journal of Social Work Education, 51*(suppl.2), S239–S251. doi:10.1080/10437797.2015.1072424

Rosenthal, J. A., & Waters, E. (2006). Predictors of child welfare worker retention and performance: Focus on Title IV-E funded social work education. *Journal of Social Service Research, 32*(3), 67–85.

Ryan, J., Garnier, P., Zyphur, M., & Zhai, F. (2006). Investigating the effects of caseworker characteristics in child welfare. *Children and Youth Services Review, 28*(9), 993–1006.

Scannapieco, M., & Connell-Carrick, K. (2003). Do collaborations with schools of social work make a difference for the field of child welfare? Practice, retention and curriculum. *Journal of Human Behavior in the Social Environment, 7*(1/2), 35–51.

Scannapieco, M., & Connell-Carrick, K. (2007). Child welfare workplace: The state of the workforce and strategies to improve retention. *Child Welfare, 86*(6), 31–52.

Scannapieco, M., & Painter, K. (2014). Barriers to implementing a mentoring program for youth in foster care: Implications for practice and policy innovation. *Child and Adolescent Social Work Journal, 31*(2), 163–180. doi:10.1007/s10560-013-0315-3

Stolin-Goltzman, J., Kollar, S., & Trinkle, J. (2010). Listening to the voices of children in foster care: Youth speak out about child welfare workforce turnover and selection. *Social Work, 55,* 47–553.

United States General Accounting Office (USGAO). (2003). *Health and Human Services could play a greater role in helping child welfare agencies recruit and retain staff.* Washington, DC: US General Accounting Office.

Westbrook, T. M., Ellis, J., & Ellett, A. J. (2006). Improving retention among public child welfare workers: What can we learn from the insight and experiences of committed survivors. *Administration in Social Work, 30,* 37–62. doi:10.1300/J147v30n04_04

Wilson, S. E., Nichols, Q. I., Kirk, A., & Wilson, T. (2010). A recent look at the factors influencing workforce retention in public child welfare. *Children and Youth Services Review, 33,* 157–160. doi:10.1016/j.childyouth.2010.08.028

Yankeelov, P. A., Barbee, A. P., Sullivan, D., & Antle, B. F. (2009). Individual and organizational factors in job retention in Kentucky's child welfare agency. *Children and Youth Services Review, 31,* 547–554. doi:10.1016/j.childyouth.2008.10.014

Zlotnik, J. L. (2003). The use of Title IV- E training funds for social work education: An historical perspective. *Journal of Human Behavior and the Social Environment, 7*(1/2), 5–20.

Zlotnik, J. L., & Corneilius, L. J. (2000). Preparing social work students for child welfare careers: The use of Title IV-E training funds in social work education. *The Journal of Baccalaureate Social Work, 5*(2), 1–13.

Factors affecting turnover rates of public child welfare front line workers: C omparing cohorts of title IV-E program graduates with regularly hired and trained staff

Anita Barbee ⓞ, Corrie Rice, Becky F. Antle, Katy Henry, and Michael R. Cunningham

ABSTRACT
The purpose of the study is to examine the impact of a state-wide intervention (BSW level Title IV-E Program) on both the workers' intent to leave the job and their actual exit from a state administered public child welfare agency. Employees completed an extensive survey including scales assessing individual, team, and organizational variables that might impact turnover. Results show that more Title IV-E graduates stay with the agency than do regular hires and leave at a slower rate. Different variables impact intent to leave compared to actual exit and vary across type of employee. Implications for the workforce are discussed.

Recruiting and retaining a competent and committed workforce is crucial for public child welfare agencies to achieve child safety, permanency, and well-being (e.g., Strolin-Goltzman, Kollar, & Trinkle, 2010). Child welfare agencies are beginning to adopt research-based strategies and interventions for recruiting, hiring, training, and retaining the best frontline workers. These front-end strategies include three main approaches. First is carefully recruiting appropriate applicants by using such strategies as providing realistic job previews (Breaugh, 2017; Faller et al., 2009). Second is utilizing tools to enhance employee selection such as testing, situational judgment or simulation tasks, and behavioral interviewing (Ellett, Ellett, Ellis, & Lerner, 2009; Goldstein, Pulakos, Passmore, & Semedo, 2017). Third is enhancing the onboarding, initial training, coaching, and supervision processes for new employees (e.g., Yankeelov, Barbee, Sullivan, & Antle, 2009). All of these strategies are aimed at helping those who are truly suited for the job to join and remain with the agency.

Another child welfare recruitment and selection intervention that incorporates and extends many aspects of the three strategies noted above has been in place for over 35 years since the passage of the

Adoption Assistance and Child Welfare Act of 1980 (P.L. 96–272). This intervention is referred to as the Title IV-E Child Welfare Educational Program (hereto referred to as Title IV-E; Barbee, Antle, Sullivan, Dryden, & Henry, 2012; Zlotnik & Pryce, 2013). In a Title IV-E program, funds are expended to financially support students, sometimes vetted through a rigorous selection process, for between 1 and 2 years in a Council on Social Work Education (CSWE) accredited Bachelor of Social Work (BSW) or Master of Social Work (MSW)-level educational program. Students usually take specialized courses on child abuse and neglect, and conduct a field placement in a public child welfare agency. Social work is likely the best background for child welfare jobs (e.g., Ellett & Leighninger, 2007), due to overlap between social work curricula and child welfare work duties. However, the social work degree has not always been found to sufficiently prepare employees for complex child welfare work (e.g., Perry, 2016). Thus, investing in child welfare specializations within social work programs may be a way to not only bring talent into the field, but to give them both the broad and specific knowledge and skills necessary to thrive in child welfare. To retain this talent, there is a stipulation that graduates are required to work in public child welfare to "payback" the cost of their tuition and stipend payments. This essentially locks graduates into the job for several years.

Several studies support the notion that both BSW and MSW Title IV-E graduates of social work programs can outperform those hired through a regular process on short-term outcomes like gains in knowledge after training (Bagdasaryan, 2012; Franke, Bagdasaryan, & Furman, 2009; Gansle & Ellett, 2002) and transfer of knowledge to the field (Scannapieco & Connell, 2003). Furthermore, BSW Title IV-E graduates, more than others, have been found to engage in best practices on the job such as intervening proactively in cases, placing more children with relatives and fewer in residential settings, completing more adoptions, and visiting children more regularly (Barbee et al., 2009a). Finally, MSW Title IV-E graduates have been found to have better outcomes than others in shortening the length of time from removal of children to reunification with parents, and moving children to adoption (Leung & Willis, 2012).

Study purpose

The purpose of the current study is to replicate and extend previous research on the effectiveness of BSW Title IV-E programs in retaining these competent frontline workers in public child welfare agencies. The study longitudinally follows, across a 4-year period of time, cohorts of (a) workers who had completed a Title IV-E stipend program at the BSW level and (b) workers who had not completed a Title IV-E stipend program (regular hires).

Findings from previous Title IV-E turnover outcome studies

Impact of Title IV-E on turnover

A small group of studies have tested the efficacy of the Title IV-E intervention on actual turnover. Studies have found that both BSW and MSW Title IV-E graduates versus regular hires had lower turnover at the 1-year mark (Barbee et al., 2009a; Fox, Miller, & Barbee, 2003; Gansle & Ellett, 2002; Robin & Hollister, 2002), and a lower risk for turnover overall (among BSW graduates) (Rosenthal & Waters, 2006). Other studies found Title IV-E graduates were retained for longer than a year (Altman & Cohen, 2016; Barbee et al., 2009b; Dickinson & Perry, 2002), but few studies examining multi-year retention contrasted IV-E graduates with non-graduates (e.g., Jones, 2002; Madden, Scannapieco, & Painter, 2014).

Studies of why Title IV-E graduates remain beyond the payback period

Several studies also sought to understand why MSW Stipend graduates intended to or actually stayed on the job longer. A number of individual and team variables have been shown to have an impact on which Title IV-E graduates are more likely to intend to or actually remain in the agency. The individual variables include: having higher levels of organizational commitment (O'Donnell & Kirkner, 2009), and lower rates of burnout (Dickinson & Perry, 2002). The team variables include supervisory support (Morazes, Benton, Clark, & Jacquet, 2010; O'Donnell & Kirkner, 2009). Another study of BSW IV-E graduates examined predictors of intent to stay with the agency and mirrored findings with MSW IV-E graduates (Barbee et al., 2009a). Barbee's team found that intention to stay was predicted by social support from supervisors, organizational commitment, job satisfaction, as well as lower levels of job stress and absenteeism. Finally, in a follow-up qualitative exit interview study with 15 Title IV-E graduates who had exited the agency (Barbee et al., 2009b), it was found that these specially trained workers left after their commitment was fulfilled due to receiving poor-quality supervision, working for supervisors with unrealistic expectations for them due to their educational experience (e.g., believing that they needed little support or additional training). Finally, they felt unsupported by coworkers even as they felt high levels of stress from mounting caseloads.

Gaps in the literature addressed in the current study

While this literature is growing, there are some gaps in our knowledge to date. First, there have been few published studies that have longitudinally compared cohorts of Title IV-E graduates with regular hire cohorts from the same time period on turnover rates at multiple points across several years (Madden et al., 2014). This type of analysis will tell us precisely when different types of workers leave the agency. Knowing the rates of leaving across time can potentially unearth different reasons why the leaving is occurring so that solutions can be generated. This type of analysis could examine if (1) Title IV-E graduates stay longer than regular hires at the 1-year mark, (2) if Title IV-E graduates are retained longer than their payback period (in this case, the 2-year mark), and (3) if Title IV-E graduates stay long beyond the payback period (up to 4 years) compared to regular hires. Such outcomes have implications for how to lower financial and emotional turnover costs for both remaining staff and children.

Second, only a few studies have simultaneously attempted to understand what drives Title IV-E graduates not only to intend to leave the agency, but what factors drive *actual* turnover in these workers. Digging deeper into the turnover question will give agencies a better idea of whether or not IV-E graduates bring more stability to the workforce and what keeps them in place. Such analyses will also illuminate the different motivations of the various types of workers so that more tailored turnover reduction interventions can be applied to each group.

Finally, when designing the study and choosing potential variables that could affect intended or actual leaving behavior, we utilized both an Ecological Framework (Moos, 1973) and a Resiliency and Growth Framework (see Bonanno, 2004). Turnover can be influenced by individual/intrapsychic, team, organizational, and community or sociocultural level variables. These may include factors such as low stress, team cohesion, learning, and support for families. Further, since intending to leave the job or actually quitting may include dissatisfaction or distress, we also consider risk and resilience factors such as secondary trauma and commitment.

Hypotheses and research questions

In this study we sought to understand the trajectories of employment of both groups over time while also comparing the two groups regarding patterns in the timing of actual exits from the agency. We also sought to understand what variables predicted both intention to leave the agency as well actual exits from the agency for each group. Finally we compared the two groups to better understand if the same or different variables predicted these two outcomes of intent to leave and actual leaving. The overall goal of the study was to compare the impact of the different recruitment strategies (hiring new employees via investment in specialized social work education versus business as usual) along with other key variables on worker retention.

Based on past research noted above, we hypothesized that H1: More Title IV-E graduates than regular hires would intend to remain with the agency.

H2: More regular hires will leave the agency than Title IV-E graduates overall and will do so at a faster rate during in the first and second years of employment. H3: More Title IV-E workers will remain with the agency than leave the 2 years following their payback period and more will remain at the 4-year mark than regular hires. H4: Less organizational commitment, less supervisory support, more stress, and more secondary trauma will influence intent to leave the agency for both groups. H5: Employees from both groups who leave the agency will be less committed to the organization, perceive less supervisory support, and feel more stressed and traumatized than those who stay with the agency. Research Question 1: Do any patterns of leaving for the two groups emerge? If so, what other factors may be driving those patterns besides how they were hired into the agency? Research Question 2: What other variables predict Title IV-E graduate intent to leave, and are any of these variables different from what predicts regular hire intent to leave? Research Question 3: How do those who stay versus those who leave the agency differ on key variables and do any of those variables overlap between Title IV-E graduates and regular hires? Research Question 4: Do different variables influence intent to leave than actual exits?

Method

Participants

Two types of employees hired into the department that houses the child welfare function across an entire Southern state between June, 2012 and June, 2016 were enlisted as part of a program evaluation. A cross-university evaluation has continuously assessed the impact of the Title IV-E program during its entire 20-year history (e.g., Fox et al., 2003). A new approach to evaluation that differed from the approach taken from 1998–2012 occurred from 2012–2016. During the first 14 years of evaluation, Title IV-E graduates completed follow-up surveys at 6 months and 2 years (after their obligation to the state was completed). In addition, supervisors of the graduates were surveyed at the 6-month mark. Graduate turnover rates were tracked and periodically exit interviews with those who left the agency were conducted. One comparison study with non-Title IV-E graduates was conducted regarding 11 practice behaviors. For the second phase of evaluation starting in 2012, the study was expanded in that the turnover of all new employees was tracked across time, and all employees were surveyed 6 months after completion of their Academy Training. These two changes allowed Title IV-E and regularly hired employees to be compared. Future efforts will link these employee data to case data in a larger study comparing different types of employees on both practice behaviors and outcomes.[1]

The first type of employees in the study was comprised of new frontline workers hired through normal hiring channels rather than through a special program. A total of 1081 people were hired during this period in this conventional manner (regular hires). A follow-up survey was sent out 6 months after the workers completed a child welfare academy training that lasted 4 months. A total of 126 employees had already left the agency by the time of the follow-up survey. So, out of the 955 eligible participants (1081 minus 126), 598 completed a follow-up survey for a 63% response rate.

The second type of employees were graduates of the state's Title IV-E program aimed at BSW students. In the program, college students at 11 universities across the state with CSWE-accredited BSW programs are carefully vetted to become part of the program. The vetting process incorporates most components of the three key evidence based recruitment and selection strategies mentioned on page one. The vetting process consists of an assessment of (1) intelligence and hard work (observed in the transcript with the expectation of high performance in rigorous classes and an overall GPA above a 3.25, sample of written work from a college class and under pressure during the interview, and letters of recommendation from faculty and employers attesting to both traits), (2) commitment to working with children and families, in general, and public child welfare, in particular, expressed in the personal essay, letters of recommendation, and the interview, (3) demonstration of empathy toward families who are poor and oppressed based on experience working with diverse, vulnerable populations and ability to talk about specific situations during the behavioral interview. The intense behavioral interview process is led by a group of panelists consisting of professors and public child welfare supervisors/managers. Those who are accepted into the program receive up to 2 years of tuition and a stipend for books and other expenses. Beyond all of their regular classes in the BSW major, these students take several classes in their child welfare specialization. The syllabi and content of these classes is consistent across all 11 BSW programs. The students conduct a year-long field practicum in a public child welfare agency which serves as a realistic job preview as well as more experience working with vulnerable clients. They also attend program retreats each semester where they meet students from across the state and key leaders in the agency so as to deepen connections and build a professional network within the statewide agency. In addition, they receive training on emerging issues in child welfare practice. Upon successful completion of all aspects of the program and graduation, students apply for employment with the state agency. Most have been hired into the public child welfare system. In return, they are obligated to work for the state for 2 years after hiring; otherwise, they have to pay back tuition and stipend funds. Two years was chosen for fiscal and practical reasons. It is a widely held belief that it takes 2 years of child welfare practice to master the job. So the program development team believed that it was important to incentivize workers to remain on the job even when their limited skill was being challenged by difficult case-work so as to stay until they felt more competent.

During the time period 2012–2016, 198 Title IV-E students graduated from the program, were hired by the agency, and were followed for retention tracking purposes. When the 6-month follow-up survey was administered, 18 graduates had already left the agency, for a total of 180 eligible participants. Of those eligible participants, 135 completed the survey for a 75% response rate. Thus, to summarize, 1,279 employees were part of the retention portion of the study ($n = 1,081$ regular hires and 198 Title IV-E graduates) and 733 of these employees participated in the survey component of the study ($n = 598$ regular hires and 135 IV-E graduates).

Procedure

The study received approval from the Cabinet for Health and Family Services Institutional Review Board in 2012. Because the study is part of an evalua-tion, the University IRB exempted the chart file review study. The research team had access to participant identification, so all data were not anonymous, but were kept confidential and stored on secured computers using standard protocols for encryption.

All of these new frontline workers were sent an e-mail invitation from a researcher at the lead state University to complete a survey evaluating their preparation for the job and the context in which the job took place. The e-mail contained a link to an online survey housed on a private and secure University server. For the regularly hired employees, the e-mail was first sent approximately 6 months after the completion of their orientation to the agency (initial onboarding period) and completion of an Academy which includes several Masters level courses. These courses also serve as new employee training classes that are delivered across a 4-month period of time. For those employees who did not complete the survey within a week, reminder e-mails were sent weekly for a month (Dillman, Smyth, & Christian, 2014). Thus, most of these regularly hired employees who com-pleted the survey had been with the agency between 10 and 12 months at the time of the survey administration.

For the Title IV-E graduates, the e-mail was first sent approximately 6 months after the completion of the second course in the Academy (which they completed within the first two months of employment). For those graduates who did not complete the survey within a week, reminders were sent weekly for a month. Thus, most of these graduates who completed the survey had been with the agency between 8 and 10 months at the time of the survey administration. While the two groups had been agency employees for different lengths of time, both were working at full capacity for between 6 and 8 months.

Measures

The measures for this particular analysis were part of a larger battery of measures administered as a survey. Only details of measures germane to this study are described here.

Demographic questions

The questionnaire consisted of individual demographic and background items including gender, age, race, ethnicity, education, type of team they worked on (e.g., Intake, Investigations, Ongoing, Recruitment & Certification of Foster Homes, and Adoption), and number of hours worked per week. The questionnaire included 15 scales, all with high reliability and most with high levels of validity[2] (See Table 2 for all scales, means, standard deviations, and Cronbach's alpha reliability scores in this study for each scale for each group of employees). The scales were categorized according to the framework described on page 5 including individual risk and resiliency factors, team-level resiliency factors, and organizational resiliency factors. No community/sociocultural factors were assessed in this study.

Individual risk and resiliency measures

Included were measures of stress (TCU, 2011), secondary trauma (Secondary Traumatic Stress Scale (STSS), Bride, Robinson, Yegidis, & Figley, 2004), organizational commitment, voicing concerns (Lijegren, Nordlund, & Ekberg, 2008), and job satisfaction (Spector, 1994). The measure of *human service job satisfaction* included 36 items divided into four items each across nine subscales (verified through factor analysis) assessing satisfaction with pay, promotion, supervision, benefits, contingent rewards, operating procedures, coworkers, nature of work, and communication (Spector, 1985, 1994). In this study, a 5-point rather than a 6-point scale of 1 (disagree very much) to 5 (agree very much) was utilized. The *organizational commitment* scale includes 15 items, while the *voicing concerns* scale includes 10 items and the *TCU stress measure* includes 4 items – all three utilizing a 5-point Likert type scale expressing levels of agreement from 1 (disagree) to 5 (agree). The STSS has 17 items with three sub-scales to assess the frequency of intrusion, avoidance, and arousal symptoms associated with secondary trauma resulting from working with traumatized populations. Respondents indicate how frequently (on a 5-point Likert-type scale ranging from never to very often) each item was true for them in the past seven days. Each item on the STSS corresponds to one of the 17 post-traumatic stress disorder symptoms as delineated in the Diagnostic and Statistical Manual of Mental Disorders (4th ed., text revision) (DSM-IVTR)

(APA, 2000). Scores are obtained by summing the items assigned to each subscale and the entire instrument.

Reational/team measures

Team-level scales included measures from an earlier version of the Comprehensive Organizational Health Assessment (COHA) developed by the team at the Butler Institute at the University of Denver (Potter, Leake, Longworth-Reed, Altschul, & Rienks, 2016). All scales have acceptable levels of reliability. Validity studies are in process, but all scales have good face validity. Three subscales of the COHA measuring *supervisor quality* (10 items), *supervisor support* (6 items), and *team cohesion* (14 items) using Likert-type scales were created and tested for reliability by the Butler Institute team. Two other subscales of the COHA measuring *coworker support* (5 items) and *shared vision* (6 items) were both developed and validated by Ellett (2009). In the current study, all Likert-type scales were on a 1 (not at all) to 5 (very much) continuum.

Organizational measures

Two other subscales from the COHA measuring *leadership* (14 items), and *perceptions of professional development* (assesses perceptions that the organization supports worker competency) (14 items) were utilized along with a measure of *role overload* (assesses perceptions that the organization creates stress for workers) (12 items) created and validated by the TCU team (2011). Also included were 30 items developed by the evaluation team focused on *preparation for the job* in key child welfare practices (Barbee et al., 2009a). Participants rated on a 1 (not at all) to 5 (very much) scale about how prepared they felt they were in conducting specific behaviors of engagement, intake, assessment, case planning/casework, legal, and case closure. This scale is similar to a self-efficacy scale created by Chen and Scannapieco (2010), thus is labeled as both preparedness and self-efficacy.

Outcome measures

Finally outcome measures included an *intent to leave* scale (6 items; Lijegren et al., 2008) and a measure of actual turnover. All employees hired in the specified time period were tracked over time by the agency to determine if and when any actually exited the agency (date of termination).

Results

Descriptive results

Title IV-E graduates were younger and less diverse than regular hires who came from a variety of educational backgrounds (see Table 1). The type of

Table 1. Demographics: percentage of participants in each dimension.

| | Gender | | Race | | | Age | | | | | | Degrees | | | | | Position type | | | |
	Female	White	Black	Other	20s	30s	40s	50s	60s	BA	MA	BSW	MSW	Intake	Invest	Ongoing	FC/Adopt
Regular hires	85	83	12	5	50	31	13	5	1	64	5	25	6	2	47	44	4
Title IV-E	88	91	8	5	73	19	5	3	0			100		1	47	51	1

teams the two groups worked on was fairly similar. Overall, 47% of both groups worked on investigative teams. But far more Title IV-E graduates worked on ongoing teams and more regular hires worked on intake and foster care or adoption teams. Finally, both groups worked similar numbers of hours: 67% of both IV-E and regular hires were extremely overworked (working more than 49 hours per week).

As noted in Table 2, Title IV-E graduates experienced significantly more role overload, less shared vision, and lower preparedness on specific practice behaviors than did others.

Analyses to test hypotheses regarding intent to leave and actual turnover

Hypothesis 1 (intention to leave): In spite of the stress on Title IV-E graduates, their intent to leave (see Table 2) and actual exits from the agency (see Tables 2 and 3 and a fuller discussion below) were significantly lower than regular hires. Thus, Hypothesis 1 was supported.

Hypothesis 2 (regarding turnover in years one and two and comparisons between groups) and *Hypothesis 3 (regarding retention past the payback period and up to 4 years)*. Of all regular hires (those who stayed and left among 1081 participants), 11% left in the first year, another 14% left within 2 years (25% cumulatively) by the end of 2 years, and another 8% left in the third year of employment. A total of 33% had left within 3 years of hire. Only 2% left after 3 years on the job for a total of 35% departing within 4 years. Of the 198 Title IV-E graduates hired between March 2012 and September 2016, only 9.5% left in the first year and 5% left by the end of the second year for a total of 14.5% leaving after 2 years with the agency, which was within the payback period. These percentages of retention through the 2-year mark have been stable for 20 years. In the third year, another 8.5% Title IV-E hires left the agency for a total of 23% leaving by the end of 3 years with the agency and 2% more leaving by the 4-year mark. So over a 4-year period, only 25% of Title IV-E graduates left the agency which was equal to the exit rate for non-Title IV-E participants at the 2-year mark.

Examination of timing of exit

To examine when regular hires who left did so, we found that 33% left in the first year and another 38% left in the second year. So cumulatively, 71% of leavers were gone by the end of the second year of employment. The rate of leaving was cut in half by the third year when only 14.5% additional people left. But, another interesting finding was uncovered when examining the data in 6 month increments. It was found that of regular hires who left the agency, 20% did so between 7 and 11 months after they were hired. This is the period of time when the new worker training and coaching in the field has ended and the caseloads of new employees grow to a typical size (somewhere

Table 2. List of scales, items, means, standard deviations, and ANOVAS comparing non-Title IV-E employees with Title IV-E graduates.

	Cronbach's alpha	Regular Hires Means (S.D.) or Percentage	Title IV-E Means (S.D.) or Percentage	ANOVA Significance (p)	Chi Square Significance (p)
Individual risk and resilience factors (# items)					
Stress (4)	.88	15.09 (3.57)	15.66 (3.21)	ns	n/a
Secondary trauma (17)	.89	36.85 (12.01)	38.09 (13.75)	ns	n/a
Job satisfaction (36)	.90	110.25 (16.25)	112.35 (16.25)	ns	n/a
Org commitment (15)	.86	48.99 (7.15)	47.68 (8.30)	ns	n/a
Voicing concerns (10)	.95	40.13 (5.87)	40.72 (5.51)	ns	n/a
Team factors (# items)					
Supervisor quality (10)	.91	37.54 (7.47)	37.10 (7.06)	ns	n/a
Supervisor support (6)	.97	24.21 (5.16)	24.93 (5.05)	ns	n/a
Coworker support (5)	.95	20.45 (3.75)	20.62 (4.44)	ns	n/a
Team cohesion (14)	.87	49.00 (7.52)	48.46 (4.99)	ns	n/a
Shared vision (6)	.89	21.26 (4.22)	20.37 (4.99)	$p < .04$	n/a
Organizational factors (# items)					
Role overload (12)	.94	43.71 (10.17)	45.96 (9.11)	$p < .02$	n/a
Leadership (14)	.98	47.59 (11.60)	48.46 (10.45)	ns	n/a
Professional development (14)	.91	49.43 (9.00)	49.85 (10.32)	ns	n/a
Preparedness/Efficacy (30)	.98	111.29 (25.27)	105.73 (27.75)	$p < .003$	n/a
Outcome factors (# items)					
Intent to leave (6)	.95	15.48 (6.38)	14.07 (6.29)	$p < .03$	n/a
Actual exit Yes or No	n/a	35%	25%	n/a	$p < .005$

Table 3. Percentage turnover of cohorts over time (longitudinal view of cohorts).

	All regular hires N = 1080	Of regular hires who left N = 387	All Title IV-E graduates N = 198	Of Title IV-E graduates who left N = 50
Time at Exit				
<6 months	3	9	6	25**
7–11 months	7	20**	3	10
12 months	1	4	<1	2
Total through Year 1	11	33	9.5	37
13–17 months	7	19	1	4
18 months	1	3	0	0
19–23 months	5	13	<1	2
24 months	1	3	3.5	14***
Total through Year 2	25	71	14.5	57
25–29 months	3	7.5	5	20***
30 months	<1	2	1.5	6
31–35 months	2	4	2	8
36 months	<1	1	0	0
Total through Year 3	30	85.5	23	91
Over 3 years	2	5	2	9
Sometime in first 4 Years	3	9.5	—	—
Total 4 Year Turnover	35	100	25	100

** First time new employees are likely to be carrying a caseload after completing training. Note Title IV-E hit that barrier first because they have already taken the first CFL course in college, so jump into a caseload and greater job stress sooner.

*** Title IV-E students can leave after completing 2 years with the agency – so there is a spike in leaving that month and the few months following the 2 year mark. So they stay for their one or two years then leave sometime in their second (for those with 1 year obligation) or their third (for those with 2 years obligation) years.

between 15 and 30 cases depending on which region the employee worked in). The second bump in exits was at the 13–17-month mark.

When Title IV-E graduates who did leave the agency during the 4-year period left, 36% did so in the first year of employment, 20% in the second year of employment, 34% in the third year of employment, and 10% in their fourth year of employment. So cumulatively only 56% of leavers did so in the first 2 years of employment compared to 71% for regular hires. Furthermore, and in support of the notion that introduction of a full caseload is a vulnerable time for new employees to exit child welfare agencies, of the Title IV-E graduates who left the agency, 25% did so within 6 months of starting the job and another 12% did so in months 7–12 on the job. It is likely that the early introduction to a full caseload drove 37% of Title IV-E graduates who left before the penalty period had ended. So, H2 was supported. Overall, 35% of regular hires compared to 25% of Title IV-E graduates left the agency within 4 years and most regular hires left within 2 years. H3 was also supported in that 75% of Title IV-E graduates remain with the agency 4 years from hire. The turnover rate for regular hires at the 2-year mark is the same as the turnover rate for Title IV-E graduates at the 4-year mark. Thus, the same percentage of Title IV-E employees remain on the job 2 years longer than regular hires.

Predictors of intent to leave

Hypothesis 4 (regarding predictors of intent to leave). Using the *regular hires* dataset, correlation analyses were conducted which showed that all 14 variables were significantly correlated with *intent to leave* and could potentially predict the outcome. A linear regression analysis was conducted including all of these significantly correlated variables. Only five variables were significant. Thus, the regression was conducted again with only those five variables and was found to be significant while also accounting for a large portion of the variance, $R^2 = .43$, F $(5,525) = 78.48$, $p < .0001$. Regular hires who were *more committed* to the organization's mission, and perceived that their *supervisor was supportive* were less likely to *intend to leave* the organization. Furthermore, the *more prepared* they felt to do the job combined with the *more stress and secondary traumatic stress* they experienced, the more they *intended to leave* the organization.

Using the *Title IV-E graduates'* dataset, correlation analyses were conducted which showed that 11 variables were significantly correlated with *intent to leave* (supervisor quality, supervisor support, coworker support, team cohesion, shared vision, leadership, professional development opportunities, satisfied, stressed, traumatized, or experiencing role overload) and could potentially predict the intent to leave. A linear regression analysis was conducted including all of these significantly correlated variables. Only four of those variables were significant in the regression analysis. Thus, the regression was conducted again with only those four variables and was found to be significant while also accounting for a large portion of the variance, $R^2 = .49$, $F(4,109) = 26.34$, $p < .0001$ (see Table 4). The Title IV-E graduates had a slightly different pattern regarding what drove *intent to leave*. Like regular hires, Title IV-E graduates' intent to leave was partially driven by having *less commitment, more stress, and more secondary trauma*, but it was also driven by a *strong shared vision*. So, Hypothesis 4 was partially supported in that for both groups having less organizational commitment and more stress as well as secondary trauma predicted intent to leave. And for the regular hires, supervisory support buffered intent to leave, but not for Title IV-E graduates.

How do regular hires who stay differ from those who leave?

Hypothesis 5 (regarding difference between stayers and leavers in both groups). MANOVA analyses were conducted with each group (regular hires and Title IV-E graduates). The independent variable in these analyses was *actual leaving* so as to compare the *stayers versus* the *leavers*. For the regular hires who completed a survey ($N = 598$), 139 of those had left as of April of 2017. We examined those who stayed versus those who left on all of the key variables measured in the study first using individual ANOVA analyses. There were significant differences between the stayers and leavers on 11 of

Table 4. Regression table examining predictors of intent to leave for regular hires and Title IV-E graduates.

Regular hires					
Source	B	SE B	β	t	p
Organizational commitment	−.293	0.04	−.33	−8.44	.0001
Stress	.368	0.07	.21	5.27	.0001
STS	.122	0.02	.23	5.89	.0001
Supervisor support	−.194	0.04	−.19	−4.40	.0001
Prepared	.020	0.08	.08	2.38	.02
Title IV-E graduates					
Source	B	SE B	β	t	p
Organizational commitment	−.336	0.07	−.43	−4.59	.0001
Stress	.620	0.17	.31	3.67	.0001
STS	.098	0.04	.21	2.46	.01
Shared vision	.224	0.11	.18	2.04	.04

Regular hires R^2 = .43 (p < .0001) Title IV-E Graduates R^2 = .49 (p < .0001).

14 variables tested (see Table 5). These included individual variables of *organizational commitment* (leavers felt less committed) $F(1, 570)$ = 6.12, p < .0001, *stress* (leavers felt more stressed), $F(1, 570)$ = 4.28, p < .0001, *likely to leave* (leavers had higher intentions of leaving), $F(1, 570)$ = 8.30, p < .0001, *preparedness* (leavers felt less prepared), $F(1, 570)$ = 7.67, p < .0001, and *job satisfaction* (leavers felt less satisfied), $F(1, 570)$ = 5.36, p < .0001. But, also included team variables such as *supervisory support* (leavers felt less support), $F(1, 570)$ = 4.36, p < .04, *coworker support* (leavers felt less support), $F(1, 570)$ = 4.17, p < .04, *team cohesion* (leavers felt less cohesion), $F(1, 570)$ = 5.66, p < .0001, *shared vision* (leavers saw less shared vision), $F(1, 570)$ = 8.14, p < .0001, and organizational variables such as *positive leadership* (leavers perceived less positive leadership), $F(1, 570)$ = 7.85, p < .0001 and *professional development opportunities* (leavers perceive fewer), $F(1,570)$ = 4.41, p < .04.

Then a MANOVA was conducted to see which variables were most different between the two groups of leavers and stayers. In the significant MANOVA $F(7, 582)$ = 2.69, p < .01, seven variables remained significant including *organizational commitment, intent to leave, overall perceptions of preparedness, job satisfaction, team cohesion, shared vision,* and *leadership.*

Do Title IV-E stayers differ from Title IV-E leavers?

For the IV-E hires who completed a survey (N = 135), 13 had left as of April of 2017. We examined those who stayed versus those who left on all of the key variables measured in the study. We found in the individual ANOVA analyses that there was a significant difference between the two groups on 7 out of 14 variables tested. These included individual variables like *preparedness* (leavers felt less prepared), $F(1, 122)$ = 4.00, p < .05 and

Table 5. Means and standard deviations on key differences in stayers versus leavers for regular hires and Title IV-E graduates.

	Regular hires Stayers Mean (S.D.)	Regular hires Leavers Mean (S.D.)	Title IV-E Stayers Mean (S.D.)	Title IV-E Leavers Mean (S.D.)
Individual risk and resilience factors				
Stress	14.92 (3.69)	15.68 (3.09)	15.56 (3.37)	16.15 (2.52)
Secondary trauma	36.67 (12.16)	37.50 (11.68)	37.66 (13.72)	40.30 (14.58)
Job satisfaction	111.09 (16.70)**a	107.19 (14.26)	113.53 (16.64)	106.40 (14.49)
Org commitment	49.39 (7.09))**a	47.54 (7.28)	48.19 (8.43)	45.16 (8.01)
Voicing concerns	40.16 (5.63)	40.06 (6.77)	41.33 (5.37)**b	37.55 (6.51)
Team factors				
Supervisor quality	37.82 (7.47)	36.53 (7.34)	37.88 (7.12)**b	33.05 (5.97)
Supervisor support	24.45 (5.03)	23.33 (5.57)	25.35 (5.13)**b	22.85 (4.89)
Coworker support	20.63 (3.72)	19.83 (3.85)	21.04 (4.20)**b	18.50 (5.81)
Team cohesion	49.40 (7.68)**a	47.54 (6.98)	49.06 (8.56)	45.45 (8.20)
Shared vision	21.13 (4.28)**a	20.28 (3.68)	20.88 (4.99)**b	17.80 (4.22)
Organizational factors				
Role overload	40.51 (10.50)	44.42 (9.15)	46.04 (8.79)	45.55 (10.31)
Leadership	48.32 (11.27)**a	44.93 (11.72)	49.75 (10.12)**b	44.42 (11.81)
Professional development	49.86 (9.02)	47.88 (8.58)	49.04 (10.10)	47.78 (12.48)
Preparedness/Efficacy	112.87 (24.75)**a	105.79 (28.91)	105.89 (28.05)**b	92.50 (21.49)
Outcome Factors				
Intent to Leave	15.07 (6.32)**a	16.96 (6.43)	13.99 (6.35)	14.50 (5.90)

a Denotes significant difference between regular hire leavers and stayers.
b Denotes significant difference between Title IV-E graduate leavers and stayers.
** $p < .0001$.

willingness to voice concerns (leavers voiced concerns less), F $(1,119) = 8.35$, $p < .05$. But, the list also included team variables such as *supervisor quality* (leavers felt supervisors were of lower quality), F $(1,121) = 8.33$, $p < .005$, *supervisory support* (leavers felt less support), F $(1, 119) = 4.19$, $p < .04$, *coworker support* (leavers felt less support), F(1, 119) = 5.67, $p < .03$, and *shared vision* (leavers saw less), F(1, 119) = 6.67, $p < .01$ and the organizational variable of *positive leadership* (leavers perceived less), F(1, 116) = 4.25, $p < .04$. Then a MANOVA was conducted to see which variables were most different between the two groups. In the significant MANOVA F(7, 106) = 2.65, $p < .04$, all of the same seven variables remained significant including *overall perceptions of preparedness, voicing concerns, supervisor quality and support, coworker support, shared vision,* and *leadership all predicted retention*. Thus, H5 was partially supported. For regular hires, leavers were less committed to the organization and were more likely to intend to leave. But, supervisory support, stress, and secondary trauma were not significant in the final MANOVA analysis. For Title IV-E employees, less supervisory support was a significant predictor of retention but the other four variables were not.

Discussion

Results largely supported the five literature-based hypotheses, and also yielded interesting insights into the four research questions. As hypothesized for the first three hypotheses, fewer Title IV-E BSW graduates than others intended to leave and fewer did leave the agency, overall. When they did leave the agency, they did so at a slower rate than did regular hires. And, while the penalty for leaving before 2 years did deter most Title IV-E graduates from leaving before their obligation was due (85.5% stayed through their obligation), hanging on through 2 years led to, at least, an additional 2 year gain in employment when compared to the regular hires in that 25% of regular hires left by the 2-year mark while 25% of Title IV-E left by the 4-year mark. There was stabilization across both groups by the fourth year. So, it may be the case that if more new workers can be retained through that treacherous 2-year mark, the likelihood is high that they may remain up to four.

Some clues as to what drove workers away were revealed through the patterns of exits. For both groups, there was a spike in exits in the period immediately following completion of training when the employees were given a full caseload. Even for the Title IV-E graduates who come with much more preparation regarding the job and a realistic view of what it will entail, moving to a full caseload so early in one's tenure can be a precarious venture that makes some of them vulnerable to leaving. Future research needs to directly verify the impact of moving to a full caseload on new workers to understand the ideal pacing of caseload assignment, especially for those hired under varying circumstances. Another clue emerged. For regular hires not initially deterred by the full caseload, more than a third who left did so between their first and second year of employment. It may be the case that many employees have the attitude that if they can persevere in a difficult or undesirable job for at least a year, they will look stable to other employers and can quit without undue penalty in the job market. While this phenomenon did not happen with Title IV-E graduates, the incentive to "stick it out" another year until the financial obligation was met after the 2-year mark seemed to work for most in the program, but soon after the obligation there was a bump in exits. Further research is needed to understand if today's employees believe quitting a job within a year of employment is stigmatizing and if this notion is a motivator to stay in a stressful position until after the 1-year mark.

Variables impacting intent to leave

When examining the variables affecting intent to leave the agency, our hypothesis was largely supported in that for both groups having more organizational commitment, less stress, and secondary trauma did predict less intent to leave. And for regular hires, supervisory support also predicted less intent to leave. These findings largely replicate previous research on the importance of organizational commitment (Boyas, Wind, & Kang, 2012), supervisory support (e.g., Chenot, Benton, & Kim, 2009), and lower stress levels (e.g., Kim & Mor Barak, 2015) in elevating the will to persevere. This is the first study showing a link between secondary trauma and intent to leave. This finding, thus, extends the literature that overall stress levels, burnout, and now secondary trauma can impact the intent to leave a child welfare position (e.g., Boyas, Wind, & Ruiz, 2013). More research is needed to understand the mediators and moderators that influence links between these related, but slightly different reactions to a difficult job, and intent to leave.

With regard to our research question about differences in variables that predicted Title IV-E graduates' and regular hires' intent to leave, we found that regular hires who felt prepared but lacked supervisory support wanted to leave the agency. These two variables did not impact the intent to leave for Title IV-E graduates. For them sensing that there was a shared vision in the agency made them want to leave. This paradoxical finding could mean that when employees are trained in best practices, feel that they have the tools they need to do the job and enter a workplace with a strong shared vision they should feel empowered, but these feelings are undermined by a highly stressful organizational context which is full of clients experiencing extremely traumatic events. So, unless they have a strong personal commitment to the organization and a supportive supervisor, they will want to leave the organization. This finding may be an anomaly thus would need to be replicated and explored further in future research.

Interestingly, our final hypothesis about correspondence between intent and actual leaving was only partially supported, meaning that the variables that impact intent to leave do not always correspond to the variables that impact actual exits from the agency. In terms of actual exits from the agency, for regular hires, intent to leave and organizational commitment predicted actual turnover along with feeling less prepared or self-efficacious, and less satisfied, inspired, and connected. There are other studies which find that each of these variables impacts actual turnover (Cahalane & Sites, 2008; Chen & Scannapieco, 2010), but none of these studies examined this entire configuration of variables with intent to leave and actual exits as outcomes.

The pattern was decidedly different for Title IV-E graduates. Intent to leave and organizational commitment did not predict actual leaving. Instead, what mattered most was a lack of self-efficacy and not voicing their concerns about the workplace along with a profound sense of not getting the kind of supervision they felt they needed, nor social support from supervisors or colleagues. If the context was also devoid of a shared vision and positive leadership then those organizational variables helped to launch them out of the agency. This finding with a larger sample using validated measures largely mirrored what the authors found in their 2009b small qualitative exit study and what other authors have found for MSW IV-E graduates (Altman & Cohen, 2016; Benton, 2016; Willis, Leung, & Chavkin, 2016). What was shared between the two groups was feeling unprepared and uninspired. What differed was that IV-E graduates who were disempowered (no voice) and working on a team without quality supervision or support was important for exiting whereas for regular hires, having high dissatisfaction while already having made up their minds that they would leave the agency, along with no connections to keep them at the agency catapulted their exits. The implications for these findings are numerous.

Implications of the findings regarding intentions and actual exits

Organizational commitment and self-efficacy were robust predictors of both outcomes and for both types of employees. The strength of these variables in differentiating those who stay from those that leave builds on the growing literature showing the primacy of these variables for staff retention (e.g., O'Donnell & Kirkner, 2009). There are people in the world who are motivated to work with children and families and will easily believe in the mission of a child welfare organization. Recruitment efforts that target these types of potential employees and use of selection tools that tap into the level of commitment a person has regarding this field may lead to higher retention of staff. Certainly the Title IV-E program does this by looking for social work students with a commitment to children and utilizing essays and interview questions targeted toward this predictor. But the program does not use testing to ascertain levels of commitment. This would strengthen the selection process. However, the program goes further by also increasing the odds that a person will ultimately be more competent in their job by providing general social work knowledge, specialized knowledge and skills in child welfare policy and practice, and extended time working in the field during a practicum and once employed. Commitment coupled with competence is a strong buffer against wanting to leave and doing so.

But, the results also show that stress and secondary trauma can undermine this resolve to remain with the agency for all types of workers. And, while these variables did not directly impact actual exits from the agency, both may have contributed to exits of regular hires since intent to leave was predictive of actual leaving. Future research needs to conduct path analyses to determine the paths among all of these variables. And we may need to add other individual resilience measures to see for whom stress and secondary trauma derail the most. Finally, while stress and secondary trauma were not directly related to turnover for IV-E graduates, the fact that for those who felt unprepared and were unwilling to voice their concerns, lack of quality supervision, lack of support, and lack of inspiration all predicted actual exits. Title IV-E graduates may come into the agency with higher expectations for a shared mission and camaraderie with others. And, once they actually handled casework by themselves (unlike in a field placement), they may have been more aware of what they did not know because of their education, and thus felt less prepared or self-efficacious. Others may have felt less prepared because of their younger age and lack of life experience. A lowered sense of self-efficacy, for whatever reason, may have triggered the seeking of guidance and support from coworkers and supervisors who may have believed they should not need such direction, given their specialized education and training. If the graduates' pleas for help were rejected, then they may have felt alienated and left the agency in spite of their great commitment and capacity to engage in best practices (Barbee et al., 2009b).

Future research needs to unpack the interplay between Title IV-E graduates and others in the workplace to better understand where the interactions go awry and test possible ways to mitigate this problem. In the meantime, these results support a strategy of slowing down the flow of work and increasing guidance and support for new workers, even those from a Title IV-E program. The strategy to overload new Title IV-E workers because they come in with more knowledge is ill-advised because some of them cannot cope, especially without support, and the investment in them will be lost. Taking a bit more care of these employees might yield even better retention rates and certainly better case outcomes.

The child welfare/retention literature is full of studies that examine either the outcome of intention to leave the agency or the outcome of actual exits from the agency. There is an assumption that these two outcomes are synonymous. However, examining both outcomes in the same study revealed that intent to leave does not always translate into actual leaving. Thus, the child welfare literature on retention and turnover needs to be viewed with caution by paying careful attention to what outcome is being measured and grouping results accordingly.

The retention model used for this study conceptualizes predictors of turnover by examining the intersection of risk and resilience with an ecological model. The intersection is important because there is a tendency to operationalize risk and resilience at an individual level rather than at all levels of the ecology. The current study showed that for both intent to leave and actual exits, all variables at all levels of the system predicted outcomes. In addition, many of the team and organizational-level variables served as resilience factors in the face of stress and low self-efficacy. This interactional model can be utilized more fully in future research with larger samples to examine the buffering effects of such things as supervisor support on mitigating the effects of stress on outcomes of intended or actual turnover. Conversely, operationalization of organizational culture and climate into interactional patterns between workers and supervisors or between workers and other teammates could demonstrate the impact of strained relationships or specific punitive actions by bosses on the feelings of stress of workers and their ultimate decisions to remain with the agency or leave it.

How do these results speak to the efficacy of Title IV-E programs?

Results from this study and much of the work in the literature on evaluations that compare Title IV-E graduates with regular hires find evidence supporting the program's efficacy in terms of reducing turnover and enhancing practice (e.g., Leung & Willis, 2012; Madden et al., 2014). However, because the Title IV-E Program bundles a number of recruitment, selection, and retention strategies into one intervention, it is impossible to determine which strand in the intervention is responsible for the outcomes. In fact, it is not even clear what the standard is in terms of operationalizing the Title IV-E Intervention. For example, we know that there are at least two versions of the model, one aimed at BSW education and one aimed at MSW education. Without the articulation and wide dissemination of those standard models of a BSW and an MSW IV-E Stipend Program, it is difficult to know whether any given evaluation or research study on the topic is studying one of the standard programs or an adaptation or enhanced version of the program. Thus, the Title IV-E program we describe in this paper is either a standard BSW version or an enhanced version (with multiple embedded strategies laid out on pages 8–9). The results may be unique to our setting or may be generalizable across the nation. Until the work is conducted to clarify the Title IV-E models nationally, confusion will continue to plague this area of research. Future studies need to be careful to specify exactly which recruitment, selection, and retention strategies are embedded in their Title IV-E program when reporting results, especially as more researchers move to conduct national studies (e.g., Leake, de Guzman, Reinks, Archer, & Potter, 2015).

Many argue that studies like this one "prove" that a component like social work education is the key ingredient (e.g., Dickinson & Perry, 2002) to the success of the program; however, some studies find the social work degree is not sufficient for positive outcomes in child welfare (e.g., Perry, 2016). The fact that in many studies Title IV-E graduates outperform or outstay those from a regular social work program intimates that the child welfare specialization may be the important difference, but it may be any of the other strands that intersect with social work education such as choosing committed students, that makes the difference. So, moving forward, we offer several recommendations: (1) Scholars in this area need to be clearer about what we know – that the Title IV-E program interventions are complex bundles of multiple recruitment, selection, and retention strategies and show some evidence that they are efficacious in improving practice and lowering turn-over. But more clarity about what constitutes each intervention is needed. (2) If we want to understand the essential ingredients of a Title IV-E program, we need to disentangle the strands that make up Title IV-E programs and study those using rigorous evaluation techniques (e.g., RCTs or Quasi-Experiments). For example, one empirical question involves the importance of social work education in the model. Does a Title IV-E program need to embed the child welfare specialization in a social work program or could a Family Studies major take some foundation courses on social work policy and practice then the specialized child welfare courses along with a year-long practicum and do just as well? Similarly, once the basic model is defined, the addition of other enhancements could be tested to see if outcomes improve. If caseload management or the problem of unsupportive supervisors and coworkers changed, would either of those lead to a bump in retention?

Limitations

While this study had many strengths, there were some limitations. While we were able to extract the date of exits from the organization, we were unable to discern whether the exit was voluntary or involuntary. Were some of these employees fired or let go before the probationary period was completed due to unethical conduct or poor performance? Or, did the majority leave because of other opportunities or because they simply did not like the job or the agency enough to stay? How many of those voluntary exits were due to life changes out of their control like moving to another state or experiences with health pro-blems? These distinctions are actually missing from the entire child welfare turnover literature. Thus, future research needs to attend to the different types of reason for exit so that the research focuses on voluntary and dysfunctional exits only. In addition using largely self-report data is a weakness.

Conclusion

In conclusion, these findings are in line with the broader literature on child welfare that finds that it is essential to get the right person in the job in order to stem the tide of turnover. The data from this study and past studies are intimating that the right person may be someone with a combination of a BSW degree, and child welfare specialization, who is smart, hardworking, and committed to the mission of the organization. In addition, it is important to educate and train workers so that they will be competent. What the Title IV-E program may not emphasize enough is how to manage the stressors of the job, toxic work environments, or how to advocate for themselves. This study does give one more piece of evidence to the efficacy of a BSW Title IV-E program in preparing a set of workers who are likely to remain with the agency 4 years or more. It is time for researchers to step up their game and operationalize the Title IV-E Intervention and begin to tease out the various strands that contribute to its success.

Notes

1. This final phase of the new design is being constructed and analyses will be conducted when the size of the Title IV-E group reaches 300 so that SEM and other sophisticated analyses can be conducted.
2. See references for each scale for previous reliability and validity study results.

Funding

This work was supported by Federal and State funds awarded to Eastern Kentucky University by the Kentucky Cabinet for Health and Family Services [PON2 736 1400001493 1].

ORCID

Anita Barbee ⊙ http://orcid.org/0000-0002-3951-1276

References

Adoption Assistance and Child Welfare Act of 1980, Pub. L. No. 96-272. (1980).

Altman, J. C., & Cohen, C. S. (2016). I could not have made it without them: Examining trainee cohort perspectives on MSW education for public child welfare. *Journal of Public Child Welfare, 10*(5), 524–541. doi:10.1080/15548732.2016.1181022

American Psychiatric Association. (2000). *Diagnostic and statistical manual of mental disorders* (4th ed., text rev.). Washington, DC: Author.

Bagdasaryan, S. (2012). Social work education and Title IV-E program participation as predictors of entry-level knowledge among public child welfare workers. *Children and Youth Services Review, 34*(9), 1590–1597. doi:10.1016/j.childyouth.2012.04.013

Barbee, A. P., Antle, B., Sullivan, D., Huebner, R., Fox, S., & Hall, J. C. (2009b). Recruiting and retaining child welfare workers: Is preparing social work students enough for sustained commitment to the field? *Child Welfare, 88*, 69–86.

Barbee, A. P., Antle, B. F., Sullivan, D., Dryden, A. A., & Henry, K. (2012). Twenty-five years of the Children's Bureau investment in social work education. *Journal of Public Child Welfare, 6*, 376–389. doi:10.1080/15548732.2012.705237

Barbee, A. P., Sullivan, D. J., Antle, B. F., Moran, E. B., Hall, J. C., & Fox, S. (2009a). The Public Child Welfare Certification Program: Worker retention and impact on practice. *Journal of Social Work Education, 45*, 427–444.

Benton, A. (2016). Understanding the diverging paths of stayers and leavers: An examination of factors predicting worker retention. *Children and Youth Services Review, 65*, 70–77. doi:10.1016/j.childyouth.2016.04.006

Bonanno, G. A. (2004). Loss, trauma, and human resilience: Have we underestimated the human capacity to thrive after extremely aversive events? *American Psychologist, 59*(1), 2028. doi:10.1037/0003-066X.59.1.20

Boyas, J., Wind, L., & Kang, S. (2012). Exploring the relationship between employment-based social capital, job stress, burnout, and intent to leave among child protection workers: An age-based path analysis model. *Children and Youth Services Review, 34*, 50–62. doi:10.1016/j.childyouth.2011.08.033

Boyas, J., Wind, L., & Ruiz, E. (2013). Organizational tenure among child welfare workers, burnout, stress and intent to leave: Does employment-based social capital make a difference? *Children and Youth Services Review, 35*(10), 1657–1669. doi:10.1016/j.childyouth.2013.07.008

Breaugh, J. A. (2017). The contribution of job analysis to recruitment. In H. W. Goldstein, E. D. Pulakos, J. Passmore, & C. Semedo (Eds.), *The Wiley Blackwell handbook of the psychology of recruitment, selection and employee retention* (pp. 12–28). Malden, MA: John Wiley & Sons, Ltd.

Bride, B. E., Robinson, M., Yegidis, B., & Figley, C. R. (2004). Development and validation of the secondary traumatic stress scale. *Research on Social Work Practice, 14*(1), 27–35. doi:10.1177/1049731503254106

Cahalane, H., & Sites, E. (2008). The climate of child welfare employee retention. *Child Welfare, 87*, 91–114.

Chen, S.-Y., & Scannapieco, M. (2010). The influence of job satisfaction on child welfare worker's desire to stay: An examination of the interaction effect of self-efficacy and supportive supervision. *Children and Youth Services Review, 32*(4), 482–486. doi:10.1016/j.childyouth.2009.10.014

Chenot, D., Benton, A. D., & Kim, H. (2009). The influence of supervisor support, peer support, and organizational culture among early career social workers in child welfare services. *Child Welfare, 88*(5), 129–147.

Dickinson, N. S., & Perry, R. E. (2002). Factors influencing the retention of specially educated public child welfare workers. *Journal of Health and Social Policy, 15*, 89–103. doi:10.1300/J045v15n03_07

Dillman, D. A., Smyth, J. D., & Christian, L. M. (2014). *Internet, phone, mail and mixed-mode surveys: The tailored design method.* Hoboken, NJ: John Wiley & Sons.

Ellett, A. J. (2009). Intentions to remain employed in child welfare: The role of human caring, self-efficacy beliefs, and professional organizational culture. *Children and Youth Services Review, 31*(1), 78–88. doi:10.1016/j.childyouth.2008.07.002

Ellett, A. J., Ellett, C. D., Ellis, J., & Lerner, B. (2009). A research-based child welfare employee selection protocol: Strengthening retention of the workforce. *Child Welfare, 88*(5), 49.

Ellett, A. J., & Leighninger, L. (2007). What happened? An historical analysis of the deprofessionalization of child welfare with implications for policy and practice. *Journal of Public Child Welfare, 1*, 3–34. doi:10.1300/J479v01n01_02

Faller, K. C., Masternak, M., Grinnell-Davis, C., Grabarek, M., Sieffert, J., & Bernatovicz, F. (2009). Realistic job previews in child welfare: State of innovation and practice. *Child Welfare, 88*(5), 23.

Fox, S., Miller, V., & Barbee, A. P. (2003). Finding and keeping child welfare workers: Effective use of Title IV-E training funds. *Journal of Human Behavior in the Social Environment, 7*, 67–82. doi:10.1300/J137v07n01_06

Franke, T., Bagdasaryan, S., & Furman, W. (2009). A multivariate analysis of training, education, and readiness for public child welfare practice. *Children and Youth Services Review, 31*(12), 1330–1336. doi:10.1016/j.childyouth.2009.06.004

Gansle, K. A., & Ellett, A. J. (2002). Child welfare knowledge transmission, practitioner retention, and university-community impact: A study of Title IV-E child welfare training. *Journal of Health and Social Policy, 15*(3/4), 69–88. doi:10.1300/J045v15n03_06

Goldstein, H. W., Pulakos, E. D., Passmore, J., & Semedo, C. (2017). *Handbook of employee recruitment, selection and retention.* New York, NY: Wiley Blackwell.

Jones, L. (2002). A follow-up of a Title IV-E program's graduates' retention rates in a public child welfare agency. *Journal of Health and Social Policy, 15*(3/4), 39–51. doi:10.1300/J045v15n03_04

Kim, A., & Mor Barak, M. (2015). The mediating roles of leader-member exchange and perceived organizational support: A longitudinal analysis. *Children and Youth Services Review, 52,* 135–143. doi:10.1016/j.childyouth.2014.11.009

Leake, R., de Guzman, A., Reinks, S., Archer, G., & Potter, C. (2015). NCWWI traineeships: A national cross-site evaluation of child welfare stipend programs for ethnically diverse students. *Journal of Social Work Education, 51*(2), S299–S316. doi:10.1080/10437797.2015.1072419

Leung, P., & Willis, N. (2012). The impact of Title IV-E training on case outcomes for children serviced by CPS. *Journal of Family Strengths, 12*(1), 1–16. Article 9.

Lijegren, M., Nordlund, A., & Ekberg, K. (2008). Psychometric evaluation and further validation of the Hagedoorn et al. modified EVLN measure. *Scandinavian Journal of Psychology, 49*(2), 169–177. doi:10.1111/j.1467-9450.2007.00620.x

Madden, E. E., Scannapieco, M., & Painter, K. (2014). An examination of retention and length or employment among public child welfare workers. *Children and Youth Services Review, 41,* 37–44. doi:10.1016/j.childyouth.2014.02.015

Moos, R. H. (1973). Conceptualizations of human environments. *American Psychologist, 28* (8), 652–665. doi:10.1037/h0035722

Morazes, J., Benton, A., Clark, S., & Jacquet, S. (2010). Views of specially-trained child welfare social workers: A qualitative study of their motivations, perceptions, and retention. *Qualitative Social Work, 9,* 227–247. doi:10.1177/1473325009350671

O'Donnell, J., & Kirkner, S. L. (2009). Title IV-E programs: Preparing MSW students for public child welfare practice. *Journal of Teaching in Social Work, 29,* 241–257. doi:10.1080/08841230903022050

Perry, R. E. (2016). Let's stop playing monopoly with the child welfare workforce. *Research on Social Work Practice, 26*(5), 498–509. doi:10.1177/1049731515619234

Potter, C. C., Leake, R., Longworth-Reed, L., Altschul, I., & Rienks, S. (2016). Measuring organizational health in child welfare agencies. *Children and Youth Services Review, 61,* 31–39. doi:10.1016/j.childyouth.2015.11.002

Robin, S. C., & Hollister, C. D. (2002). Career paths and contributions of four cohorts of IV-E funded MSW child welfare graduates. *Journal of Health and Social Policy, 15*(3), 53–67. doi:10.1300/J045v15n03_05

Rosenthal, J. A., & Waters, E. (2006). Predictors of child welfare worker retention and performance: Focus on title IV-E-funded social work education. *Journal of Social Service Research, 32*(3), 67–85. doi:10.1300/J079v32n03_04

Scannapieco, M., & Connell, C. K. (2003). Do collaborations with schools of social work make a difference for the field of child welfare? Practice, retention and curriculum. *Journal of Human Behavior and the Social Environment, 7,* 35–51. doi:10.1300/J137v07n01_04

Spector, P. E. (1985). Measurement of human service staff satisfaction: Development of the job satisfaction survey. *American Journal of Community Psychology, 13*(6), 693–713. doi:10.1007/BF00929796

Spector, P. E. (1994). *Job satisfaction survey.* Tampa, Florida: University of South Florida.

Strolin-Goltzman, J., Kollar, S., & Trinkle, J. (2010). Listening to the voices of children in foster care: Youths speak out about child welfare workforce turnover and selection. *Social Work, 55*(1), 47–53. doi:10.1093/sw/55.1.47

Texas Christian University. (2011). *Organizational readiness for change 4 domain assessments Texas Christian University.* Fort Worth, Texas: Institute for Behavioral Research.

Willis, N., Leung, P., & Chavkin, N. (2016). Finding "health" and "meaning" in Texas-sized turnover: Application of seminal management principles for administration and research in U. S. public child welfare agencies. *Advances in Social Work, 17*(2), 1–18.

Yankeelov, P. A., Barbee, A. P., Sullivan, D. J., & Antle, B. (2009). Retention of child welfare workers. *Children and Youth Services Review, 31,* 547–554. doi:10.1016/j.childyouth.2008.10.014

Zlotnik, J., & Pryce, J. A. (2013). Status of the use of Title IV-E funding in BSW and MSW programs. *Journal of Public Child Welfare, 7*(4), 430–446. doi:10.1080/15548732.2013.806278

Views on workplace culture and climate: Through the lens of retention and Title IV-E participation

Sandhya Rao Hermon, Michael Biehl, and Rose Chahla

ABSTRACT
Retention of public child welfare (PCW) workers is the focus of much scholarly research. Examinations of the topic have ranged from assessments of workers' background to job factors and attitudinal components about the workplace. Unlike most studies, the present study uses agency administrative data on retention. In it, 502 PCW workers responded to a point-in-time survey covering a wide range of topics including job satisfaction, commitment to child welfare, perceptions of culture and climate, Title IV-E status, and demographic variables. While Title IV-Es were more likely to leave the agency, several significant interactions between Title IV-E and retention status showed that Title IV-Es who left the agency had significantly lower supervisor satisfaction and influence than Title IV-Es who stayed; and lower efficacy scores than non-Title IV-Es who left. No such differences were found for non-Title IV-E stayers and leavers. Implications for these differences for county agencies and universities are discussed.

Introduction

High turnover plagues the public child welfare (PCW) system nationally (Cyphers, 2001; U.S. General Accounting Office [GAO], 2003). Turnover rates for child welfare workers have stayed depressingly constant between 20% and 40% for several decades despite many preventative initiatives (Willis, Chavkin, & Leung, 2016). High costs associated with PCW worker turnover include economic costs incurred in the recruitment and training of new workers, increased workload and decreased morale of workers, and negative client outcomes (DePanfilis & Zlotnik, 2008).

Reasons for turnover

Mor Barak, Nissly, and Levin (2001) identified three overarching groups of turnover antecedents including workers' demographic background (e.g., age), cognitive appraisals/reactions (e.g., stress), and organizational conditions (e.g., work

---

Color versions of one or more of the figures in the article can be found online at www.tandfonline.com/wpcw.

demands). Job satisfaction, organizational commitment (Landsman, 2001), supervisor support (e.g., Dickinson & Perry, 2002), and positive organizational support and climate (Claiborne, Auerbach, Zeitlin, & Lawrence, 2015) are among the top reasons PCW workers credit for intending to stay. Worker attitudes and traits such as higher self-efficacy and lower emotional exhaustion affect retention positively (i.e., resulting in longer stays; DePanfilis & Zlotnik, 2008). In a study of MSW Title IV-E graduates, organizational commitment was the most consistent predictor of Title IV-E workers' staying past their contract commitment (O'Donnell & Kirkner, 2009). In terms of demographics, age has emerged as one of the more consistent predictors of PCW worker job stress, burnout, and retention, with younger workers reporting higher levels of job stress and emotional exhaustion than their older counterparts (Boyas, Wind, & Kang, 2012).

Several of the aforementioned variables connected to intent to stay have been shown to impact PCW workers' intent to leave, including poor salary and benefits (e.g., Benton, 2016; Zlotnik, DePanfilis, Daining, & Lane, 2005) and lack of supervisor support (Augsberger, Schudrich, McGowan, & Auerbach, 2012; DePanfilis & Zlotnik, 2008). Other factors such as large caseloads (O'Donnell & Kirkner, 2009; Zlotnik et al., 2005), perceived lack of respect, and poor organizational communication (Augsberger et al., 2012) also hasten departure from the agency.

Reading through the litany of reasons for staying or leaving can be overwhelming, but some factors such as agency culture and climate, workload, and quality of supervision are consistently implicated in turnover. Building this knowledge allows agencies and educators invested in stabilizing, professionalizing, and strengthening PCW services to isolate factors that predict turnover with a goal of tailoring solutions to help alleviate this problem.

Strategies to address turnover

Much attention has been paid to how PCW workers might be better recruited and trained for long careers in child welfare (Gansle & Ellett, 2003; Jones, 2003; O'Donnell & Kirkner, 2009; Smith, Prichard, & Boltz, 2016). While some worker-centric strategies (Earnest, Allen, & Landis, 2011), have been linked to retention, it is increasingly clear that implementing organizational strategies and interventions (e.g., increasing transparency) conducive to retention plays a critical role as well (Kruzich, Mienko, & Courtney, 2014; Strolin-Goltzman, Kollar, & Trinkle, 2010). Of course, such strategies are challenged by multiple demands on agencies' time, tight budgets, and the lack of validated interventions (Collins-Camargo, Ellett, & Lester, 2012)

Title IV-E stipend program and its role in professionalizing the workforce

One recruitment strategy for improving the quality of the PCW workforce has been through the Title IV-E stipend program. The Title IV-E stipend program incentivizes the attainment of social work degrees and provides students with federal monetary support, specialized field internships and curricula in exchange for completing a work obligation at a qualifying PCW agency (National Association of Social Workers, 2004). Therefore, it is argued that one indicator of the program's success is the longer-term retention of these specially trained PCW workers, which, ideally, should result in higher-quality care and continuity of care for children and families. Several studies suggest that this is indeed the case, and that graduates of Title IV-E programs tend to be more competent than non-Title IV-E recipients (Dickinson & Perry, 2002; Gansle & Ellett, 2003; Jones & Okamura, 2000), are retained longer (Jones, 2003; Jones & Okamura, 2000; Rosenthal & Waters, 2006), and have more positive client outcomes as evidenced by reductions in recurrence of maltreatment and greater stability of foster care (Leung & Willis, 2012). Other studies that have conducted research with Title IV-E populations indicate that former stipend recipients may not necessarily be more satisfied with their jobs than nonrecipient workers, but are more satisfied with the respect they receive from others (Jones & Okamura, 2000). However, more scholarly work is needed to understand the differences in attitudes, perceptions, work performance, and retention of former Title IV-E stipend recipients.

Challenges in the retention research

Although retention is the focus of much of the child welfare workforce literature, identifying general trends in PCW retention research can be challenging because of the definition of retention across the literature (DePanfilis & Zlotnik, 2008; Mor Barak et al., 2001). Few studies capture actual departure from the agency. One typical way the construct is operationalized is by capturing workers' intention to stay in the PCW agency and/or in child welfare as opposed to a documented departure from the job and agency. Mor Barak and colleagues (2001) contend that it is reasonable to use intent to leave as a meaningful outcome variable as it avoids the hindsight bias that comes with retroactive assessments and because the construct has proved to be the strongest predictor of actual turnover in their meta-analytic review of 25 articles. Other researchers disagree noting that while there are numerous intent to leave scales in the literature, their validity as a proxy for actual turnover may vary (Auerbach, Schudrich, Lawrence, Claiborne, & McGowan, 2013).

The present study seeks to make valuable additions to the existing literature on retention and Title IV-E. One unique contribution of the present study is the use of administrative retention data collected independently by county agencies' human resource systems. Another is to look at different but related aspects of organizational culture and climate, and understand how the differences in these perceptions vary among those who are retained at the agency (stayers) and those who leave (leavers). These differences will be studied in a sample of PCW workers including both former Title IV-E participants (IV-Es) and non-Title IV-E workers (non IV-Es).

Research questions

(1) How are Title IV-E workers different from non-IV-E workers in terms of their perceptions of job satisfaction, commitment to child welfare, commitment to agency, and agency culture and climate?

(2) How are Title IV-E workers different from non-IV-E workers in terms of their retention within their PCW agencies?

(3) How do Title IV-E stipend status and retention status interact in terms of their perceptions of job satisfaction, commitment to child welfare, commitment to agency, and agency culture and climate?

Method

Description of the county workforce study

The California Social Work Education Center (CalSWEC) Title IV-E stipend program seeks to professionalize the social work workforce (a) by increasing the numbers of current county/state child welfare workers with social work degrees, (b) through the incorporation of Title IV-E-specific competencies in university curricula, and (c) by increasing the ethnic and linguistic diversity of child welfare workers to better reflect the children and families who use this system.

Since 1993, CalSWEC has offered stipends to MSW students at its participating schools (currently numbered at 22). Receipt of the stipend contractually obliges the recipient to work in a PCW (county, state, or Tribal) agency upon graduation for a period of time at least equal to the period for which she or he received support. An important part of CalSWEC's mission is the longer-term retention of child welfare workers in public agencies, ideally beyond the period of their mandated employment obligation.

The current County Workforce study gathered information from 10 child welfare staff at different county agencies in CalSWEC between 2014 and 2016. CalSWEC researchers proposed the study at a state-held child welfare committee meeting and recruited a convenience sample of 10 counties who volunteered to participate. The survey included a number of attitudinal, organizational, and demographic factors (e.g., commitment to the agency and child welfare, perceptions of organizational culture and climate, respondent age, respondent gender, and Title IV-E status). CalSWEC researchers coordinated data gathering at the counties with help from county management. In addition, retention data was collected from county agencies in December 2016. As some counties had completed the survey earlier in the study, their retention time frames were longer than others; the authors describe how they control for this in the analysis section.

Participants

The sample included PCW workers from 10 different counties in CalSWEC. Two large counties accounted for 68.3% of the cases ($n = 343$); the four medium-sized counties made up 24.9% of the respondent sample ($n = 125$), while the four small counties accounted for only 6.8% of the same ($n = 34$). The counties included a mix of large, medium, and small counties in both urban and rural areas. Survey administration was conducted at county agency offices, and participants completed the surveys online via Qualtrics survey link.

Measures

Job satisfaction

PCW staff were presented with survey items similar to ones developed by Buckley, Fedor, Veres, Wiese, and Carraher (1998), except they were modified for time frame and some additional items were added. The final set of items included "My expectations for this job were met," "I have had opportunities to get ahead in this job," "This job has been outstanding," "This job has NOT helped me improve myself (reverse coded)," "I have NOT been satisfied with this job (reverse coded)," "I find enjoyment in my job," "Most days I am enthusiastic about my job," and "I am usually satisfied with my client outcomes." For each item, respondents were asked their level of agreement on a Likert scale (1 = strongly disagree to 5 = strongly agree). The scale included eight items with very good reliability (Cronbach's alpha = 0.89).

Commitment to child welfare

This scale included four items, and has been used in past CalSWEC research (Jacquet & Rao Hermon, 2017) with items including "By continuing to serve as a child welfare social worker, I feel I can make a difference in people's lives," "I became a social worker because I knew it was meant to be," "I believe that my work as a child welfare social worker is important to society," and "Social work is my calling." The scale included four items with good reliability (Cronbach's alpha = .75).

Commitment to agency

This scale included eight items based on past research at CalSWEC with items including "I am proud to tell others I am part of this county agency," "This county agency is the best of all possible places to work," "There is a good chance I will search for another job (outside this agency) within the next year" (reverse coded), "I plan to leave this agency as soon as possible" (reverse coded), "Under NO circumstances will I voluntarily leave this agency," "I speak highly of this agency to my friends," "Turnover at this agency is too high" (reverse coded), and "I plan to stay in this county agency as long as possible." These eight items had strong reliability (Cronbach's alpha = .88).

Satisfaction with supervisor

This scale included six items based on past research at CalSWEC with items including "My supervisor gives me good advice on case-related problems," "My supervisor is very knowledgeable about child welfare," "I can/did rely on my supervisor when the going gets/got tough," "My supervisor focuses on my strengths and positive characteristics," "My immediate supervisor listens to my work-related problems," and "My supervisor helps me think about how to apply things I learn in training to my work with families." These six items had excellent reliability (Cronbach's alpha = .92).

Culture and climate

Culture and climate measures were captured through the TCU Survey of Organizational Functioning (SOF; Lehman, Greener, & Simpson, 2002). These measures have been used in previous research in other fields (e.g., substance abuse counselors) and have shown to have very good psychometric properties (Lehman et al., 2002). All items were adapted for PCW workers and their agency. The following culture and climate measures (and subscales) were included in this study: resources: training (four items); staff attributes: growth (five items), efficacy (four items), influence (six items); organization climate: mission (five items), cohesion (five items), communication (five items), stress (four items), change (five items); job attitudes: burnout (three items), leadership (nine items); workplace practices: focus on outcomes (five items), and reflective dialogue (two items). One other scale assessing unit staffing and cohesion (seven items) was created from items in both the staffing and cohesion subscales that were adapted specifically to assess staffing and cohesion within workers' specific unit. Reliability for these scales were good ranging from .68-.95 with an average Cronbach's alpha of .80 across the 14 TOC-SOF scales. Respondents rate items on a scale from 1 (strongly disagree) to 5 (strongly agree). Each scale is averaged and multiplied by 10, resulting in mean scores ranging from 10 to 50 (Lehman et al., 2002).

Title IV-E status

Title IV-E status was assessed on the survey where participants indicated yes or no to the question, "Were you a IV-E stipend recipient?"

Retention status

Staff turnover was assessed from administrative data provided by each of the 10 participating counties. This information was collected approximately 1–2 years after the survey was completed. The information provided indicated either "yes" or "no" if they had left their position since the time of the survey completion. This administrative data was then linked with the survey data.

Years as social worker

We also assessed the time each participant had been social worker with the following question, "How long have you been a social worker?" in both months and years. Scores were converted to the number of years as a social worker with months computed into partial years (e.g., 6 months = 0.5 years). This variable served as a covariate in the analyses.

Time between survey completion and retention

As time between survey completion and turnover varied from agency to agency (i.e., staff at some agencies completed the survey months before staff at others), the time (in days) between the survey completion and the collection of the administrative data on retention from the county agencies was computed. This variable served as a covariate in the analyses.

Data analysis

Given the nested nature of these data, a multilevel analytic approach, which accounts for this nesting across counties, would have been ideal. However, this approach was not appropriate for two reasons: (a) varying sample size within the counties and (b) the small number of counties (or clusters). There were large variations in sample size by county with the four smaller counties having few as 6 or 11 cases each. A multilevel analysis with such a small sample within counties would likely have yielded unreliable parameter estimates (McNeish & Stapleton, 2016). More importantly, because only 10 counties were included in this study a multilevel approach would also yield unreliable parameter estimates, which typically requires a minimum of 20 clusters for reliable estimates (McNeish, 2014; McNeish & Stapleton, 2016). All analyses were conducted in SPSS version 24. We chose analysis of variance (ANOVA) to test our research questions since we wanted to test the main effects of both Title IV-E status, retention status, and their interaction. In addition, we also conducted analysis of covariance (ANCOVA) to see if controlling for other relevant factors (years as social worker and time between survey completion and retention) would affect any findings. Chi-square analyses compared differences in demographics, Title IV-E status, and retention status, and t tests were conducted to compare differences in tenure as social workers by Title IV-E and retention status separately.

Results

Demographics

The sample include 502 PCW workers from 10 different counties in CalSWEC including a mix of large, medium, and small counties in both urban and rural areas. Approximately 84% were female and 15% were male. The participants ranged from 22 to 65 in age. Approximately 56% were between the ages of 31 and 49, followed by 26.5% who were between 50 and 65, 15% were between 22 and 30, and 2% over 65. The ethnicity of the participants included White/Caucasian (48%), followed by Hispanic (26%), African-American (10%), Asian/Pacific Islander (9%), and multiracial/other (8%).

t-Test analyses

We conducted two t tests to examine differences between IVEs and non-IVEs, and leavers and stayers in terms of years as social worker. Results showed that Title IV-E workers had significantly ($t(487) = 3.83$, $p< .001$) fewer years of social work experience ($M= 9.56$) compared to non-Title IV-E workers ($M = 13.40$). Results also showed that leavers had significantly ($t(467) = 2.57$, $p < .05$) fewer years of social work experience ($M = 9.70$) compared to stayers ($M = 12.61$).

Chi-square analyses

We also conducted chi-square analyses for both Title IV-E and retention status by demographic characteristics and found no significant differences for gender and ethnicity. However, differences in age groups were significant for both Title IV-E status ($X^2(6) = 38.50$, $p < .001$) with participants ages 25–30 more likely to be Title IV-Es. Looking at retention status leavers were more likely to be ages 22–30 or over 65 ($X^2(6) = 29.10$, $p < .001$). We then examined differences in Title IV-E status and retention status and results showed that Title IV-Es were more likely to be leavers ($X^2(6) = 5.9$, $p < .05$; see Table 1).

Table 1. Demographic information.

Demographic	Category	N	%	IV-E status χ^2	df	p	Retention status χ^2	df	p
Gender	Male	76	15.10	2.79	1	ns	0.67	1	ns
	Female	413	82.30						
	Transgender	1	0.20						
	Missing	12	2.40						
	Total	502	100.00						
Age range	22–25	17	3.40	38.54	6	***	29.05	6	***
	26–30	58	11.60						
	31–40	138	27.50						
	41–49	137	27.30						
	50–58	92	18.30						
	59–65	37	7.40						
	65+	9	1.80						
	Missing	14	2.80						
	Total	502	100.00						
Ethnicity	African-American/Black	46	9.20	10.79	6	ns	2.74	6	ns
	Asian/Pacific Islander	41	8.20						
	Hispanic	127	25.30						
	Multiracial	18	03.60						
	Native American	3	0.60						
	White/Caucasian	232	46.20						
	Other	20	4.00						
	Missing	15	3.00						
	Total	502	100.00						

		Retention status				
		Stayers	**Leavers**	χ^2	df	p
Title IV-E status	Yes	127 (77.40%)	33 (20.60%)	5.97	1	*
	No	300 (87.60%)	42 (12.30%)			

Note: * $p < .05$, ** $p < .01$, *** $p < .001$; ns = not significant.

Analytic approach

In order to test our research questions, we conducted a two-way ANOVA with both Title IV-E status (A) and retention status (B) and their interaction (A × B) on our dependent variables (i.e., job satisfaction, commitment to child welfare, commitment to agency, supervisor satisfaction, and culture and climate variables). Results of the ANOVA analyses showed several significant differences (see Table 2).

Differences between Title IV-Es and non-IV-Es

The results for the main effects of Title IV-E status showed significant differences in five of the dependent measures (see Table 2), including commitment to child welfare and four of the culture and climate measures (efficacy, influence, stress, and burnout). Specifically, results showed that Title IV-Es had higher scores on commitment to child welfare but lower

Table 2. Two-way ANOVA on Title IV-E status and retention status on DVs.

| | Title IV-E status (A) | | | | | | Retention status (B) | | | | | | A × B | |
| | Title IV-E (n= 159) | | Non-Title IV-E (n= 339) | | | | Stayers (n= 421) | | Leavers (n= 75) | | | | | |
Scale	Mean	SD	Mean	SD	F	p	Mean	SD	Mean	SD	F	p	F	p
Job satisfaction	29.36	5.39	29.64	5.41	1.12		29.95	5.27	27.30	5.63	16.79	***	2.20	
Commitment to child welfare	21.06	2.71	20.12	3.24	4.99	*	20.45	3.10	20.27	3.21	0.71		0.09	
Commitment to agency	25.87	6.26	27.20	6.32	0.93		27.42	6.08	23.08	6.49	27.20	***	0.19	
Supervisor satisfaction	22.94	5.13	23.33	5.30	3.40		23.39	5.15	22.14	5.69	4.69	*	4.79	*
Training resources	33.96	8.29	33.72	8.45	0.19		33.95	8.25	32.91	9.13	1.43		1.28	
Growth of staff	32.24	7.73	32.92	7.23	1.63		32.88	7.24	31.67	8.17	1.79		1.05	
Efficacy of staff	40.89	5.29	41.55	5.30	4.54	*	41.34	5.20	41.32	5.84	0.03		3.13	
Influence of staff	36.41	7.65	37.52	7.49	5.80	*	37.49	7.25	35.38	8.93	5.70	*	4.80	*
Mission of agency	33.20	6.49	33.70	6.73	0.56		33.78	6.51	32.16	7.30	3.58		0.25	
Cohesion of agency	32.66	8.42	33.53	7.97	1.06		33.47	7.78	32.03	9.78	1.76		0.23	
Communication of agency	27.71	8.25	28.62	7.75	1.61		28.75	7.61	25.89	9.18	8.16	**	0.86	
Stress of agency	39.08	7.42	36.48	8.64	8.55	**	37.38	8.04	36.93	10.01	0.49		0.38	
Change of agency	30.79	6.28	30.83	6.10	0.00		31.22	6.10	28.55	6.01	12.10	*	0.11	
Burnout	29.44	8.41	26.99	8.46	8.44	**	27.52	8.35	29.18	9.33	1.99		1.32	
Leadership	33.21	7.91	32.98	9.10	0.23		33.43	8.66	30.88	8.87	6.29	*	1.63	
Focus on outcomes	31.82	6.52	32.57	6.21	1.72		32.56	6.18	31.01	6.98	3.45		0.73	
Reflective dialogue	34.94	8.94	35.59	7.99	2.61		35.46	8.18	34.93	9.02	0.47		2.51	
Unit staffing and cohesion	31.93	7.04	32.74	6.59	0.69		32.49	6.63	32.44	7.37	0.01		0.03	

Note: * p< .05, ** p< .01, *** p< .001.

scores on efficacy and influence scales than non-IV-Es. They also reported being significantly more stressed and burned out than their non-IV-E counterparts.

Differences between leavers and stayers

Results for the main effects of retention status indicated significant differences in eight of the outcome measures (see Table 2) in the expected direction. Specifically, stayers had higher scores on job satisfaction, commitment to agency, supervisor satisfaction, and some culture and climate variables (influence, communication, ease of change in agency, and agency leadership) than leavers.

Interactions between retention and Title IV-E status

The interaction of Title IV-E and retention was tested in the two-way ANOVA (see Table 2). Two significant interactions for both supervisor satisfaction and influence scales emerged, which led to simple effects analyses for these two scales. Results of these analyses showed that Title IV-E stayers had higher supervisor satisfaction scores than Title IV-E leavers, while among non-Title IV-E stayers and leavers no significant differences in supervisor satisfaction were observed. For influence in the agency, simple effects analyses revealed that Title IV-E stayers had higher influence scores than

Title IV-E leavers, while non-Title IV-E recipients had no significant differences between stayers and leavers on influence scores.

ANCOVA analyses

We then conducted a two-way ANCOVA with Title IV-E status (A) and retention status (B) and their interaction (A × B) on our dependent variables, but included two covariates (years as a social worker and time between survey completion and retention), to test if the previous ANOVA effects were still significant after controlling for those variables. Results of the ANCOVA analyses showed nearly all the effects were still significant even after controlling for these variables (see Table 3).

The results for the main effects analyses of Title IV-E status still showed significant differences for commitment to child welfare, stress, and burnout scales, but no significant differences were found for the efficacy and influence scales. However, the main effect for supervisor satisfaction was significant. Again, results indicated that Title IV-Es had higher scores on commitment to child welfare, stress, and burnout scales; and they had lower scores on supervision satisfaction.

The main effects of retention status revealed an identical pattern of results. Specifically, stayers had higher scores on job satisfaction, commitment to

Table 3. Two-way ANCOVA on Title IV-E status and retention status on DVs controlling for (1) years in social work and (2) retention time frame.

| Scale | Title IV-E status (A) | | | | | | Retention status (B) | | | | | | A × B | |
| | Title IV-E (n= 151) | | Non-Title IV-E (n= 311) | | | | Stayers (n= 389) | | Leavers (n= 73) | | | | | |
	Mean	SD	Mean	SD	F	p	Mean	SD	Mean	SD	F	p	F	p
Job satisfaction	28.44	5.39	29.24	5.41	1.27		30.17	5.27	27.51	5.63	14.29	***	2.19	
Commitment to child welfare	21.14	2.71	20.06	3.24	7.10	**	20.69	3.10	20.52	3.21	0.17		0.03	
Commitment to agency	24.78	6.26	25.82	6.32	1.64		27.39	6.08	23.21	6.49	26.78	***	0.12	
Supervisor satisfaction	21.84	5.13	23.56	5.30	6.45	*	23.43	5.15	21.97	5.69	4.71	*	6.86	**
Training resources	33.18	8.29	33.91	8.45	0.43		34.20	8.25	32.90	9.13	1.40		2.01	
Growth of staff	31.70	7.73	33.05	7.23	1.89		32.97	7.24	31.77	8.17	1.52		1.46	
Efficacy of staff	40.89	5.29	42.00	5.30	2.57		41.51	5.20	41.39	5.84	0.03		3.99	*
Influence of staff	36.40	7.65	37.30	7.49	0.96		37.77	7.25	35.93	8.93	4.06	*	4.43	*
Mission of agency	32.55	6.49	33.54	6.73	1.25		33.64	6.51	32.45	7.30	1.80		0.44	
Cohesion of agency	31.99	8.42	33.56	7.97	2.19		33.51	7.78	32.05	9.78	1.90		0.38	
Communication of agency	26.60	8.25	28.16	7.75	2.26		28.69	7.61	26.07	9.18	6.40	*	0.92	
Stress of agency	39.13	7.42	35.91	8.64	8.46	**	37.89	8.04	37.15	10.01	0.46		0.62	
Change of agency	29.76	6.28	30.01	6.10	0.10		31.24	6.10	28.53	6.01	11.40	**	0.03	
Burnout	30.04	8.41	26.93	8.46	7.41	**	27.81	8.35	29.16	9.33	1.40		1.66	
Leadership	31.63	7.91	32.55	9.10	0.63		33.64	8.66	30.55	8.87	7.22	**	1.53	
Focus on outcomes	31.08	6.52	32.28	6.21	2.02		32.40	6.18	30.95	6.98	2.98		0.80	
Reflective dialogue	34.26	8.94	35.91	7.99	2.35		35.51	8.18	34.66	9.02	0.63		1.68	
Unit staffing and cohesion	32.24	7.04	32.85	6.59	0.49		32.57	6.63	32.52	7.37	0.00		0.00	

Note: * p < .05, ** p < .01, *** p< .001.

agency, supervisor satisfaction, and several culture and climate variables (influence, communication, change agility in agency, and agency leadership) than did leavers.

Results for the interaction between Title IV-E and retention status again showed significant interactions for supervisor satisfaction and influence. In addition, a third significant interaction was found for efficacy scores. Simple effects analyses showed Title IV-E leavers had significantly lower satisfaction with supervisors ($M = 20.23$) when compared with Title IV-E stayers ($M = 23.45$), non-Title IV-E stayers ($M = 23.42$), and leavers ($M = 23.70$). A similar pattern was found for influence scores, with Title IV-E leavers having significantly lower influence scores ($M = 34.53$) compared to Title IV-E stayers ($M = 38.27$), non-Title IV-E stayers ($M = 37.26$), and leavers ($M = 37.33$). Results for efficacy scores showed that Title IV-E leavers had significantly lower efficacy scores ($M = 40.15$) than non-Title IV-E leavers ($M = 42.76$). As can be seen in Figures 1a–c, Title IV-E leavers had significantly lower scores than Title IV-E stayers, both on supervision satisfaction and influence scores, and lower scores on efficacy compared to non-Title IV-E leavers. This is in contrast to non-Title IV-E recipients who were not significantly different between stayers and leavers.

Overall, findings showed that there were significant differences by both Title IV-E and retention status. In addition, several significant interactions were found. Moreover, these findings were still significant even after controlling both years in social work and time between survey completion and retention.

Discussion

This study adds considerably to previous research on retention in PCW workers, particularly as it relates to Title IV-E participation. An important contribution of the study is the use of actual turnover data, not intent to leave, which is a staple of much PCW scholarship (e.g., Ellett, 2000).

As expected, and consistent with past research (e.g., Cahalane & Sites, 2008; Jones, 2003; O'Donnell & Kirkner, 2009) differences between stayers and leavers were in a predictable direction with leavers significantly more dissatisfied on a variety of measures including job satisfaction, commitment to agency, supervisor satisfaction, influence, and culture and climate measures (i.e., change, communication, leadership). This finding is of importance for a couple of reasons. One, it is probable that less satisfied employees are less effective in their jobs. Support for this notion comes from other fields (e.g., Judge, Thoresen, Bono, & Patton, 2001), although there are no data in PCW linking this measure to work performance. While any turnover in staff is keenly felt at the agency, both in terms of increased workload for remaining workers (e.g., Graef & Hill, 2000) and disruption of services for children

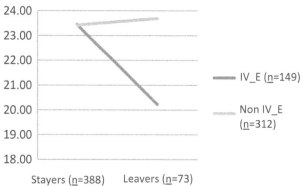

Satisfaction with Supervisor by Title IV-E and Retention

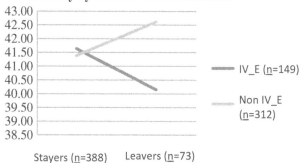

Efficacy by Title IV-E and Retention

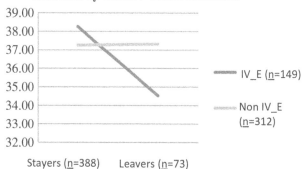

Influence by Title IV-E and Retention

Figure 1. (a–c) Satisfaction with supervisor, efficacy, and influence by Title IV-E and retention status.

and families served (e.g., Cicero-Reese & Black, 1998), if a dissatisfied employee stays on the job, the quality of services provided is likely to be lower than those of a more satisfied employee. Another reason for the significance of this finding is that these attitudinal variables serve as predictors for turnover. Agencies are constantly looking for actionable ways in which to stem turnover, and assessments of culture and climate—if employed at the right time—could give agencies a way to identify strong workers most at risk of leaving, and find creative ways of making them stay.

It was disheartening to find Title IV-Es significantly more prevalent among the leavers. Given the huge investments in their education and professionalization, it is natural to want them to be retained. However, what is not known is what opportunity Title IV-Es are leaving for. Are they leaving the agency for another PCW position? Or are they leaving PCW altogether? The answer to such questions changes the interpretation of turnover quite dramatically. The measure utilized in this study lacked the sensitivity to address such subtleties. In fact, this appears to be a shortcoming in the PCW literature at large. Turnover is captured rather crudely either by intent to leave or actual departure from the agency, while a more nuanced view of turnover (e.g., leaving one agency for a better position at another PCW agency) would be very beneficial to the social work practitioners and researchers alike.

It was, however, encouraging to find that Title IV-Es were more committed to child welfare. This is consistent with past research by Jacquet (2012) and Jacquet and her colleagues (2008). The findings suggesting Title IV-Es are less satisfied with agency life—demonstrated by significantly higher negative attitudes around efficacy and influence of staff, and higher stress—is also consistent with some past research (Jones & Okamura, 2000). The reasons for this are less well known. Possibly, the strong theoretical grounding that Title IV-Es receive through their education might result in significantly higher expectations for the job. Previous research by Jacquet and Rao Hermon (2017) shows that higher expectations for the job translate into lower satisfaction. Universities who play a key role in educating Title IV-E students would do well to manage the expectations of their students for the realities of PCW work.

The interaction effects from this study merit particular interest. Briefly, among non-IVEs there were no significant differences in terms of job satisfaction, commitment to child welfare, and culture and climate variables. However, among the Title IV-Es there were noticeable differences among stayers and leavers. While only three interaction effects were significant, taken as a whole, the pattern of findings across all dependent variables was similar. Satisfaction with supervisor was significantly higher for Title IV-E stayers than Title IV-E leavers, whereas no such pattern was seen among non-IV-Es. Identical patterns were observed with perceptions of influence. These interaction effects provide more context around the main effects that show Title IV-Es more likely to leave the agency. The implication from these findings is that Title IV-Es have specific needs and are more sensitive to the effects of poor culture and climate than non-IV-Es. Addressing the quality of supervision, making space for Title IV-Es to have influence and to be efficacious will likely stem their turnover.

Why, one might ask, should such special efforts be made for Title IV-Es, especially after all the investments made in their education? While the research on Title IV-Es is not robust, several differences have been noted between Title IV-E and non-IV-E workers. Title IV-E stipend students tend to have higher levels of commitment to child welfare (e.g., Jacquet, 2012; Jacquet et al., 2008), a desire for mission-driven work, concern for clients, and are more likely to have tenure predicted by organizational commitment (O'Donnell & Kirkner, 2009). In terms of performance, knowledge and skills between Title IV-E workers and their counterparts suggest that Title IV-Es are more competent (Gansle & Ellett, 2003; Jones & Okamura, 2000) and have better case outcomes (i.e., fewer instances of recurrence of maltreatment and improved stability in foster care) (Leung & Willis, 2012). Finally, at CalSWEC we receive anecdotal reports that Title IV-Es make better workers, and that they are more likely to rise through the ranks of the agency. However, more conclusive evidence is needed on the links between Title IV-E participation and outcomes for children and families.

One finding of interest is a demographic finding that leavers tend be younger than stayers. There is some support for this finding from other PCW researchers (e.g., Boyas et al., 2012). Stories abound in the popular press about the "job hopping" nature of millennials. The empirical evidence is sparse but there is some evidence to show that work is less central to the lives of millennials, that they report having a weaker work ethic than previous generations, and that work stability is less important to them (Twenge, 2010). While the evidence doesn't warrant special interventions to ameliorate turnover in millennials, PCW agencies would be wise to better understand the specific needs of this demographic so they might be able to effectively respond to a changing workforce.

One question unanswered by these findings, and unanswerable by our data, is what does it mean to be a former Title IV-E stipend recipient? Across the nation, different schools have different criteria for hiring, and different curricular and field experiences. While Title IV-E serves as a proxy for a higher caliber of student, in reality it is a combination of monetary support, specialized curriculum, and select background and demographic variables of the student. To be truly able to understand the impact of Title IV-E, what that experience means and how it translates into work experiences, more research is clearly needed to unpack the construct.

Limitations

While these findings are of much value, the authors would be remiss not to mention the study's limitations. First, this study has limited generalizability because of the use of convenient sampling. Only 10 out of a possible CalSWEC counties participated in this study. While the sample size is adequate, generalizations to the entire state of CalSWEC cannot be extrapolated. Additionally, given the small sample size in several counties and the total number of counties, it was not possible to control for the effects of clustering using a multilevel modeling approach (McNeish, 2014; McNeish & Stapleton, 2016). Future studies could adopt a sampling approach that is adequate for controlling for the effects of clustering across counties. Second, the survey deployed was cross-sectional in nature, making it impossible to establish any causality among the attitudinal factors on the survey, and the possibility of nonresponse bias contaminates the results. However, linking these survey data with retention data obtained at a later point considerably strengthens the study. And while the inclusion of true retention data is important, this study still takes a binary view of turnover, equating staying at an agency as a desirous outcome. As discussed previously, future research needs to better delineate "leaving an agency" from "leaving PCW." This echoes recent calls by Willis et al. (2016) for the field to change long-held narrowly defined views on turnover.

One last limitation of this study is that links from attitudes and background variables halt at retention and do not go beyond, to outcomes for children and families. This is also a limitation in the field, and more collaborative work between agencies and universities needs to establish what success looks like for a case worker.

In conclusion, findings from this study significantly advance knowledge on retention by taking a more nuanced view of the different needs of stayers and leavers, particularly as it relates to Title IV-E stipend participation.

References

Auerbach, C., Schudrich, W. Z., Lawrence, C. K., Claiborne, N., & McGowan, B. G. (2013). Predicting turnover: Validating the intent to leave child welfare scale. *Research on Social Work Practice, 24*(3), 349–355.

Augsberger, A., Schudrich, W., McGowan, B. G., & Auerbach, C. (2012). Respect in the workplace: A mixed methods study of retention and turnover in the voluntary child welfare sector. *Children and Youth Services Review, 34*(7), 1222–1229.

Benton, A. D. (2016). Understanding the diverging paths of stayers and leavers: An examination of factors predicting worker retention. *Children and Youth Services Review, 65*, 70–77.

Boyas, J., Wind, L. H., & Kang, S. Y. (2012). Exploring the relationship between employment-based social capital, job stress, burnout, and intent to leave among child protection workers: An age-based path analysis model. *Children and Youth Services Review, 34*(1), 50–62.

Buckley, M. R., Fedor, D. B., Veres, J. G., Wiese, D. S., & Carraher, S. M. (1998). Investigating newcomer expectations and job-related outcomes. *Journal of Applied Psychology, 83*(3), 452–461.

Cahalane, H., & Sites, E. W. (2008). The climate of child welfare employee retention. *Child Welfare, 87*(1), 91–114.

Cicero-Reese, B., & Black, P. (1998). Research findings suggest why child welfare workers stay on job. *Partnerships for Child Welfare Newsletter, 5*, 5.

Claiborne, N., Auerbach, C., Zeitlin, W., & Lawrence, C. K. (2015). Climate factors related to intention to leave in administrators and clinical professionals. *Children and Youth Services Review, 51*, 18–25.

Collins-Camargo, C., Ellett, C. D., & Lester, C. (2012). Measuring organizational effectiveness to develop strategies to promote retention in public child welfare. *Children and Youth Services Review, 34*(1), 289–295.

Cyphers, G. (2001). *Report from the child welfare workforce survey: State and county data and findings.* Washington, DC: APHSA.

DePanfilis, D., & Zlotnik, J. L. (2008). Retention of front-line staff in child welfare: A systematic review of research. *Children and Youth Services Review, 30*(9), 995–1008.

Dickinson, N. S., & Perry, R. E. (2002). Factors influencing the retention of specially educated public child welfare workers. *Journal of Health and Social Policy, 15*(3/4), 89–103.

Earnest, D. R., Allen, D. G., & Landis, R. S. (2011). Mechanisms linking realistic job previews with turnover: A meta-analytic path analysis. *Personnel Psychology, 64*(4), 865–897.

Ellett, A. J. (2000). *Human caring, self-efficacy beliefs, and professional organizational culture correlates of employee retention in child welfare* (Unpublished doctoral dissertation). Louisiana State University, Baton Rouge, Louisiana, USA.

Gansle, K. A., & Ellett, A. J. (2003). Child welfare knowledge transmission, practitioner retention, and university-community impact: A study of Title IV-E child welfare training. *Journal of Health & Social Policy, 15*(3–4), 69–88.

Graef, M. I., & Hill, E. L. (2000). Costing child protective services staff turnover. *Child Welfare, 79*(5), 517–533.

Jacquet, S. E. (2012). Successful student recruitment for public child welfare: Results from California's Title IV-E MSW stipend program evaluation. *Journal of Public Child Welfare, 6*(4), 405–424.

Jacquet, S. E., Clark, S. J., Morazes, J. L., & Withers, R. (2008). The role of supervision in the retention of public child welfare workers. *Journal of Public Child Welfare, 1*(3), 27–54.

Jacquet, S. E., & Rao Hermon, S. (2017). Job expectations and career goals of Title IV-E child welfare social workers with varying levels of work experience: How do they differ? *Journal of Public Child Welfare, 12*(1), 42–59. doi:10.1080/15548732.2017.1311289

Jones, L. (2003). A follow-up of a Title IV-E program's graduates' retention rates in a public child welfare agency. *Journal of Health & Social Policy, 15*(3–4), 39–51.

Jones, L., & Okamura, A. (2000). Reprofessionalizing child welfare services: An evaluation of a Title IVE training program. *Research on Social Work Practice, 10*(5), 607–621.

Judge, T. A., Thoresen, C. J., Bono, J. E., & Patton, G. K. (2001). The job satisfaction–Job performance relationship: A qualitative and quantitative review. *Psychological Bulletin, 127* (3), 376–407. doi:http://dx.doi.org/10.1037/0033-2909.127.3.376

Kruzich, J. M., Mienko, J. A., & Courtney, M. E. (2014). Individual and work group influences on turnover intention among public child welfare workers: The effects of work group psychological safety. *Children and Youth Services Review, 42*, 20–27.

Landsman, M. J. (2001). Commitment in public child welfare. *Social Service Review, 75*(3), 386–419.

Lehman, W. E., Greener, J. M., & Simpson, D. D. (2002). Assessing organizational readiness for change. *Journal of Substance Abuse Treatment, 22*(4), 197–209.

Leung, P., & Willis, N. (2012). The impact of Title IV-E training on case outcomes for children serviced by CPS. *Journal of Family Strengths, 12*(1), 9.

McNeish, D. M. (2014). Modeling sparsely clustered data: Design-based, model-based, and single-level methods. *Psychological Methods, 19*(4), 552.

McNeish, D. M., & Stapleton, L. M. (2016). The effect of small sample size on two-level model estimates: A review and illustration. *Educational Psychology Review, 28*(2), 295–314.

Mor Barak, M. E., Nissly, J. A., & Levin, A. (2001). Antecedents to retention and turnover among child welfare, social work, and other human service employees: What can we learn from past research? A review and meta-analysis. *Social Service Review, 75*(4), 625–661.

National Association of Social Workers. (2004). *Fact sheet: Title IV-E child welfare training program.* Retrieved from http://www.socialworkers.org/advocacy/updates/2003/081204a.asp

O'Donnell, J., & Kirkner, S. L. (2009). A longitudinal study of factors influencing the retention of Title IV-E master's of social work graduates in public child welfare. *Journal of Public Child Welfare, 3*(1), 64–86.

Rosenthal, J. A., & Waters, E. (2006). Predictors of child welfare worker retention and performance: Focus on Title IV-E-funded social work education. *Journal of Social Service Research, 32*(3), 67–85.

Smith, B. D., Prichard, C., & Boltz, L. D. (2016). Do child welfare job preview videos reflect evidence on retention and turnover? *Children and Youth Services Review, 71*(12), 210–216.

Strolin-Goltzman, J., Kollar, S., & Trinkle, J. (2010). Listening to the voices of children in foster care: Youths speak out about child welfare workforce turnover and selection. *Social Work, 55*(1), 47–53.

Twenge, J. M. (2010). A review of the empirical evidence on generational differences in work attitudes. *Journal of Business and Psychology, 25*, 201–210.

U.S. General Accounting Office. 2003. *Child welfare: HHS could play a greater role in helping child welfare agencies to recruit and retain staff.* Retrieved from http://www.gao.gov/assets/260/252443.pdf

Willis, N., Chavkin, N., & Leung, P. (2016). Finding "health" and "meaning" in Texas-sized turnover: Application of seminal management principles for administration and research in U.S. Public Child Welfare Agencies. *Advances in Social Work, 17*(2), 116–133.

Zlotnik, J. L., DePanfilis, D., Daining, C., & Lane, M. (2005). *Factors influencing retention of child welfare staff: A systematic review of research.* Washington, DC: Institute for the Advancement of Social Work Research. Retrieved from http://hdl.handle.net/10713/74

An effective pedagogy for child welfare education

Virginia C. Strand and Marciana Popescu

ABSTRACT
Preparing social workers for child welfare practice with the complexly traumatized children now in the system has created the need for schools of social work to integrate trauma content into the curriculum. This article presents findings of an evaluation of a child welfare course designed to prepare MSW level trauma-informed child welfare practitioners. Findings indicate that students in 29 schools of social work not only significantly increased their confidence in working with traumatized children and families but also are significantly more prepared to work toward these three child welfare goals of safety, permanency, and well-being.

Introduction

It is becoming increasingly apparent that for social workers to address the challenges currently facing the child welfare system, schools of social work need to prepare practitioners for trauma-informed child welfare practice. Trauma-informed child welfare practice is defined by SAMHSA as one that "realizes the widespread impact of trauma and understands potential pathways for recovery; recognizes the signs and symptoms of trauma in clients, families, staff and others involved with the system; and responds by fully integrating knowledge about trauma into policy, procedures, and practices and seeks to actively resist retraumatization" (SAMHSA, 2014, p. 9).

Children under three experience the highest frequency of first exposure to abuse, causing an increased number of infants and preschool children coming into care. (Wulcyzn, Barth, Yuan, Harden & Landseer, 2005). Young children exposed to trauma have both posttraumatic distress combined with significant disruptions in multiple domains of development, such as attachment and affect regulation problems. On the other end of the spectrum, adolescents aging out of foster care had higher rates of posttraumatic stress disorder (PTSD) than Vietnam veterans (Pecora, 2010).

Schools of social work have been engaged in preparing students for child welfare practice for a considerable time through federal Title IV-E funding for student stipends. The program was inaugurated in 1980 but it was not until the 1990s that schools of social work began to use Title IV-E funds more widely. A 2009 study of four universities preparing MSWs for child welfare found that students indicated they felt prepared for practice through a quality education experience (O'Donnell & Kirkner, 2009). By 2011, 147 schools used Title IV-E funds for Bachelor of Social Work (BSW) education, and 94 were using these funds for Master of Social Work (MSW) education. A recent survey of the 94 social work education programs found positive outcomes, including the development of a more professionalized workforce with degree-holding staff, increased collaboration between schools of social work and child welfare agencies, and a positive impact on the social work curriculum and program, including the ability to recruit more ethnically diverse student bodies. There is no specific evidence, however, that moving toward a more trauma-informed child welfare professional has been a focus of Title IV-E training (Zlotnik & Pryce, 2013).

The effort to prepare social workers for child welfare practice with difficult complexly traumatized children now in the system has created the need to integrate trauma content into the curriculum. This article presents findings of an evaluation of a child welfare course designed to prepare MSW-level trauma-informed child welfare practitioners. The purpose of the evaluation was to determine how effective the course was in increasing students' confidence in working with traumatized children and their families. The course was offered 57 times at 29 different schools of social work across the country between 2010 and 2015. The findings are discussed within the framework of the child welfare goals of safety, permanency, and well-being.

Literature review

The Adoption and Safe Families Act of 1997 (Public Law 105-89) clearly identified goals for child welfare as safety, permanency, and well-being in stating "that the health and safety of children served by child welfare agencies must be their paramount concern". For the next 15 years, safety and permanency guided child welfare intervention. In 2012, against a backdrop of research findings highlighting the impact of trauma on children's developing brains, attending to well-being became critical for states. A memo from the Administration for Children and Families (ACF) Children's Bureau Commissioner not only advanced well-being to the forefront, but expanded the definition to include multiply abused children's untreated traumatic stress disorders (Samuels, 2011).

Achieving trauma-informed child welfare systems and services is a major challenge facing child welfare at the beginning of the 21st century. In a study of over 16,000 children in the Illinois child welfare system, findings indicated that children exposed to both interpersonal violence and attachment-based (non-violent) traumas were more likely to exhibit symptoms of emotional, attentional, or behavioral dysregulation in addition to posttraumatic stress symptoms when compared to children with either type of trauma alone (Kisiel et al., 2014). Children in child welfare have a greater propensity of mental health problems when compared to others (Pecora, White, Jackson, & Wiggins, 2009), and removal from home in and of itself may exacerbate the effects of an original trauma (Cook et al., 2005; Ko et al., 2008).

Other researchers have found that cumulative exposure to trauma increases the risk of problematic behaviors in adolescents (attachment difficulties, skipping school, running away from home, substance abuse, suicidality, criminality, self-injury, alcohol use, and victim of sexual exploitation), with the addition of each trauma exposure increasing the likelihood of risk-taking behavior and functional impairment (Layne, Greeson, Ostrowski, Kim, Redding, Vivrette, Pynoos, 2014). In the same ACF informational memo cited above, the Children's Bureau director maintained that

"Identifying the trauma-related symptoms displayed by children and youth when they enter care is critical for the development of a treatment plan. It is also important to have a complete trauma history for each child." (Samuels, 2011, p.6).

Child welfare agencies face considerable dilemmas, such as the increased difficulty in working with children affected by complex trauma, and the workforce challenges engendered by secondary traumatic stress among staff that fuels high staff turnover rates. These issues have frustrated attempts to establish a stable workforce and resulted in the call to develop trauma-informed practitioners and trauma-informed agency cultures. Challenges identified in the literature include: developing the ability to undertake a trauma-focused assessment of a child welfare system (Hendricks, Conradi & Wilson, 2011); changing practitioner's paradigms from a specific event-focus (i.e., child abuse) to consideration of the impact of the trauma on the child and caregiving system; the difficulty of integrating a trauma framework and evidence-based practices into child welfare systems; and the need for consistent organizational support for new practices (Henry et al., 2011).

Specific areas of need for training include understanding (1) the impact of trauma on the child; (2) the underlying neurobiology that affects the child's ongoing preoccupation with danger and safety; (3) the role of the family/caregiving system and the impact of secondary traumatic stress on the worker; and (4) the contribution of culture to child and families' experience of and reaction to traumatic events. Initiatives are underway in all four areas that either illustrate effective training or point to crucial worker attitudes and skills. Conners-Burrow and colleagues (2013), for example, found that the implementation of a trauma-informed training program with frontline child welfare staff improved knowledge of trauma-informed care practices at the end of the training program and in a three-month follow-up.

Much has already been written about both 'the need for' and the 'how to' of training child protective workers regarding secondary traumatic stress.

Pryce, Schackelford, and Pryce (2007) devoted a chapter in their book solely to making child welfare staff more knowledgeable about the impact of secondary traumatic stress. The Resilience Alliance, available on the NCTSN web site (http://www.nctsn.org/products/nctsn-affiliated-resources/ resilience-alliance-promoting-resilience-and-reducing-secondary-trauma- handbook), is a workbook developed for training child welfare workers not only on secondary traumatic stress but also on resilience. Less widely explored is the role of MSW programs in preparing students for child welfare practice.

Description of the course

A course entitled the *Core Concepts of Trauma Informed Child Welfare* was developed by the National Center for Social Work Trauma Education and Workforce Development to prepare MSW students specifically for trauma- informed child welfare practice. Two conceptual frameworks underlie this course. The first is a trauma paradigm based on 12 Core Concepts articulated by the National Child Traumatic Stress Network (http://www.nctsn.org/pro ducts/12-core-concepts-understanding-traumatic-stress-responses-children- and-families), which offers an effective lens through which to view and understand the overwhelming and often-enduring effects of adverse life experiences on children and adolescents. The second is the use of problem- based learning (PBL) as the key pedagogical framework.

The 12 *Core Concepts for Understanding Traumatic Stress Responses in Children and Families* reflect an expert consensus about the issues needing attention to fully understand the child and family's experience of traumatic events. They highlight the need for a moment-to-moment understanding of the child's experience, as well as an understanding of its impact on development, the family caregiving system, the influence of the family's culture, and on how the child and family experience the traumatic event. In addition to understanding the impact of trauma on children and families, child welfare staff must attend to child safety, permanency and well-being. Therefore, in the following chart (Table 1), the 12 concepts are grouped according to their emphasis on safety, permanency, and well-being. Core Concepts 2, 3, and 5 emphasize the way trauma directly affects a child's safety. Once a child is stabilized, permanency can be addressed through intervention and treatment that attend to the disruptive impact of trauma on the child and family (Core Concept 6), and identification of adverse effects (Core Concept 8). Intervention to solidify permanency needs to take into consideration culture (Core Concept 10), legal and ethical issues (Core Concept 11), and the potential distress evoked in providers (Core Concept 12). The complexity of trauma (Core Concept 1), wide-ranging interactions to trauma (Core Concept 4), and the role of preexisting and protective factors (Core Concept 7), all contribute to challenges to establishing well-being, not the

Table 1. Core concepts of trauma by child welfare goals.

Child welfare main goals	Core concepts of childwood trauma
Safety	CC2: Emphasizes that trauma occurs within a broad context that includes both extrinsic and intrinsic factors that affect a child's safety, such as their appraisal of traumatic events; expectations about danger, protection, and safety; their temperament; and prior trauma. In addition, trauma and the course of posttrauma events can increase adversity due to vulnerability factors, such as a history of loss and poverty. CC3: Focuses on the child's increased posttrauma distress due to family separation, relocation, injury, and legal proceedings, and trauma and loss reminders that can tax the child's coping capacity, producing fluctuations in daily emotional and behavioral functioning that affects safety. CC5: Highlights that danger and safety are core concerns for traumatized children since trauma can undermine their sense of protection and safety and magnify their concerns about danger, as well as increase their difficulty in knowing the difference between safe and unsafe conditions
Permanency	CC6: Emphasizes trauma's disruptive impact on the child's family interactions and attachment, from losses and ongoing danger, or their caregiver's own distress that may impair their ability to support the child. Trauma can also disrupt broader caregiving systems, such as the functioning of schools and other community institutions and interfere with the caregiver and child's needed support. CC8: Explores how trauma and post-trauma adversities undermine well-being by strongly influencing children's acquisition of developmental competencies and delaying their reaching milestones in cognitive functioning, emotional regulation, and interpersonal relationships. All of which can lead to regressive behavior, reluctance, or inability to participate in developmentally appropriate behavior or developmental accelerations. CC10: Examines the way cultural factors and processes may profoundly influence trauma exposure. CC11: Exploring how interventions with trauma-exposed children and adolescents need to address ethical and legal issues as these arise. CC12: Explore how working with trauma-exposed children and adolescents impacts the practitioner in working with these populations.
Well-being	CC1: Explains how traumatic experiences are inherently complex and reactions can be influenced by prior experiences and developmental level. CC4: Understand that children can exhibit a wide range of reactions to trauma and loss, including posttraumatic stress and grief reactions. CC7: Understand how preexisting protective and promotive factors (e.g., positive attachment relationship with primary caregiver, family cohesion, social support, adaptive coping, social competence) can reduce the adverse impact of trauma exposure across development. CC9: Underscores the neurobiological consequences of exposure to trauma that last over time.

least of which is the underlying neurobiological consequences (Core Concept 9) that impact the child's recovery.

The course content is built around five case vignettes developed by a panel of national child trauma experts. Each case presents a trauma history (client problem) that is contextualized developmentally and culturally. The cases vary in age from 18 months to 13 years; represent urban, suburban, and rural living environments; include a variety of ethnic and racial groups; and illustrate many different trauma types, including interpersonal trauma such as physical, emotional, and sexual abuse, refugee trauma, community violence, and witnessing domestic violence. Each case is set in the context of either child protective services, preventive services, kinship foster care, or pre-adoption services.

In class, students work in small groups of 5–6, consistent with the PBL method described above, to answer questions posed by the case vignette. Case questions are designed to elicit understanding of the core concepts, and students develop their own questions as well. The class then reviews the small group learning before going on to the next section of the case. In addition, students generate case-based researchable questions in their small group, search the literature for evidence-based answers to the question, report back to the small group, and formulate a presentation to the class based on their findings.

The course pays special attention to secondary traumatic stress and the importance of self-care. Students as well as practitioners who work with children and families who have traumatic histories are at risk of developing secondary traumatic stress because of chronic exposure to traumatized children and their families. Engaging in work with traumatized families may also evoke strong feelings and memories of personal trauma- and loss-related experiences within the clinician. Students who enroll in trauma courses may experience secondary traumatic stress due to their exposure to trauma material. These effects highlight the important role of proper self-care as part of providing quality care and to sustaining personal and professional resources and capacities over time. Heightening students' attention to these issues through on-going discussion of Core Concept 12 – which emphasizes that the work with traumatized individuals may cause distress in the provider – constitutes a significant important learning activity in this course.

Course evaluation

This evaluation research used a mixed method approach, using the qualitative component to triangulate the quantitative research findings. Building on items measuring changes in students' confidence with the course content and related skills, the qualitative analysis focused on perceived usefulness of the course, in terms of content, teaching method, and assessments used, and its relevance for child welfare practice.

Method

The evaluation utilized a matched pretest and posttest survey format. The pretest was administered at the beginning of the first class while the posttest was given at the end of the final class. The pretest, a 33-item questionnaire, included items collecting demographics, exploring previous trauma experience/exposure, asking about confidence in working with traumatized children and their families (termed the Core Concepts Confidence Scale), and items exploring what the participants desired and expected from the course (termed the Course Design Scale). The posttest included a Course Design Scale, the Core Concepts Confidence Scale, and items garnering general feedback and recommendations for course enhancements.

The Core Concepts Confidence Scale (a 9-point Likert scale) was employed on the pretest and posttest as a matched scale measuring changes in students' confidence between the pre- and the posttests. Responses options range from 1 = "Not Confident at All", through 5 = "Somewhat Confident", to 9 = "Completely Confident". The Course Design Scale, utilized only on the posttest, was a 17-item measure asking for students' overall evaluation of course content, the learning environment, and the course process. It used a 5-point Likert scale with response options ranging from SD = "Strongly Disagree", D = "Disagree", U = "Uncertain", A = "Agree" to SA = "Strongly agree".

There were 971 students enrolled in the course. A total of 950 pretests and 845 posttests were returned and introduced in the SPSS data for analysis; 784 pretests were matched with their posttests for a survey return rate of 80.7%. Scale reliability was determined using Cronbach's alpha coefficient. The pretest Core Concepts Confidence Scale yielded an alpha of .960 and the posttest version of the scale yielded an alpha of .955; the Course Design Scale on the posttest returned an alpha of .935. All these scores indicate high statistical reliability.

There were two open-ended response items on the pretest and four on the posttest. The responses received to these items were reviewed and coded for common elements, using a thematic content analysis framework. The identified codes were aggregated into major themes, further elaborating on the findings from the quantitative data. The quantitative and qualitative data were combined and used to determine how the course affected participant trauma-oriented knowledge, skills, and confidence.

Findings

Most students enrolled in this course were women (87.9%). Most of the students identified themselves as White (72.6%); 13.6% were Black, and another 7.6% were Hispanic/Latino. Over half of the students (61.9%) were in the Advanced Year of their MSW program. Most students were not employed at a social work agency at the time of the pretest (58.8%). Participants ranged in age from 19 to 68 years old. The average age was 29.8 years, with a standard deviation of 8.78 years. The most frequently noted age was 23. Prior to pursuing their MSW degrees, students reported having between 0 and 35 years of work experience in a social work agency. The average length of experience was 3 years, with a standard deviation of 4.77 years. Most students (53.2%) reported no prior work experience in the field.

Of the 623 students that answered the question related to the percentage of trauma cases in their current caseload, over one-third of the students reported that more than half of their caseloads were comprised of children/adolescents with a history of trauma (43.1%). Many students currently in field placements reported that they were unsure whether their field instructors had received formal trauma training (36%), yet despite their uncertainty, most students reported that their field instructors were trauma resources for them (53.9%) during their field placement.

Students were provided with trauma training opportunities by their field placements (18.9%), their agency of employment (20.2%), or both (11.1%). Training in evidence-based trauma treatment (EBTT) was unavailable to many of the students. Those that did have access reported training at their field placement (10%), their agency of employment (10.1%), or both (4.6%). Most respondents reported that they had never attended a trauma-related conference, seminar, or other training opportunity (71.6%).

Students were asked to identify their main learning expectations/priorities. For students enrolled in the course offerings taught between 2010 and 2015, the primary theme that emerged from the responses was the desire to gain specific intervention skills. This was followed by an expressed interest in learning about neurobiology and general information regarding trauma and the role of trauma within the child welfare system. The quotes below reflect these common themes:

> I would like to gain skills in different interventions while dealing w/kids who suffer from trauma. I would like to gain knowledge on how to properly handle those different situations. (Student, 2012)

> [I would like to know how the brain is affected, how to recognize trauma in individuals, and about tools to adapt individually to survivors. (Student, 2013)

> [I expect to] learn skills and interventions that can be utilized when working with people who have experienced trauma [and to] learn what will help families of children that have been traumatized. (Student, 2014)

> [I hope to] learn [about] Child Welfare practices and ways to help in traumatic situations. (Student, 2015)

The posttest was administered at the end of the final class session. Some of the items included on this survey were intended to explore what aspects of the course participants found most useful along with those they found least useful. For the item asking about the most useful aspects of the course (Table 2), students' responses were grouped under five major themes: (1) case studies/class discussion; (2) conceptual foundation; (3) course materials/activities; (4) self-care techniques; and (5) system approaches to trauma work.

When asked about the least useful aspects of the course, most students agreed that the course was highly effective in its entirety, and fully relevant for the child welfare field of practice. The other responses were coded and

Table 2. Most useful experiences.

Theme	Common codes	In their voice
Case studies/Class discussions	Applying the 12 CCs to specific cases increased relevance for practice Using case discussions to prepare for practice	"The 12 Core Concepts will be very useful in the future." "The cases examples really helped my learning and awareness."
Conceptual foundation	General trauma knowledge Impact/Neurobiology of Trauma Using the trauma concepts as a framework for assessment/interventions	"Learning about trauma should be part of the required MSW curriculum." "I enjoyed discussing the trauma concepts and the neurobiology aspect of trauma. It is important to take into consideration how the trauma can affect a child's development and what ways we can cope with the trauma". "It was very clear on the proper ways to assess a traumatized child and develop a treatment plan."
Course materials/ Activities	Group work Readings/handouts	"The group participation and sharing of feelings helpful to digest some of the difficult materials." "The reading material was diverse and informative. It covered neurobiology, child development, and touched on social determinants of health."
Self-care techniques Systems approach to trauma work	Information/application of self-care techniques Understanding how systems interact and how trauma affects the functionality of the whole Safe systems	"Self-care strategies are extremely important and crucial when dealing with this population." "The Core Concepts really helped me understand the many layers of trauma and how it impacts the child and their system of care."

grouped under three main themes: (1) overuse of case studies; (2) minimal effectiveness of some group activities/projects; and (3) the lack of time allocated for more in-depth discussions of the core concepts learned in this class.

Course impact

The primary objective of the course is to increase the students' trauma knowledge, skills, and associated confidence; as reflected in the 12 Core Concepts of Trauma. As noted above, these concepts are specifically relevant to the achievement of safety, permanency, and well-being in the child welfare system. Changes between pre- and posttests were measured using a matched t test. The analysis determined that there was a statistically significant increase in confidence from the pretest mean of 5.27 to a posttest mean of 7.79 ($df = 674$, $p < .0001$). The effect size (r) value is .6813, indicating a significant change in the predicted direction.

The core concept item that saw the largest increase between pretest and posttest averages was CC6 ($M_{Pre} = 4.12$, $M_{Post} = 7.41$), which pertains to providing a framework for interventions which address the level of functioning of the primary caregiving environments. This item also recorded the lowest pretest average score among all core concepts. Core Concept 9, which pertains to understanding the neurological consequences of exposure to trauma, had the lowest posttest average score ($M = 7.20$).

Findings in the context of safety, permanency, and well-being

The core concepts were grouped into three clusters for this analysis (See Table 1): Cluster 1 – Safety, consisted of Core Concepts 2, 3 and 5; Cluster 2 – Permanency, consisted of Core Concepts 6, 8, 10.11, and 12; and Cluster 3 – Well-Being, consisted of Core Concepts 1, 4, 7, and 9. Table 3 provides the content of each core concept by cluster. Reliability scores were calculated for each of these clusters throughout the child welfare data set. Results indicate high reliability for all three clusters.

To determine the changes in students' confidence with each of these clusters, a paired sample t-test analysis was conducted. Findings show significant differences for all three clusters between the pretests and posttests. For the Safety Cluster, scores increased from 17.19 to 24.03 ($df = 681$, $p < .0001$),

Table 3. Reliability scores for cluster analysis.

Cluster	Alpha coefficient	
	Pretest	Posttest
Safety	.888	.883
Permanency	.921	.914
Well-being	.874	.848

suggesting that students understand that traumatized children are preoccupied with danger and safety, and that increased posttrauma distress due to family separation, relocation, injury, and legal proceedings – and trauma and loss reminders – can tax the child's coping capacity. For the Permanency Cluster, scores increased from 24.77 to 38.33 ($df = 678$, $p < .0001$). These scores reflect students' expanding knowledge and awareness there are many challenges to increasing traumatized children's emotional readiness for attachment and permanency, including the way cultural factors and processes may profoundly influence trauma exposure and how post-trauma adversities can influence trauma recovery.

There was also a large jump in the Well-Being scores. Pretest WB scores were 20.54 and increased to 30.93 ($df = 772$, $p < .0001$). These findings underscore students' increased understanding that the neurobiological consequences of exposure to trauma last over time and need to be addressed. However, well-being is also affected by preexisting protective and promotive factors (e.g., positive attachment relationship with primary caregiver, family cohesion, social support, adaptive coping, social competence) that can reduce the adverse impact of trauma exposure across development.

Effect sizes were large, indicating significant changes in the expected direction, attributable to the course, for all three clusters (Table 4). Finally, of interest is the finding that students' prior experience in child welfare is significantly correlated with higher confidence scores, for each core concept, and for all three clusters.

Limitations

This study uses a self-report measure and thus is at risk for subjectivity and threats to internal validity. The findings would have been strengthened by independent reports from field instructors, for example, to determine students' level of confidence and effectiveness in working with traumatized clients. In addition, the creation of the clusters of core concepts aligned with safety, permanency, and well-being was based on the authors' interpretation of the relevance of a given core concept for the cluster. The high reliability of the subscales lends support to the cluster divisions, but this is an area that could be strengthened by further analysis.

Table 4. Changes in students' confidence with safety, permanency, and well-being clusters.

Clusters	N	Pretest		Posttest		t	df	p	ES
		M	SD	M	SD				
Safety	682	17.19	5.322	24.03	2.913	−32.768	681	.000	.6233
Permanency	679	24.77	8.720	38.33	5.506	−38.225	678	.000	.6809
Well-being	773	20.54	6.886	30.93	4.015	−40.916	772	.000	.6777

Discussion and implications

Considering the findings in the current literature regarding the prevalence of trauma in child welfare and the related need for practitioners that understand and can identify and assess trauma and make effective referral, it is suggested that the course may be extremely valuable for social workers preparing for child welfare practice at the MSW level. The evaluation findings presented here demonstrate that the course was effective in significantly increasing students' confidence in working with traumatized children and their families.

When clustering the core concepts around the three main goals for child welfare of safety, permanency, and well-being, students are not only indicating that they are more confident with trauma knowledge in general, but more importantly, that they are more prepared to work toward these three child welfare goals. The course design scale indicates that students found the course to be not only relevant for the field of child welfare practice, but also significantly contributing to their ability to identify and search for new knowledge as needed.

Preparing MSW students for child welfare practice remains a challenge that social work education needs to embrace and address. This evaluation study showed that a PBL methodology, relying on extensive case analysis, shows promise for engaging students and increasing their knowledge and preparedness for work with traumatized children and their families. Both the course content and the learning method should be considered as important resources for further enhancing social work education and preparing students for practice.

References

Conners-Burrows, N. A., Kramer, T. L., Siegel, B. A., Helpenstill, K., Sievers, C., & McKelvey, L. (2013). Trauma-informed care training in a child welfare system: Moving it to the front line. *Children and Youth Services Review, 35*, 1830–1835. doi:10.1016/j.childyouth.2013.08.013

Cook, A., Spinazzola, J., Ford, J., Lanktree, C., Baumstein, M., Cloture, M., ... VanDer Kolk, B. (2005). Complex trauma in children and adolescents. *Psychiatric Annals, 35*(5), 390–398. doi:10.3928/00485713-20050501-05

Hendricks, J., Conradian, L., & Wilson, C. (2011). Creating trauma-informed child welfare systems using a community assessment process. *Child Welfare, 90*(6), 187–206.

Henry, J., Richardson, M., Black-Pond, C., Sloane, M., Atchinson, B., & Hyter, Y. (2011). A grassroots prototype for trauma-informed child welfare system change. (2011). *Child Welfare, 90*(6), 169–186.

Kisiel, C. L., Ferenbach, T., Torgersen, E., Stolbach, B., McClelland, G., Griffin, G., & Burkman, K. (2014). Constellations of interpersonal trauma and symptoms in child welfare: Implications for a developmental trauma framework. *Journal of Family Violence, 29,* 1–14. doi:10.1007/s10896-013-9559-0

Ko, S. J., Kassam-Adams, N., Wilson, C., Ford, J. D., Borowitz, S. J., Wong, M., ... Layne, C. (2008). Creating trauma-informed system: Child welfare, education, first responders, health care, juvenile justice. *Professional Psychiatry, 39*(4), 396–404.

Layne, C. M., Greeson, J. K. P., Ostrowski, S. A., Kim, S., Redding, S., Vivrette, R. L., ... Pynoos, R. S. (2014). Cumulative trauma exposure and high-risk behavior in adolescence: Findings from the national child traumatic stress network core data set. *Psychological Trauma: Theory, Research, Practice, and Policy, 6*(S1), S40–S49. doi:10.1037/a0037799

O'Donnell, J., & Kirkner, S. L. (2009). Title IV-E Programs: Preparing MSW students for public child welfare practice. *Journal of Teaching in Social Work, 29,* 241–257. doi:10.1080/08841230903022050

Pecora, P. J. (2010). Why current and former recipients of foster care need high quality mental health services. *Administration and Policy in Mental Health and Mental Health Services Research, 37*(102), 185–190. doi:10.1007/s10488-010-0295-y

Pecora, P. J., White, C. R., Jackson, L. J., & Wiggins, T. (2009). Mental health of current and former recipients of foster care: A review of recent studies in the USA. *Child & Family Social Work, 14*(2), 132–146. doi:10.1111/j.1365-2206.2009.00618.x

Pryce, J. G., Schackelford, K. K., & Pryce, D. H. (2007). *Secondary traumatic stress and the child welfare professional.* Chicago, IL: Lyceum Books.

Samuels, B. (2011). Testimony of Bryan Samuels, commissioner administration on children, youth and families administration for children and Families U.S. Department of Health and Human Services before the subcommittee on human resources Committee on ways and means U.S. House of Representatives. June 16, 2011. Retrieved April 24, 2012 from http://waysandmeans.house.gov/UploadedFiles/Bryan_Samuels_Testimony.pdf

Substance Abuse and Mental Health Services Administration (2014). *SAMHSA's concept of trauma and guidance for a trauma-informed approach.* Prepared by Samhsa's trauma and justice strategic initiative. HHS Publication No. (SMA) 14-4884. Rockville, MD: Substance Abuse and Mental Health Services Administration, 2014. Retrieved August 2016 from: http://store.samhsa.gov/shin/content/SMA14-4884/SMA14-4884.pdf

Wulcyzn., F., Barth, R. P., Yuan, -Y.-Y. T., Harden, B. J., & Landsverk, J. (2005). *Beyond common sense: Child welfare, child well-being and the evidence for policy reform.* New Brunswick, NJ: Aldine Transaction.

Zlotnik, J., & Pryce, J. A. (2013). Status of the use of title iv-e funding in BSW and MSW programs. *Journal of Public Child Welfare, 7,* 430–446. doi:10.1080/15548732.2013.806278

The future of online social work education and Title IV-E child welfare stipends

Kate Trujillo, Lara Bruce, and Ann Obermann

ABSTRACT

In this concept paper, the authors explore online learning in social work and how IV-E education has been and will continue to be impacted. An empirical estimate of the national prevalence of online IV-E social work degree options is presented. Using Colorado as a case example, the authors share some of the opportunities and challenges presented by online education. Universities in Colorado have realized that online education connects rural and indigenous communities, reduces the need for students to relocate, and promotes a well-prepared, qualified child welfare workforce, but online options also challenge programs with localization issues. With connectivity increased and the physical location of students becoming less and less relevant, IV-E child welfare education providers need a proactive national dialogue to further assess the benefits and barriers to IV-E partnerships across state lines and the development of promising approaches in this area. The recruitment and retention of a well-educated and prepared child welfare workforce is critical for positive outcomes for children and families. Online social work education continues to grow nationwide. Now is the time for a national workgroup, including a broad group of stakeholders, to explore how the IV-E community will respond to online delivery of social work education.

Introduction

Recruiting and retaining qualified child welfare professionals is of utmost concern across the nation; child welfare agencies and the children and families they serve are severely impacted by high turnover rates and the challenge of adequately training professional staff (Zlotnik, DePanfilis, Daining, & McDermott Lane, 2005). One mechanism that states use to recruit, prepare, and retain a strong child welfare workforce is providing higher education opportunities to the existing and potential workforce. Higher education partnerships, often referred to as university–agency partnerships, help address the challenges of recruitment, preparation, and retention in the child welfare workforce by reinforcing worker competencies, providing stipends for undergraduate and graduate education (i.e., Title IV-E stipends, stipend programs, IV-E programs), providing specialized continuing education to address local concerns, informing university child welfare curriculum, facilitating professional communities, and training leaders (NCWWI, 2013; Strand, Dettlaff, & Counts-Spriggs, 2015). Stipend programs are made available through Title IV-E of the Social Security Act, in combination with matched state funds. Social work education and specialized IV-E stipend training have been shown to predict retention among child welfare workers (Zlotnik et al., 2005). Research has demonstrated that child welfare workers with an MSW (Master of Social Work), especially students who participated in a IV-E program, perform better on objective tests related to child welfare knowledge, such as permanency planning, case planning, and management, than child welfare workers without an MSW (Bagdasaryan, 2012).

Though the success of these partnerships has been well researched, less research has been done on how the trend of higher education being offered in online and distance education formats is impacting child welfare education, specifically IV-E stipend recipients and programs. As online programs and hybrid options make pursuing a degree more feasible, it is all the more critical that child welfare considers the influence of these options on career paths so that agencies can attract, train, and retain professional social workers to child welfare positions. IV-E workforce development considerations need to reflect changes in the educational needs and modalities and the ever-changing demographics of the child welfare workforce. This article, using Colorado as a case example, seeks to set the stage for a formal national dialogue regarding what's possible for the future of IV-E programs and online social work education, as this mode of higher education continues to impact our programs, our students, and ultimately the children and families served by public child welfare agencies.

The growth of online education

In a recent report produced by Babson Survey Research Group, it was reported that in 2014 there were 5.8 million distance education students in the United States, with 2.85 million taking all their courses online and 2.97 million taking some of their courses online (Allen & Seaman, 2016). Students enrolled in a fully online education program represent 14% of all higher education students, and this percentage has consistently grown over the past 8 years. Though enrollment trends in higher education have been shrinking, online enrollment grew 9% at US-based public institutions from 2012 to 2014 (Allen & Seaman, 2016).

Online education has been reported as the chosen method of higher education for adults aged 25–50 years old (Moore & Kearsley, 2005). The average age and gender of online students were 25–29 years of age and female, with 57% of students between the ages of 18 and 39 years old (Rivard, 2013; Sheehy, 2013). In a 2010 study, Eaton (2016) found that students chose online education to accommodate work schedules, to access specific educational programs that were not available in the regions in which they lived, and to improve skills that facilitated job promotion and work development for job retention.

Though faculty approval of online learning remained low in 2015, 71.4% of academic leaders rated the learning outcomes in online education as the same or superior to those of face-to-face instruction, an improvement from the 2003 rate of 57.3% (Allen & Seaman, 2016). In a meta-analysis of quasi-experimental and experimental studies, results indicated that online students performed the same or better than face-to-face students (US Department of Education, 2009). However, blended/hybrid education, where components of course work are completed online with a classroom-based element, continues to be rated higher with regard to superior outcomes than both fully online and face-to-face instruction (US Department of Education, 2009).

In addition to student performance outcomes and perceptions of academic leaders, online learning has been demonstrated to contribute to forming effective learning communities (Schwen & Hara, 2004; Vrasidas & Glass, 2004) and student self-reflection (Hiltz & Goldman, 2004; Jaffe, Moir, Swanson, & Wheeler, 2006), resulting in significant learning. This will be discussed in more detail later in our exploration as it relates to IV-E education specifically.

National prevalence: initial exploration of online social work and IV-E programs

As Dawson and Fenster (2015) emphasize, the 2013 Council on Social Work Education (CSWE) survey of accredited social work programs found that among 222 master's level programs responding, 8% currently offered the entire MSW program online, 51% offered part of the program online, and another 16% were developing online offerings. Of the 471 BSW (Bachelor of Social Work) programs reporting, 2% offered full programs online, 38% had online courses, and 14% were developing online options (CSWE, 2013). Just 2 years later, the 2015 CSWE survey found that 33% of programs offering an MSW program have an online component, and 18% of programs nationally have an online option and also offer IV-E stipends (CSWE, 2015a).

To further examine the prevalence of online programs and gain insight to the availability of IV-E education within those programs, we compared the list of CSWE-accredited online programs that is available on the CSWE website (CSWE, 2017) to the list of IV-E programs that is maintained by the University of Houston (Cheung, 2017). It is important to note that neither of these websites are designed to be an exhaustive list of programs, so the data generated are not an ideal measurement of US-based, accredited online IV-E programs and, thus, our comparison is likely to underrepresent the many programs that are offering BSW, MSW, and IV-E education in online, hybrid, or distance models.

However, based on our examination of the 2 lists, there are currently 79 CSWE-accredited online programs, 44 of which have an IV-E program. The programs are distributed nationally, with at least one online IV-E program in each of the federal regions, with the exception of region seven. Most of the online programs were available to students from all over the country, with the exception of five programs that were designed to meet the needs of in-state students only. Four of the programs specifically mentioned that they were open to international students.

Case example—Colorado

The Colorado Department of Human Services (CDHS) contracts with accredited universities to provide educational stipends, and other benefits of the program, to students who are committed to meeting the child welfare needs of the state and its workforce. The Stipend Program in Colorado is overseen by a Stipend Committee that comprises representatives from the child welfare training division at the CDHS; Metropolitan State University of Denver, University of Denver, Colorado State University—Fort Collins, and Colorado State University—Pueblo (CSU Pueblo); and staff from the county departments of human/social service, including internship coordinators and field instructors. The Stipend Committee meets regularly to determine standard operating procedures for the Stipend Program, evaluate training requirements and needs, discuss specific student and agency needs, plan evaluation methods, and support the recruitment and retention of future students and graduates (CDHS, 2016). All committee members, regardless of affiliation, have a strong shared interest in developing a robust workforce to serve Colorado's children, youth, and families. Students who receive a stipend are required to complete a specified term of "payback"—employment in a Colorado county or Tribal department of human/social services in a child welfare position serving Title IV-E eligible children and their families—after they graduate (CDHS, 2016).

Table 1 represents a summary of the online program options found at each of the four universities in Colorado that are a part of the IV-E stipend committee and program.

These online options continue to grow and expand from year to year. Many are new (within the past 5 years) in their implementation, and therefore, considerations for additional educational opportunities are just now being considered. University staff have continued to ask the question, "Can child welfare stipends be awarded to students who are completing their BSW or MSW education online?" To date, the Stipend Committee has settled on the policy that online students who reside in Colorado, whose professional goals include remaining in Colorado and whose time frames for acceptance into the university match the application process for the Stipend Program,

Table 1. Colorado universities that offer stipend programs.

	Public or private	IV-E BSW stipend	IV-EMSW stipend	Online option
University of Denver	Private		X	Online MSW option available to US and international students. Distance learning options available in Glenwood Springs and Durango (rural, native-serving regions of Colorado). Distance learning options include some online courses
Colorado State University—Pueblo	Public	X	Anticipated for fall, 2018	Online available for many classes, including hybrid, but not for all
Colorado State University—Fort Collins	Public	X	X	Hybrid option available for MSW only (hybrid program requires 2 weekends per semester face to face)
Metropolitan State University of Denver	Public	X	X	Online option available for BSW and MSW

are eligible to receive a child welfare stipend. Questions remain regarding what missed opportunities exist. How can we best serve both students and agencies? How does this process contribute to or inhibit recruitment and retention opportunities for child welfare in Colorado and nationally?

Beginning a national dialogue

The National Title IV-E Roundtable Conference created an opportunity for understanding the implications of online education and IV-E training programs. This event is held annually to support educational providers and child welfare agencies alike. The 2017 conference theme was *Examining Efficiency and Increasing Access Across Systems Through Collaboration*. During the conference, held May 23–25, 2017, in Phoenix, Arizona, 32 states were present to discuss the many changes facing Title IV-E programs (A. Hightower, personal communication, May 2017). Representatives from the Colorado Stipend Committee offered a roundtable presentation entitled: *The Future of Online Learning and Title IV-E Child Welfare Stipends: Sharing Opportunities and Challenges*. During this session, the following questions were posed: (a) How might states and universities collaborate to offer field placements and IV-E payback opportunities that are not specific to state boundaries?; (b) What gets in the way of this collaboration?; and (c) What online education programs already exist (Trujillo & Bruce, 2017)?

Benefits of online education

The conversations from the roundtable overwhelmingly affirmed many of the benefits of IV-E online education we have experienced in Colorado and also helped shine a light on some additional concerns explored throughout this article. These benefits are described in the following sections.

Reaching rural communities

It has long been a difficult challenge to recruit, train, and maintain students who are willing to work in child welfare in more remote areas of Colorado. Mackie and Lips (2010) report that for every 10 mi outside an urban area, the hiring of social workers is 3% more difficult. Colorado's population is primarily located in 11 counties along the front range, but 27 Colorado counties have fewer than 10,000 people. It is especially difficult in many of the rural counties of Colorado to find well-educated and prepared social workers to work in child welfare (Colorado Health Foundation, 2010).

In 2009, the National Advisory Committee on Rural Health and Human Services found that less than a third of social work schools are located in rural areas (National Advisory Committee on Rural Health and Human Services, 2009). Before online options were available, students in Colorado were forced to relocate in order to pursue an education. Stipend Committee members have noticed that after years of residing in a more urban setting while pursuing their degrees, graduates often did not want to move back to their towns of origin and could find employment at an agency in a more urban setting. Even when the committee agreed to pay a stipend incentive for graduates to accept jobs in rural areas, stipend recipients often chose not to work in those settings. One major benefit of programs being offered online is that students who are inclined to work in child welfare from a rural community do not need to leave their community to receive the necessary education. Rural supervisors reported a preference for hiring workers from rural areas due to the worker's already existing interest, residence, and livelihood within those rural areas and their knowledge of rural culture. They felt that this targeted hiring increased retention and satisfaction of their workers (Mackie, 2012; Mackie & Lips, 2010).

Collectively, we now have nine IV-E stipend students who are living in rural communities and able to access an online social work degree because of the online and distance options available in Colorado (Kathy Clark, personal communication, September 22, 2017). Online options have created access for students who want to pursue a degree without relocating (Reamer, 2013). The opportunity to study without a major increase in living expenses because of relocation to more urban areas is another dimension of access that online options provide students in our state.

Increased access—beyond state boundaries

While online opportunities opened possibilities to students living in rural communities within Colorado, it also opened opportunity to students across the globe. Universities suddenly have students who are interested in degrees from Colorado-based universities, but whose lives might be physically located elsewhere. Students from across state lines and across the globe are now equally able to attend classes. Qualified students who are living outside of Colorado could care for aging parents, serve in the military or reside with a partner serving in the military, or pursue any number of additional activities outside of the state while pursuing a degree.

Online options have also created access to degrees for students who are working professionals or parents, who have other commitments in life, or who may not have been able to complete a face-to-face degree program (McAllister, 2013; Oliaro & Trotter, 2010; Wilke & Vinton, 2006). The ability to pursue a degree online, reducing travel time to campus and offering flexibility for scheduling, also creates access within our state borders. For many of our IV-E stipend recipients, online options have helped increased access to professional development and career advancement opportunities.

Serving military communities

There is a large military community in Colorado, which includes the US Air Force Academy, Fort Carson, and Lowry, among others. Many service members and their families might be stationed in Colorado for a few years but are then transferred elsewhere. Social work students with a military connection are currently discouraged from the Stipend Program because of the requirement to work within the state following graduation. At the same time, there are specialized units that serve military families within the state because of the unique relationship to trauma that service members and their families face. The military community's need for trained social workers and expanded understanding of trauma creates a unique opportunity for partnership with the Stipend Program. Online social work programs might be one option for students located on military bases in Colorado or potential students whose military partners may end up relocating here. Online social work programs can help bridge the gap that can exist in services for military personnel while also creating a stronger community for the program participants. One study "found that asynchronous computer conferencing [e.g., e-mail or discussion boards] can enhance a sense of community through developing camaraderie, connectedness, and sense of accomplishment among military students" (Liu, Magjuka, Bonk, & Lee, 2007). Opening the IV-E Stipend Program to talented social workers with a military commitment or connection by allowing them to repay the stipend in other states or jurisdictions may be a good idea for the child welfare workforce in Colorado and nationwide because of the unique culture of military families and how these families experience trauma.

Increased community

Another benefit that online learning in IV-E education offers is the possibility for support and the formation of specialized communities. An online community has been defined in the literature to include shared goals, membership, trust, connectedness, collaboration, social capital, and community boundaries (Liu, Magiuka, Bonk, & Lee, 2007; Shea, Li, Swan, & Pickett, 2002).

The use of online environments to form specialized communities that understand and care about child welfare may help increase students' feeling of support and socioemotional well-being due to members having shared values, behaviors, and mutual understandings regarding child welfare (Rovai, 2001). For example, students who are interested in discussing the realities of working in a small community and the lack of anonymity can find camaraderie with other students in small communities hundreds of miles away. Individuals who remain in child welfare value professional growth, self-actualization, purpose and mission, and the importance of their work; these factors are arguably more important to retention than the benefits a particular agency can provide, such as financial incentives, the work environment, and the realities of the workplace (Ellet & Millar, 2004). If recent graduates from IV-E programs see themselves committed to a cause, such as children and families, safe communities, and a purpose, rather than a specific agency, perhaps a challenge for our field is to determine how to create camaraderie with IV-E stipend programs nationally, instead of focusing on agency commitment. This opportunity to develop groups of IV-E online students who can encourage each other, support each other, and hold the vision of the importance of their work could be an untapped resource for our retention efforts post-graduation.

In addition to connectivity with a student's online community, online learning also fosters connections with other individuals, groups, research authors, ideas, larger university or educational systems, professional communities, related or diverse educational fields (e.g., psychology, sociology, public health, etc.), and society at large (Siemens, 2004). This broader connection to child welfare nationally, and potentially internationally, will foster new ideas and innovation helping to meet the demands of the workforce and the children and family served by the system.

Digital literacy

Social workers are now required to have a base level of digital literacy in order to competently do their job. Resources; paper work for agency requirements; paperwork for health care, benefits, and other public services; accessing evidence-based and best practices; and digital practice (e.g., telehealth, text reminders, peer support groups) are located online and require a practitioner with competent digital literacy (Reamer, 2013). Learning in an online format helps prepare social workers to practice in a similar online world and helps foster innovation in service accessibility and provision for the child welfare system.

Concerns of online influences in IV-E education

While there are clearly a number of benefits to IV-E programs being offered online, there are also new challenges and concerns that these program options create. Some of the most notable concerns that we have considered to date are described here.

Federal oversight, state implementation

The Title IV-E section of the social security act allows for federal oversight and state-level implementation (Stoltzfus, 2012). Of the 2.85 million students taking all online courses, 41% live in a different state than the university or college in which they are enrolled, and this especially impacts private versus public institutions (Allen & Seaman, 2016). Because of this high percentage of students attending universities outside of their resident state, federal oversight and state implementation can pose challenges to administering the IV-E stipend. With this in mind, regional interpretations of federal regulations vary from one region or state to another, and the laws in each state pertaining to the implementation of the stipend programs may be different—if they exist at a state level at all. This program variety might include various job requirements for stipend graduates, as well as differing requirements for the workforce. These varying requirements might create challenges for IV-E graduates completing work payback and create opportunities for state-university partnerships to address and meet the needs of the local child welfare agencies where students complete their work payback.

The concept of crossing state lines is not new to child welfare. The Interstate Compact on the Placement of Children (ICPC) is a federal mandate that is enacted in all 50 states, including the District of Columbia and the US Virgin Islands. Its purpose is to comply with the goal of permanency, well-being, and safety of children (APHSA, 2013). The American Public Human Services Association has called the ICPC process "antagonizing, antiquated, and burdensome" because, while in concept sharing resources to provide better services for children across state lines makes sense, the ICPC process lacks state or federal funding but imposes federal regulation. The IV-E community would be wise to anticipate how changes in education will affect changes in preparation of child welfare workers. There are lessons the IV-E community could learn from ICPC in terms of how resources are shared among and between agencies for online and distance IV-E stipend students, universities, and child welfare agencies. Many opportunities exist to explore how existing funding policies and procedures within Title IV-E could contribute to more interstate collaboration for students seeking to advance their education online and the programs that serve them.

Staff retention

There is a concern that stipend graduates, if allowed to do payback in other states, would leave, further complicating agency struggles to retain qualified staff. If graduates were not required to do their work payback in the state or area where they completed their field placement or education, what does that mean for staffing the agency long-term and the agency's short-term investment in the student?

In addition, because child welfare salaries vary across the country and even county to county within some states, like Colorado, there is a concern that students would not stay in the rural area where they received their degree and completed their field placement. Rather, they would graduate and then relocate to a more desirable place to work and live. Some research has shown that establishing and maintaining a professional culture with a clear vision, professionalism, and commitment is especially important to maintaining new workers in the field (Ellett & Millar, 2004). In rural places where a child welfare social worker may be the only social worker for hundreds of miles, a strong professional community is not available. (Conversely, as previously discussed, perhaps online communities that share a professional culture with a clear vision and commitment could support retention efforts.)

Another issue with regard to online education is the retention in online programs themselves. The rate of attrition for online can be 10–50% higher than face-to-face attrition rates, which undermines the mission of the IV-E stipend and creates further complications with interstate payback and the need to collect already received stipend money due to the recipient dropping out of the program (Park & Choi, 2009; Tirrell & Quick, 2012).

Quality field placements

Field placement is a cornerstone of social work education and child welfare workforce development (CSWE, 2015b). One study interviewed 20 recent graduates, and while some could articulate benefits of their coursework, all of them believed that their field placement was beneficial to their current job (Bates & Bates, 2013). The universities and state or county partnerships that are critical to current IV-E programs' abilities to offer IV-E stipend internship placements would be greatly complicated by online/distance delivery in the need to share resources, not only dollars, but time, organization, and experience, that go into building a cohesive and consistent child welfare field placement opportunity.

Impact on tribal communities

Another consideration for discussion is the impact on tribal communities and agencies, particularly those that reside on or across state lines. Many states offer payback opportunities in their state or a tribal nation (Cheung, 2017). However, coordination among tribal governments and states requires relationship, trust, and cultural competence, which could be difficult to build from a distance (Cross, Day, Gogliotti, & Pung, 2013).

The question of how IV-E stipends are disbursed to students who reside in tribes that cross state borders and how students do their work payback within a Tribal nation could be enhanced or complicated by online learning opportunities. One study that surveyed 47 American Indian/Alaskan Native (AI/AN) social workers found that there were 7 major barriers associated with recruitment and retention: (a) a lack of AI/AN clients, (b) a shortage of field placements that serve AI/AN clients, (c) conflicting responsibilities between student obligations and family and tribal obligations, (d) students' feelings of cultural isolation, (e) the need for AI/AN role models and mentors, (f) a lack of understanding by universities of cultural customs and traditional values, and (g) racism (Cross et al., 2013). Online options might be able to reduce or mitigate some of these barriers for AI/AN students and increase access to opportunity for students living in Tribal nations. At the same time, the online delivery could also complicate the experience for the AI/AN student, and how online options are conceptualized and delivered for an increasingly diverse student population warrants thoughtful consideration.

Recommendations

Our initial exploration of the prevalence of online options for IV-E education indicates that online BSW and MSW programs continue to grow nationwide, which will undoubtedly raise questions within IV-E programs throughout the country as more and more students prepare for professional education and positions in child welfare. At this point in time, there are more questions than answers about how offering online options for social work education will affect IV-E students. The formation of a national work group to proactively explore the benefits and challenges of building specific and intentional partnerships between online social work and IV-E programs will help to promote best practices in this arena and will have a lasting impact on the recruitment and preparation of the child welfare workforce nationwide. Recruiting qualified students to child welfare careers is essential to meet the demands of the workforce, and IV-E child welfare education programs should pay attention to the national trends of education delivery in order to be responsive to the needs of the child welfare workforce and remain an attractive choice for social work professionals.

We believe that this national work group should include, at a minimum, representatives from IV-E-funded universities from each federal region, both urban and rural; AI and AN students and faculty; students and faculty from military bases; federal administrators from the Department of Health and Human Services; national IV-E subject matter experts; and representatives from the IV-E states that rely on IV-E funds for workforce development. A natural place for these discussions to occur may be the IV-E Roundtable Conference that already has broad participation from social workers and IV-E programs across the nation. However, a future conference, or even series of conferences over a number of years, could engage a broad group of stakeholders in this discussion to develop guiding principles and best practices for how states might respond to the influence of changing educational deliveries.

Questions this group could consider include, but are not limited to:

(a) How could or should states and universities partner across state lines?
(b) How would we develop these partnerships? What resources would be needed?
(c) How does current policy support or inhibit delivery of online options in education and stipend allocation in cross-state partnerships?
(d) What changes in policy might the group recommend?
(e) How can we target locally specific worker competencies or local educational programming needs from distance educational institutions?
(f) How can we recruit and retain students when they have greater choices in where and how to pursue their social work education and where to work?
(g) What additional communities (e.g., AI/AN students, students serving in the military, students in rural communities) could online program options connect and support in way that traditional deliveries do not?
(h) Would it be feasible, both financially and logistically, to utilize other universities in different states to provide field placement supervision?
(i) What would it take to collaborate with other states and universities to provide supervision to IV-E students?
(j) How can we assure quality education for future child welfare workers in online delivery formats?

In addition to asking these questions, increased research is needed regarding social work education in online delivery formats. With the prevalence of CSWE-accredited programs offering online formats, research needs to show that these online formats are working and how. Specifically, research needs to look at IV-E stipend recipients who received their degree online to see if their online training has the same outcomes as their face-to-face peers with regard to preparation, retention, and job satisfaction.

Conclusion

How we structure our IV-E opportunities needs to keep pace with the structure of our educational options. The possibilities and opportunities of online social work education for IV-E students are vast and are met with challenges that require our collective, creative attention. As we began exploring a national dialogue about IV-E opportunities for online students, we quickly realized that this is a new conversation for many universities and states alike. Continuation of this dialogue will require true partnerships between states, universities, and IV-E programs and the communities they serve. Through collaboration, attention to this emerging opportunity may lead to increased retention of a well-prepared child welfare workforce and, in turn, to better outcomes for the children, youth, and families that they serve.

Acknowledgments

We wish to thank Kathy Clark, Colorado Department of Human Services, and Dr. Walter LaMendola, Professor Emeritus, University of Denver, for their thoughtful contributions and earlier reviews of this paper.

References

Allen, I. E., & Seaman, J. (2016). Online report card: Tracking online education in the United States. *Babson Survey Research Group*.

American Public Human Services Association. (2013). *Interstate compact on the placement of children: A pathways policy brief—April 25, 2013*. Retrieved from: http://www.aphsa-ism.org/content/dam/aphsa/pdfs/Pathways/2013-04-Interstate-Compact-Placement-Children-PolicyBrief.pdf

Bagdasaryan, S. (2012). Social work education and Title IV-E program participation as predictors of entry-level knowledge among public child welfare workers. *Children and Youth Services Review, 34*(9), 1590–1597. doi:10.1016/j.childyouth.2012.04.013

Bates, A., & Bates, L. (2013). Work-integrated learning courses: An essential component for preparing students to work in statutory child protection? *Asia-Pacific Journal of Cooperative Education, 14*(1), 45–58.

Cheung, M. (Ed.), (2017). *National survey of IV-E stipends & paybacks.* Houston, TX: University of Houston. Retrieved from http://www.uh.edu/socialwork/New_research/cwep/title-iv-e/Stipends-Paybacks/

Colorado Department of Human Services. (2016). *Title IV-E Child Welfare Stipend Program, standard operating procedures.* Denver, CO: Author.

Colorado Health Foundation. (2010). *The behavioral healthcare workforce in Colorado: A status report.* Retrieved from: http://www.wiche.edu/info/publications/bhWorkforceColorado2010.pdf

Council of Social Work Education. (2013). *Statistics on social work education in the United States.* Retrieved from: https://www.cswe.org/getattachment/3ea00923-9d60-436d-be4a-9014b78478cc/2013-Statistics-on-Social-Work-Education-in-the-Un.aspx

Council of Social Work Education. (2015a). *Annual statistics on social work education in the United States.* Retrieved from: https://www.cswe.org/CMSPages/GetFile.aspx?guid=992f629c-57cf-4a74-8201-1db7a6fa4667

Council of Social Work Education. (2015b). *2015 educational policy and accreditation standards.* Retrieved from: https://www.cswe.org/getattachment/Accreditation/Accreditation-Process/2015-EPAS/2015EPAS_Web_FINAL.pdf.aspx

Council of Social Work Education. (2017). *Formally accredited programs, online and distance education* [data file]. Retrieved from: https://www.cswe.org/Accreditation/Distance-Education.aspx

Cross, S. L., Day, A., Gogliotti, L. J., & Pung, J. J. (2013). Challenges to recruit and retain American Indian and Alaskan natives into social work programs: The impact on the child welfare workforce. *Child Welfare, 92*(4), 31.

Dawson, B. A., & Fenster, J. (2015). Web-based social work courses: Guidelines for developing and implementing an online environment. *Journal of Teaching in Social Work, 35*(4), 365. doi:10.1080/08841233.2015.1068905

Eaton, A. (2016). Students in the online technical communication classroom: The next decade. In K. Cook & K. Grant-Davie (Eds.), *Online education 2.0: Evolving, adapting, and reinventing online technical communication.* Routledge.

Ellett, A. J., & Millar, K. I. (2004). Professional organizational culture and retention in child welfare. *Professional Development: The International Journal of Continuing, 7*(3), 30–38.

Hiltz, S. R., & Goldman, R. (2004). *Learning online together: Research on asynchronous learning networks.* New York, NY: Routledge.

Jaffe, R., Moir, E., Swanson, E., & Wheeler, G. (2006). Online mentoring and professional development for new science teachers. In C. Dede (Ed.), *Online teacher professional development: Emerging models and methods* (pp. 89–116). Cambridge, MA: Harvard Education Publishing Group.

Liu, X., Magjuka, R. J., Bonk, C. J., & Lee, S. (2007). Does sense of community matter? An examination of participants' perceptions of building learning communities in online courses. *Quarterly Review of Distance Education, 8*(1), 9–24, 87–88.

Mackie, P. (2012). Social work in a very rural place: A study of practitioners in the Upper Peninsula of Michigan. *Contemporary Rural Social Work, 4,* 63–90.

Mackie, P., & Lips, R. (2010). Is there really a problem with hiring rural social service staff? An exploratory study among social service supervisors in rural Minnesota. *Families in*

Society: The Journal of Contemporary Social Services, 91(4), 433–439. doi:10.1606/1044-3894.4035

McAllister, C. (2013). A process evaluation of an online BSW program: Getting the student perspective. *Journal of Teaching in Social Work, 33*(4–5), 514–530. doi:10.1080/08841233.2013.838200

Moore, M. G., & Kearsley, G. (2005). *Distance education: A systems view* (2nd ed.). Belmont, CA: Wadsworth.

National Advisory Committee on Rural Health and Human Services. (2009). *The 2009 report to the secretary: Rural health and human services issues.* Retrieved from https://www.hrsa.gov/advisorycommittees/rural/2009secreport.pdf

National Child Welfare Workforce Institute. (2013). *Twelve NCWWI traineeship programs: Comprehensive summary of legacies and lessons learned.* Albany, NY: Author. Retrieved from http://ncwwi.org/files/NCWWI_Traineeships_Comprehensive_Summary_Legacies_Lessons_Learned_Sept2013.pdf

Oliaro, L., & Trotter, C. (2010). A comparison of on-campus and off-campus (or distance) social work education. *Australian Social Work, 63*(3), 329–344. doi:10.1080/0312407X.2010.496866

Park, J. H., & Choi, H. J. (2009). Factors influencing adult learners' decision to drop out or persist in online learning. *Journal of Educational Technology & Society, 12*(4), 207–217.

Reamer, F. G. (2013). Distance and online social work education: Novel ethical challenges. *Journal of Teaching in Social Work, 33*(4–5), 369–384. doi:10.1080/08841233.2013.828669

Rivard, R. (2013, June 26). Survey suggests growing segment of online degree-seekers prefer online to on-campus. *Chronicle of Higher Education.* Retrieved from: https://www.chronicle.com/article/Who-Are-the-Undergraduates-/123916

Rovai, A. P. (2001). Building classroom community at a distance: A case study. *Educational Technology Research and Development, 49*(4), 33–48. doi:10.1007/BF02504946

Schwen, T. M., & Hara, N. (2004). Community of practice: A metaphor for online design. In S. Barab, R. Kling, & J. Gray (Eds.), *Designing for virtual communities in the service of learning* (pp. 154–178). Cambridge, MA: Cambridge University Press.

Shea, P., Li, C. S., Swan, K., & Pickett, A. (2002). Developing learning community in online asynchronous college courses: The role of teaching presence. *Journal of Asynchronous Learning Networks, 9*(4), 59–82.

Sheehy, K. (2013, January 8). Online course enrollment climbs for 10th straight year: A new study finds that online education continues to grow despite declining faculty support. *US News & World Report.* Retrieved from: https://www.usnews.com/education/online-education/articles/2013/01/08/online-course-enrollment-climbs-for-10th-straight-year

Siemens, G. (2004). Connectivism: A learning theory for the digital age. *International Journal of Instructional Technology and Distance Learning.* Retrieved from http://www.elearnspace.org/Articles/connectivism.htm

Stoltzfus, E. (2012). *Child welfare: A detailed overview of program eligibility and for foster care, adoption assistance and kinship guardianship assistance under Title IV-E of the Social Security Act.* Washington, DC: Congressional Research Service.

Strand, V. C., Dettlaff, A. J., & Counts-Spriggs, M. (2015). Promising innovations in child welfare education: Findings from a national initiative. *Journal of Social Work Education, 51*(2), 195–208. doi:10.1080/10437797.2015.1072411

Tirrell, T., & Quick, D. (2012). Chickering's seven principles of good practice: Student attrition in community college online courses. *Community College Journal of Research and Practice, 36*(8), 580–590. doi:10.1080/10668920903054907

Trujillo, K., & Bruce, L. (2017, May). The future of online learning and Title IV-E child welfare stipends: Sharing opportunities and challenges. In A. Hightower Ed., (Chair).

Examining efficiency and increasing access across systems through collaboration. Phoenix, AZ: Lecture conducted from Arizona State University.

US Department of Education, Office of Planning, Evaluation, and Policy Development. (2009). *Evaluation of evidence-based practices in online learning: A metaanalysis and review of online learning studies.* Washington, DC: Author.

Vrasidas, C., & Glass, G. V. (2004). *Current perspectives in applied information technologies: Online professional development for teachers.* Greenwich, CT: Information Age Publishing.

Wilke, D., & Vinton, L. (2006). Evaluation of the first web-based advanced standing MSW program. *Journal of Social Work Education, 42*(3), 607–620. doi:10.5175/JSWE.2006.200500501

Zlotnik, J. L., DePanfilis, D., Daining, C., & McDermott Lane, M. (2005). *Factors influencing retention of child welfare staff: A systematic review of research.* Washington, DC: Institute for the Advancement of Social Work Research.

Index

Note: **Bold** page numbers refer to tables and *italic* page numbers refer to figures.